Enc

Don't read this book unless you are ~~champion the Holy Spirit uses to i~~_____ _ ____ _____ _____ ___ _____.
Across communities. Doug combines fresh thought from biblical teachings on prayer with best practices on strategic corporate prayer. But, before you dive into these deep and wide waters, grab your journal, find your quiet place (no phone zone), turn to the contents listing, and pray through each of the twelve teaching topics. ASK the Holy Spirit a question about each one. "What do you want to teach me?" "What changes do I need to make in my prayer life?" "How can we mobilize this truth-practice in our church?" SEEK his leading with silence...wait for scripture...scribe your thoughts. KNOCK down every hindrance with a prayer of renewed commitment. Thank you Doug for a biblically infused strategic path toward becoming that house of prayer Jesus loves to empower by his Spirit.

Phil Miglioratti
Mission America Coalition, National Facilitator

For decades Doug Small has been a leader in the prayer movement. His life demonstrates that prayer is a relationship with God, not just another topic for discussion. His new volume emphasizes the power of prayer in transforming a local church. It is scriptural, inspirational, practical and insightful. Every pastor, prayer leader, and praying believer will be enriched by the stories, the guidelines and the wisdom contained in this volume. Read, pray, and lead. An interceding church is a transformed church.

Dr. Douglas LeRoy, Second Billion, co-chairman of Unreached People Groups;
Former Director, Church of God World Missions

Having been engaged in recruiting speakers for inter-denominational events over 35 years, Doug Small remains among the best with whom I have become acquainted. His insightful content is evidence of the most thorough thought and research. His anointed delivery is no less than that of the great leaders I have witnessed among hundreds of events. While no man holds a monopoly in any particular subject, if one must choose only one prayer leader to study under, Doug Small would be who I would recommend without reservation.

Dr. Clyde M. Hughes, Director of Global Missions
International Pentecostal Church of Christ

Our hearts are passionate to see God's House transformed into a House of Prayer where Purifying Fire is released into those who attend. As we experience this transformation, we become fire starters throughout our spheres of influence. Doug Small is a humble powerful encourager. He has gathered information so that we can glean from tried and true intercessors. This book will inspire you in your journey to bring this power into your church.

Sarah Lowe, South Central National Area Leader;
National Day of Prayer Task Force

That Christians grasp the power and possibilities of prayer, know how to pray effectively, and pray regularly are great assumptions in the Church today. Sadly, they are often faulty assumptions. In *Transforming Your Church into a House of Prayer,* Doug Small unpacks the power, possibilities, and priority of prayer, and provides powerful insights and a wealth of instruction on mobilizing prayer individually and corporately.

John T. Maempa, member of the Assemblies of God Prayer Committee, PCCNA
Prayer Commission, and former director
of the AG Office of Prayer and Spiritual Care

Transforming Your Church Into a House of Prayer

Revised Edition

Transforming Your Church into a House of Prayer
Revised Edition

ISBN: 978-0-9986034-0-7

©Copyright 2018 by P. Douglas Small

Published by Alive Publications
a division of
Alive Ministries: PROJECT PRAY
PO Box 1245
Kannapolis, NC 28082

www.alivepublications.org
www.projectpray.org

Previous edition published by Pathway Press 2006

Dedication

This book is dedicated to my late grandfather and grandmother, Hoyt and Georgia Small – and to their generation. They modeled passionate prayer in the last stages of the era of the cottage prayer meeting. The sounds of their tearful prayers still echo in my heart. May God raise up an army like them.

CONTENTS

PREFACE

We are experiencing a prayer revival around the world – a movement that is sure to change the face of the church. It is epochal. Global. Unstoppable. It is not a fad. For three decades, the steady rise of voices around the earth, lifted to heaven, has been increasing. Heaven's throne room is filling up with the sound of intercession and the smell of incense. The voices flooding into it must sound, at times, like thunder. The earth – the whole earth – is being called to prayer.

The movement has been more pronounced in majority world nations. In places like Uganda, gripped by the tyranny of heartless leaders, a national revival erupted. Across the African continent, the call to prayer has summoned millions to fill stadiums for prayer, simultaneously. Nigeria is exploding with prayer and transformation. In Cali, Colombia, under the rule of the drug cartel, two decades ago, a revival swept the city drawing thousands into prayer gatherings, after which the back of the cartel was broken in that city. Argentina has likewise been affected by national renewal. In the northern provinces of Canada, revival has warmed hearts, stabilized families, affected teens, drawn in mayors, and is not only changing communities, but also the natural environment as well.

Are such stories overblown? Or is our faith in North America so diminished, so impoverished that we no longer believe change is possible? We have not seen a great awakening in our lifetime in this nation. What would it look like? What results would come with such a move of the Holy Spirit? The results in some 300 communities around the world are quantifiable, social and moral change, not only in the church, but in the surrounding culture.[1]

What is at the heart of change in these communities being visited by God? George Otis Jr. of the Sentinel Group, producer of the Transformation videos, says the common elements are unified, persistent prayer in a context of humility. The recipe is so simple. But in North America, we don't have the ingredients. The church here is divided – not merely into denominations, but culturally and ethically. Moral and social issues fragment and divide.There is a generational disconnect. Independent churches now number between 12 and 19 percent of America's Protestant congregations.[2]

Not only is there division, there is too little prayer. We lack a healthy theology of humble and united prayer. Our pride keeps us apart and hinders us from crying out to God with a sense of holy desperation. The warfare we face is disguised. The late David Wilkerson says our prosperity has become an obstacle to revival.

Luther had a dream on one occasion. In it he saw the devil on his throne listening to the reports of his agents and ambassadors regarding the progress they had made in opposing the truth of Christ and destroying the souls of men. According to the first report, a company of Christians had been crossing the desert. "I loosed the lions upon them," reported one spirit, "and soon the sands of the desert were strewn with their mangled corpses." Satan answered, "What of that? The lions destroyed their bodies, but their souls were saved. It is their souls I am after."

Another demon made his report, "A group of Christian pilgrims were sailing on the sea. I sent a great wind against the ship that drove them onto the rocks and drowned every Christian on board." Satan answered again, "What of it? Their bodies drowned in the sea, but their souls were saved. It is their souls I am after!"

A third came forward with his report, "For 10 years I have been trying to cast a Christian into a deep sleep, and at last I have succeeded." With that report, the corridors of hell rang with shouts of malignant triumph – and Luther awoke. And so did much of the church world, in the Reformation.[3]

There is no greater and clearer indication of a sleeping church than one that does not pray!

Jesus modeled prayer. And he taught on prayer. Until recently, the Bible colleges, Christian-funded universities and seminaries did neither, with a fractional exception. The theology books used in America's seminaries in the 1970s and 1980s don't mention prayer – 800 to 900 page texts ignore the place of prayer. Yet at least 10 percent of Biblical content is prayer! The volume of text given to prayer equals that of all the Minor Prophets, plus Lamentations, Ezekiel and Daniel. Still, we languish in our prayer training efforts. Less than five percent of congregations, according to our best data, have named a prayer coordinator or pastor.

Jesus taught on prayer. When he did, three times in three verses we find the phrase *"When you pray..."* (Matthew 6:5, 6, 7, emphasis added). After all he would do for them, it was inconceivable that they would not even talk to him in prayer after he had gone. It is astonishing that the church in much of the world does not talk regularly to God. Our so-called worship events are designed so that we sing about God and hear teaching and preaching about God, but we do little talking to God in prayer. And we rarely, if ever, wait before Him to hear what He might say to us as a congregation. Luther says prayer is "the real calling of all Christians." Andrew Murray says that prayer is the "highest part of the work entrusted to us, the root and strength of all other work."[4]

FOREWORD

If all you need are a few ideas and methods to help you promote your under-attended prayer meetings, you might find a few good things in this book. Some books are designed like menus, to be read and used à la carte. And some readers, mistaking this book for a menu of methods, might merely scan through it in order to pick out a few ideas that sound good.

But if you have read this far, you are probably truly hungry for something you might not be able to describe. You are not alone if you find yourself yearning for God's transforming Presence throughout whole communities. Everything God has done so far in history is an appetizer. In these days, many are setting aside church program cookbooks and proven recipes for minor revivals. We are desperate for something massive – something global and something soon.

We are yearning to be filled with what we will never fully contain. We are bored with small doses of spiritual energy that can be conjured or captured or contained in scripted church services. We want an outpouring from heaven that is so vast it will overwhelm every house and hall, penetrate every marketplace and jurisdiction, and bring life to every circle and setting of humanity.

Instead of trying to get more of God in our churches, this book is about God filling the earth with His glory. Instead of formulas to get God to help us execute our programs, this book is a call of God to join Him in fulfilling His purposes by prayer. You will find many suggestions, a lot of ideas, an array of different models; but the heart of this book is a call of God to pray. It's not just a call to pray more. It's a call to pray sufficiently to fulfill God's purpose.

Transforming Your Church Into a House of Prayer echoes something we are all hearing: God is changing more than our circumstances. God is calling us to change. Douglas Small declares that the Reformation is still on. God is still changing His church. One of the primary changes rapidly accelerating is how we pray. You might overlook a fairly radical sentence in the earliest pages: "The whole earth is being called to prayer." If God is calling the whole earth, then He is certainly calling His church to prayer.

We are not being changed involuntarily or automatically. God honors us too greatly to force Himself on us. We are being called. We can ignore God's call, but if we respond, we can have confidence that we will become the people of prayer God has long purposed to bring forth for this amazing hour of His coming kingdom.

What kind of changes are in store for our churches? First would be the very idea of what prayer is all about. The standard notion of prayer is something that is done before we do something for God. In this book you'll find that prayer is the core of how we might ever do something with God.

Another change of our standard way of thinking is to anticipate that God is calling His entire people to pray. No longer should we be satisfied with intercessors and prayer warriors doing all the praying. A regrettable, unintended consequence of the emphasis on intercessors in recent years has been that a few expert intercessors are expected to do most of the praying in many churches. Doug Small offers helpful models and balanced ideas to strengthen the place and work of intercessors. As we respond to the compelling call of God, we can expect to be part of churches where everyone intercedes – not just a few anointed leaders.

In addition to who will be praying, another change to expect is what we'll be praying about. God is calling us to pray with persistence toward His purposes being fulfilled in our communities. It is no longer sufficient to pray about a few requests that focus prayers on emergencies and momentary needs. We are bored by praying small "answerables" that might help our churches become bigger or our crisis circumstances to become better. God is summoning us to pray for great things with a long look. We're going to find ourselves following our own prayers into tremendous fulfillments of the Great Commandment and the once-in-history finishing of the Great Commission.

Small's vision and passion are anything but small. He is always about great things. Every time I am around him, I find my heart is enlarged to act boldly in expectation that God is about to do something great. You will sense an experiential authority in what he says. This is not a dream sheet or a brainstorm. The author has been working in many cities and churches for decades. He has seen programs come and go. He has been seasoned by setbacks, but he has also been tempered to a resilient hope by the prayers and partnership of many pastors and leaders. He has seen that of which he speaks.

Hold this book close to the ears of your heart. See if you don't hear the God of all the earth calling you, along with the whole earth, to pray. As you answer the call of God with others, you will find yourself moving on mission with God by prayer.

– Steve Hawthorne

Steve Hawthorne leads a prayer and mission mobilization group called WayMakers, located in Austin, Texas. He is the author of the widely used prayer guide called *Seek God for the City,* newly written each year to guide prayers of biblical hope during the 40 days to Palm Sunday. He co-authored the book *Prayerwalking: Praying On-Site with Insight* with Graham Kendrick. He is the lead editor of the book and course called *Perspectives* on the World Christian Movement. He holds a PhD from Fuller Seminary's School of Intercultural Studies.

1   This is according to a report given at the Transform World Conference in Indonesia, May 2005, by George Otis Jr. of the Sentinel Group.

2   Hartford Institute for Religion and Research: Study by Ammerman, Lummis, Roozen & Thumma, "Organizing Religious Work Project – 1997-98," indicating the number of nondenominational/independent churches at 12 percent of all churches; Study by Mark Chaves, "National Congregations Study – 1998," indicating the number of nondenominational/independent churches at 19 percent of all churches but drawing only 11 percent of all attenders. See hirr.hartsem.edu/org/faith_congregations_nondenom_estimates.html.

3   R. Kent Hughes, *1001 Great Stories and Quotes* (Wheaton, IL: Tyndale, 1998) 122.

4   Quotes in Philip Graham Ryken, *When You Pray* (Wheaton, IL: Crossway, 2000) 12.

SEVEN MARKERS OF A PRAYING CHURCH

1. Led by *a praying pastor, aided by a prayer leadership team*, we commit to bring prayer to the heart of all we do!

2. We will encourage *at-home, daily, Jesus-be-Jesus-in-me praying.* We will reestablish our personal and family altars.

3. We will call our congregation to *regular prayer,* with the goal of establishing a regular weekly prayer meeting for the entire church.

4. We will honor those who carry a special calling to pray – *intercessors.* We will identify intercessors, encourage them, train them, team them, deploy them and debrief them.

5. We will *engage in prayer evangelism, turning prayer outward* onto the neighborhood, the city, state and nation, and we will adopt a mission field for prayer, one near and one far.

6. We will *offer regular training in the area of prayer* – for our people, leaders, intercessors, prayer evangelism, our youth and children, our families.

7. We will *work toward the creation of a prayer room or center,* a physical space dedicated to prayer at our church, and we will encourage the use of such a space by members and prayer groups.

TEN PRAYER VALUES
What we believe and how we behave:

- **We value prayer;** *therefore, we will feature prayer in our worship and make prayer a central element of all ministry.*

- **We are a praying people;** *therefore, we will nurture at-home daily prayer,* family prayer, husband-wife, parent-child prayer connections, providing resources, training and nudging new and old Christians to deepen their prayer lives.

- **We believe that we are a kingdom of priests** and that prayer and worship is our highest calling, and that as priests, we are not only recipients of blessing, but the conveyors of blessing; *therefore, in prayer, we commit to pray for the favor and blessing of God upon others;* for protective care, upon our pastor, the church staff, the church family, our city and our nation. *We bless,* we do not curse. We ask God not for what we deserve, but for blessing – for continued grace and mercy!

- **We value holiness and righteousness** as the mark of God upon a people, and we recognize that the church desperately needs revival and our nation needs a great awakening; *therefore, we regularly and consistently cry out to God for revival in the church and a great awakening* for our nation.

- **We believe in the power of petition,** that God answers when people pray rightly; *therefore, we faithfully take the needs of the church, one another, the city and the world before the throne of God and ask for grace!* We provide a means whereby requests for prayer are taken seriously and held up in prayer persistently, beseeching God expectantly for an answer.

- **We believe in the power of God through intercession;** _therefore, we identify, train, team and mobilize intercessors_ for the undergirding of the ministries of the Church, and for the support of the various mission endeavors of the congregation.

- **We believe that prayer is essential to the success of every endeavor,** that without Him we can do nothing, and whatever we do in His behalf without dependence upon Him is less than it might have been, given dependence in prayer; _therefore, our rule is no one works unless someone prays!_

- **We believe that the reception of the gospel unto salvation is a spiritual issue;** _therefore, we pray for the harvest,_ that blind eyes will be open to the gospel, ears will be enabled to hear and receive the truth of Christ: hearts may be receptive to the good news that goes forth in power out of prayer.

- **We believe that there is a definitive connection between prayer and the harvest;** _therefore, we insist that prayer must have a missional dimension,_ that we must pray for lost loved ones, for the unreached in our city and the world.

- **We believe, "God governs the world by the prayers of His people;"** _therefore, we pray for our city, state and national leaders._ We pray about world conditions and various global crises. We invite God's intervening reign. We pray, _"Thy Kingdom come, thy will be done."_

ONE
A New Reformation: Transforming Your Church Into a House of Prayer

I sincerely believe that we are now in the beginning stages of the greatest movement of prayer in living memory.

— Peter Wagner

Whenever God sets about to do a new thing, he always sets his people praying.[1]

— J. Edwin Orr

A church becomes institutionalized when its members are related primarily to it as an institution rather than to Christ.[2]

— Richard Thomas

Everywhere Paul went there was a revolution, while everywhere I go they serve tea.[3]

— An English Bishop

A new reformation is taking place around the world! The church is being called by the Holy Spirit to prayer! Five hundred years ago, Luther's reformation was developed around the rallying cries of "the priesthood of all believers," along with *"Sola Fidei"* (salvation by faith alone) and *"Sola Scriptura"* (the authority of Scripture alone contrasted with the traditions of the church).

Luther's authority for the now 500-year protest was in the high and lofty place he gave to the sacred writings we call the Bible. The Bible became the cornerstone of the Reformation in an attempt to bring the church back to the simple center of objective Scriptural authority, displacing the encumbrances of tradition and the strong and singular arm of papal rule.

But the lasting impact of the Reformation in much of the Evangelical-Pentecostal world has been to make *preaching the centerpiece* of the weekly worship event. It is doubtful that this was what Luther had in mind. Lutheran architecture and ecclesiology keeps the altar table central, not the pulpit. The manifestly transforming principle of the Reformation was, in its multiple mega-shifts – from the church to Christ, from tradition to Biblical authority and revelation, from works to grace and faith, to "the priesthood of all believers!"

Only in prayer does the Scripture ultimately come to life. And only by prayer does faith appropriate vitality and life. Prayer was at the critical center of Luther's life and the Reformation. He said,

> In a typical day I am charged with the pastorate of three congregations. I teach regularly at the seminary. I have students living with me in my house. I am writing three books. Countless people write to me. When I start each day, therefore, I make it a point to spend an hour in prayer with God. But, if I have a particularly busy day and I am more rushed than usual, I make it a point to spend two hours with God before I start the day.[4]

Such a daily practiced discipline has been lost to much of the church world. In America, surveys indicate that the average believer prays less than four minutes a day. The average time a pastor prays was an abysmal five minutes a day two decades ago. That figure is now up to 30 minutes. Robert McCheyne warns, "Give yourselves to prayer and the ministry of the Word. If you do not pray, God will probably lay you aside from your ministry, as He did me, to teach you to pray."[5]

Finishing the Reformation

Something has gone wrong with the Reformation. We have lost the intended element of every believer as a functioning priest, walking in communion with God, guided by the authority of Scripture. Sadly, some Christians allow their church to stand in the place of the personal, daily relationship with Christ.

That cannot be! It is our relationship with Christ himself, not His bride, the church, that defines us as true disciples. Luther's passion was to remove any obstacle that kept the common man from experiencing the life of God, His Word, and walking in on-going communion with Him. That must now become our passion. It is time for a new reformation.

What could the church in North America do with $500 billion? According to George Barna, that is the amount spent on ministry in the U.S. in the last 15 years.[6] With such an incredible capital outlay, half of America's churches did add one member through conversion.[7]

Win Arn has noted for years that almost 85 percent of our churches have plateaued. Barna says that only one percent grow through conversions. Another 14 percent grow through transfer from the declining and dying congregations around them.[8]

Twenty-five or so years ago we began to see a shocking rash of church closures – thousands in the course of a year. Despite an aggressive church planting effort, the net gain contrasted by the perpetual time growth shows the church losing significant ground. Congregations are graying and young pastors are not replacing them in the pews. Now, we are closing 4,000-7,000 churches annually,[9] perhaps more. One assessment suggests that as many as 40,000 churches are in the last stages of dying. Money is not our problem, nor is management or a host of other so-called fixes being offered to the struggling church. What do we need?

Making Prayer the Center

First, we need a reformation of personal Christian disciplines – one that sees daily prayer as indispensable to the life of the believer, without displacing participation in a local fellowship of believers. Christianity cannot be a solo affair. It requires participation in the body of Christ. And, yet, believers should not substitute life at the center of their own heart, in a life-nurturing church, for a personal, daily walk with God.

Second, we need a reformation that brings prayer to the heart of the church and its corporate life, without displacing the primacy of Scripture. Good prayer is linked to Scripture. It rises out of Scripture. Encounters with the Bible should lead us to pray, to cry out to God that the Spirit of the Word – Christ – would become flesh again in us. Prayer is the means by which the objective truth of Scripture becomes incarnational truth – fleshed out in our lives.

Without prayer, Scriptural knowledge remains a head issue, not a heart cry. We may attempt, by sheer will, to live as we are commanded in the Scripture, but we cannot live supernatural lives with natural energy. We read – and we pray. The more we *pray* about what we have *read,* the more what we have read is laced into our lives by the Holy Spirit. The more we *prayerfully read,* the more understanding we have when we read. Suddenly, the Scripture is no longer so difficult to understand. Its truth comes alive. We see the personal implications of behavior for our own lives. The Bible then becomes a force for the Christ-life within us.

What About Us?

Americans typically settle into a congregation for nurture and growth. But the church is not for us and our comfort alone. It also exists for the city and the sea of ethnic people who live around us. We violate Biblical principles when we make the church about us and prayer so exclusively a private privilege. The church as a house of prayer *for the nations* must engage the culture, indeed the world, around us.

We have privatized faith – making worship and prayer a personal and pietistic thing. Jesus is stretching us. Prayer belongs to the nations. The church must not only pray through its windows for the world outside but, by prayer, be thrust into the harvest to invite people to come meet the Creator, the God of Israel, the Christ of the church. We must take prayer to the streets, give the gift of prayer to unbelievers and to the city itself. We must leave the fragrance of incense on every corner in the city where we have prayed (1 Tim. 2:8).

If we, like Israel, shut up the Kingdom for ourselves (see Matthew 23:13), we will lose the blessing and favor of God. He will pack up His glory and leave. God is doing a work *in* us in order that He might do a work through us. At the heart of that transformational process is prayer. It cannot be prayer for our narrow slice of pain, but prayer that engages the cosmic and timeless purposes of God.

Worship is the heart of prayer. But neither prayer nor worship can be about styles and culture, about personal preferences for music and preaching techniques. The new reformation must bring us into a personal encounter with God in which communion with Him becomes a constant feature in our lives.

We *"pray without ceasing"* (1 Thessalonians 5:17). We live out of His Presence, in unbroken fellowship with Him. This makes life bigger than our typically narrow world. It calls us to live beyond ourselves. It centers us in Christ, seeking to honor and glorify him in word and deed. And to live with others in view! It cultivates a missional view of life.

God has purposes for each of us that can only be discovered in prayer. No seminar can teach it; no book can reveal it. Families and congregations have purposes – as do cities and nations. By mission, we do not mean only the world far away, but the friends and family around us. Prayer wakes us up to the needs of our world and beyond. It empowers us to make a difference.

A Reformation of Transformational and Missional Prayer

Seven things must change if the church is going to embrace the new reformation:

1. *The preached Word must also become the prayed Word.* We integrate truth into our lives not merely by having it proclaimed and then attempting to obey. Rather, it's by hearing and seizing it prayerfully, asking the Holy Spirit to incarnate this truth into our lives. We must teach our people to *pray Scripture* – first, for the transformation of their own lives at the level of character and godliness, and second, for direction of their lives as a witness to the resurrected Christ. The new model must allow time for congregations to process in prayer the taught Word from the Lord. Teach it. Then pray it.

Two-thirds of pastors acknowledge that revival is the most pressing need of the American church.[10] But prayer, the clearest and surest way to revival, is consistently ignored. We will never preach our way to revival. Nor can we program revival. Revival comes on the wings of prayer.

2. *Prayer must be modeled by church leadership.* The cry across America is not for more great preachers, but for "holy men of God." Nothing purifies a life more than time with a holy God. Congregations must release their pastors to prayer. The apostles appointed deacons over the encroaching daily work of the fellowship and recommitted themselves to prayer and the Word. The result was unity in the place of division, and church growth in the place of stagnation (Acts 6:1-7). A new kind of leader must emerge – pastors after God's heart, who are men of prayer.

Sadly, prayer is not a priority in congregations, in terms of what they see as important, either in their lives or the life of their pastor. Prayer does not even make the list of desirable attributes used as a measure of the ideal pastor by the typical pastoral search teams.[11] Pastors sell themselves to search committees and congregations by required skill sets – preaching, teaching, administration, leadership and more – not by their practice of spiritual disciplines. Pastors must learn not only the power of secret prayer, but also the power of prayer with other men of like heart and passion. Pastors should seek out others who are giving themselves to prayer and the Word, not only on behalf of their congregation, but on behalf of the city they are called to serve.

The era of the pastor as administrator-technician has failed. Spread over a dozen roles for which he was neither called nor equipped, the typical pastor has lost his way and his church is failing. His call was not primarily to the church office – his call was to Christ, to follow him, walk with him, learn from him and teach others the ways of God. We need, again, holy men of God who bury themselves in prayer and boldly preach a fresh word from God. Enoch, Noah, Abraham, Moses, Joshua, Hannah, Samuel, David, Elijah, Daniel, Nehemiah, Ezra, Zechariah – all were devoted to prayer. Samuel declared, *"Far be it from me that I should sin against the Lord by failing to pray for you"* (1 Samuel 12:23, NIV). The absence of prayer by leaders is not merely a weakness or a pastoral disadvantage, it is a sin![12]

"The prayer life of the church will seldom rise above the pastor's personal example and commitment" to pray.[13] There is no such thing as private prayer, only prayer in private. Prayer is a part of the public record in heaven. Prayer will never be a purely personal thing. The chief thing for a pastor is not preaching; it is prayer. It is not the pulpit, but the prayer closet. The two – prayer closet and pulpit are joined. Preaching opens doors of the prayer closet; it is the public overflow of private time with God over an open Bible. The effect of personal prayer will always spill out into the church and community. Pastors and people who pray at home will get together just to pray. The record of corporate prayer meetings decorates the Book of Acts (1:14, 24; 2:1, 42; 3:1; 4:24-31; 6:4-6; 12:5-12; 13:1-3; 14:23; 16:13, 16; 20:36; 21:5).

New believers learn to pray by being in prayer meetings (2:42). Why would Luke document such an extensive record of corporate prayer? The Holy Spirit is showing us the connection between corporate prayer and explosive church growth. In Acts, prayer is not something done at meetings, *before* or *after* meetings, *during* meetings, *for* meetings, at the *beginning* or *ending* of meetings – prayer was the *purpose* of the meeting itself.

If the church is to be a praying church, the pastor must lead by calling the church to prayer in public gatherings. There is no substitute for corporate prayer meetings.

3. *We must practice prayer publicly.* Surprisingly, few people who attend church in America have a Biblical worldview. Faith

is an additive to a lifestyle and perception that is largely secular. A significant number of our homes have few or no markings of practiced faith. These people are spiritually underdeveloped, to say the least. Many are unstable in their faith. Their kids are fleeing the church. The divorce rate among Christians in the United States is now slightly higher than nonchurch-going folks. People acknowledge that they lack a vital connection with God, even at corporate worship events.[14] Evangelical Pentecostal services settle for passive participation. They offer too few opportunities for engagement – particularly in prayer.

4. *The practice of corporate prayer should enrich the personal, private, at-home, daily habit of prayer.* The more people are praying at home, the more powerful and richer and deeper the ministry of corporate prayer will become when we gather together. The two are symbiotic. Public praying must offer models that enrich and encourage personal prayer. As people with a deepening personal prayer life gather together to cry out to God, powerful public prayer meetings will take place. The public and private are connected. You cannot have one without the other. They enrich and drive each other.

Caution! Make prayer simple. The resistance to pray by many American Christians is rooted in fear. They often feel they do not know *how* to pray. There is a reason. First, the average Christian who steps into an Evangelical-Pentecostal gathering of intercessors, may encounter a style of prayer that is bold and powerful, passionate and quite out-of-the-box. It is not a bad thing to be exposed to passionate intercession, but we should not exalt a style of prayer as either the goal for all or the optimum prayer style.

Second, public praying is sometimes flowery, loaded with theological terms and unfamiliar 'God-talk.' Our liturgy and language is strange and unfamiliar to the routine of daily life. Richly articulated prayer with the depth and breadth of good theology inspires. However, we must not make the acquisition of theological language a prerequisite for prayer, or we will place an obstruction in the pathway of those beginning their prayer journeys. Neither intercessory expertise nor theological language should be a prerequisite for a prayer life.

Practice authentic prayer in public. Use ordinary conversational language aimed at the heart of God. People learn to pray by praying and by hearing others pray. Passion should not displace rational, Scripture based praying. Nor should Biblically grounded prayers leave out the heart. If we encourage prayer language, which is little more than rhetoric, our people may learn to repeat religious phrases, thinking they are praying. This is what Jesus condemned. A mouth full of words or sounds is not prayer. Model authentic praying.

5. *We need a better theology of prayer.* In the typical Evangelical Pentecostal worship service, prayer is usually about petitioning God for personal needs – sickness, emergencies, problems. Prayer time is a recital by people who are not only riddled with needs, but are also in despair. The litany of needs, Sunday after Sunday, is depressing. It speaks of lives nearly out of control, and a God who seems foreign and uninvolved. Rather than build faith, such prayer times discourage faith. The reason? Our prayer times begin at the wrong place, and they end at the wrong place.

The best prayer begins, not with self, but with God in all of His glory. It sees Him whose hand is not shortened, whose ear is not heavy (Isaiah 59:1). Only when we climb the mountain and get a clear view of Him will we have the faith to face life's fears (40:9).

Start your prayer time with a celebration of who God is. Gratitude opens the gateway to grace. Thank God. Worship Him sincerely, not as if you were attempting to prime Him for power. Rather love Him authentically. Remember the greatest answer to prayer is not an answer, but laying hold of the One who is *the Answer.* He is the place of lasting peace. Once people sense God's Presence, faith rises. There is assurance that He is our deliverer, whether He delivers us from or through the situation. Only then should we move to petition and intercession.

Petition is the privilege of prayer, but it is not the center of prayer. Prayer, at its heart is worship; and at its edge mission, and in between, God meets our needs.

Without having the certain sense of His love in prayer, we are only making a noise. And without praying for those who have never experienced His liberating love, we have shut up the Kingdom and made it about ourselves. Begin prayer with worship of Him. Intercede for others. Find a place for your needs in between. Prayer must be worshipful at its center and missional at its edge. Close the prayer with praise that anticipates an answer. Celebrate with heartfelt assurance that we have been heard, as Jesus did (John 11:41, 42).

6. *We must embrace the discipline of prayer until we again know the delight of prayer.* This means spending regular extended times in prayer. Most of the time we rush into prayer without quieting our hearts. And then we rush through prayer. We must learn to linger in the Presence of God until He comes. And when God comes into a prayer and worship experience, both sinners and saints know His Presence. In a culture addicted to busyness, this is no small assignment.

When we are too busy to pray, we are too busy – too worldly. We characterize wordliness as a list of naughty words and phrases, images or activities, of cultural styles and paradigms. Those are manisfestations of worldliness. Its more profound hold on us is evident in our inability to break free of its grip to engage the world on top of this world. We do not take time to pray. When we do pray, it is often on the run. Escaping the 'hold' of this world to rest in God daily, to get apart from the world before we come apart, demands consistent, quality time in prayer. Such moments with God instill quiet and peace at the center of our soul. It insures a higher quality of life, not only spiritually, but in every way.

Prayer is the great equalizer for our lives. It is the means of bringing life into harmony with God, and living in heaven's rhythm. Without it, we bog down in visionless routines or we spin out of control, our lives moving far too fast with too many programs and people to track. The central discipline of our lives is prayer. But if it is only a discipline, we will have a joyless ministry. The *discipline* of prayer must become the *delight* of our lives.

Be certain of this: No relationship with a church – no matter how glorious the choir or how engaging the preacher – can take the place of a personal, intimate relationship with the living Christ. You cannot satisfy your relationship with Christ by relating to His bride, the church. Without realizing it, we have engaged in a style of Christianity in which the church has replaced personal intimacy with Christ. Loving the church is not the same as loving Christ. Going to church, even regularly, does not ensure a vital connection to Christ. It is cultural Christianity at best and apostasy at worst.

Our people must learn the power of His Presence. We cannot, with God's help, allow them to live from Sunday to Sunday. Such a church will never change the world. Short prayer times engender shallow encounters with God. Arrange for extended seasons of prayer. Don't fear quiet; don't quench passion. Dedicate whole services to prayer. Arrange for extended prayer retreats modeled on prayer summits[15] – aimed at experiencing God's Presence personally and corporately.

7. *We need to identify intercessors – those who have a special call to prayer and grace to pray.* These people have a heart-altar full of prayer-fire. Use them to encourage a culture of prayer in

the church. Don't merely foster more prayer activities. Healthy intercessors are those who have learned to live in communion with God in prayer. They move from worship to warfare, then praise to petition, from lament to resolution. That is the climate you want to see imparted to the whole of the congregation – again, a culture of prayer out of worshipful communion.

Not all intercessors are healthy. Those who are will be characterized by a spirit of humility and deep dependence upon God. Their immediate reaction to any need or crisis is to pray. They depend upon God for wisdom and guidance, for power and provision. They have a strange mixture of gentleness and grit. Their soft, steel-like character is a reflection of Christ, the Lamb who is also the Lion.

What difference would it make to identify and mobilize intercessors, partnering them with specific people? One prayer leader developed a five-hour course to train intercessors, teaching them how to pray for pastors and ministry leaders. After the course, intercessors were given a one-year assignment to pray for a ministry leader. After that year, 89 percent of the 130 pastors, evangelists and missionaries that had been prayed for indicated a positive change in ministry effectiveness. The intercessors had prayed for them only 15 minutes a day.[16]

Few congregations will make progress in prayer without identifying and training intercessors. What church can develop a choir without gathering singers and musicians? It is impossible. No church can develop a serious prayer ministry without teaming those who have a special call to prayer – intercessors.

We must add to prayer – harvest eyes! Only two percent of pastors can identify God's vision for the ministry they lead. Few members have a Biblical worldview.[17] Without a vision the people perish (Proverbs 29:18). We need a vision of the harvest that results in an intentional prayer evangelism emphasis. We cannot turn inward, making prayer about ourselves. Our cry must be that of Jesus, *"My house shall be called a house of prayer – for the nations!"* (see Mark 11:17).

Prayer must embrace those for whom Christ died who have not yet come to salvation. The church as an intercessory agency – a corporate intercessor – stands in every community as a bridge between lost men and God, between communities that carry out daily functions without God and a God who longs to bless cities, to be glorified in and by our cities. The failure of the church to bless its community and invite God's intervention is one of its major failings. We see ourselves as powerless. We are conflicted – do we become a political force to change culture? If not, what do we do? Sit helplessly by and watch? There is another way.

Peter declared that we are a *royal priesthood* (1 Peter 2:9). As priests, we pray. But what does it mean to be a royal priesthood? A *kingly* priesthood? God, it seems, governs the world by the prayers of His people. The Greek word translated intercession in 1 Tim. 2:1, means to meet a king. There is a kingly dimension to prayer to which we have failed to fulfill. On our knees, before the King of Glory, there and there alone, we call Him to His rightful place in our world. We rule by praying. And with the very act of prayer, we invite the rule of Christ. Through prayer, He asserts His rightful claim on our communities. We become, in that process alone, His ambassadors to a lost world. Andrew Murray says, "The power of the Church to truly bless rests on intercession – asking and receiving heavenly gifts to carry to men."[18]

The obligation of the kingdom of priests is to daily invite God's kingly rule into our time-space world, "Thy kingdom come, Thy will be done in our city, Lord." And of course, the greatest desire of God is that men should be saved, that they would come to know Him. *"The Lord is not slack concerning His promise, as some count slackness, but is longsuffering toward us, not willing that any should perish but that all should come to repentance"* (2 Peter 3:9).

Every Christian should be praying regularly for friends and family, neighbors and workplace associates, that they come to know God. People of influence in the community should be adopted by congregations and intercessors for prayer. Every place of pain and promise in the community should be the focus of ongoing prayer. The harvest will not come in unless it is first "prayed in!" Jesus called the Father *"the Lord of the harvest"* and commanded us *"to pray"* until we were thrust forth by the Lord, into the harvest field (Matthew 9:38). Prayer changes us for the harvest. And prayer readies the harvest for reaping.

The longing of the disciples was to learn to pray. I believe that is the secret longing of every true believer. Luther warned, "He who does not pray is no Christian!" Beware of the folks who want to hang out with the church group, be members of the board and leaders of ministries, but do not answer the call to prayer. Carnal Christians avoid prayer. Yet prayer is the distinguishing mark of a true believer. Genuine Christians will want to live in unbroken fellowship with the Father and walk "in the Spirit." True believers want *"Christ in [them], the hope of glory"* (Colossians 1:27) to break out through conversations, in life decisions, and reveal himself alive in and through them. This is prayer!

My House Shall Be Called a House of Prayer for the Nations

It was the desire of Jesus that the Temple be a house of prayer for the nations. Instead, it was full of religious activities with the priests in their rich garments, the expensive sacrificial ceremonies, the formality of the pomp and priestly procedures, the rituals and rites of cleansing and consecration, all without free repentance and restitution. In the midst of all the elaborate and sacred ceremonies – the blowing of the shofar, the fire and smoke, the blood of the altar and the water of the laver – the wonder of all the symbolic action, the simplicity of communion with God, had been lost. Getting to God had become a complicated maze.

The money changers extracted an enormous surcharge from those with foreign money who needed to make change to pay their offerings of restitution or vows of consecration. The sheep merchants had also inflated the price of the approved lambs. Those with meager means who wanted to offer a burnt or peace offering (Leviticus 1; 3), and who needed to offer a sin or trespass offering (chs. 4; 5) could hardly afford to do so.

These common and poor people wanted to get to the altar to get right with God. Some wanted to consecrate themselves and then offer to God the peace offering (ch. 3). From that offering, the priest would return to them a portion of the sacrifice, according to the Law, and allow them to eat it in the Presence of God as a symbol of their fellowship and union with Him (7:15-18). But the Temple system placed obstacles loaded with exorbitant fees between the people and God. To purchase the lamb, they needed to exchange their foreign money. Upon exchange, they met excessive fees. With reduced funds, they encountered inflated prices for the sacrificial lambs. Much of the time, the lambs they brought could not pass inspection. They didn't qualify as perfect enough for an offering. It was all a rip-off.

Jesus thunders through the Temple, overturning tables: *"My house shall be called a house of prayer"* (Matthew 21:12, 13; Mark 11:15-17). He was a prophet, crying out, not against the exchange of currency or the availability of lambs in the Temple, but against the obstacles that prevented the people from praying, against the arrangement that put a price on prayer and access to the grace of God.

But there is more! When we quote this passage, we often leave off the phrase *"for all nations."* No prayer ministry is complete unless it has a global and missional focus. It was incarnational, global and missional praying that Jesus longed for in the Temple. Jerusalem was to be a blessing for and to the nations. The call to Abraham was that through him all the nations of the earth would be blessed (Genesis 22:18).

Learning From History

We rarely mention the fact that Jesus was quoting from Isaiah 56:7. That chapter is a judgment speech, rehearsed by Isaiah for the captives returning from Babylon. It was meant to be an explanation of why the judgment came that destroyed the Temple, wasted Jerusalem and carried them into captivity, and an exhortation to not repeat the same mistake their fathers had made.

Jesus shouted loudly in the Temple, and the effect of His message was clear: "You have made the same mistake as your fathers! You will experience the same consequences as your fathers – a dismantled Temple, a decimated city, and new *diaspora* of the nation."

It all happened. The armies of Rome came, the Temple was destroyed, the city was demolished, and the Jews were scattered. Why? They had failed to make the Temple *a house of prayer for all nations.* Is the church relieved of such judgment if we fail in the same way?

Isaiah details the problem:

Israel's watchmen are blind, the whole lot of them. They have no idea what's going on. They're dogs without sense enough to bark, lazy dogs, dreaming in the sun – but hungry dogs, they do know how to eat, voracious dogs, with never enough. And these are Israel's shepherds! They know nothing, understand nothing. They all look after themselves, grabbing whatever's not nailed down. "Come," they say, "let's have a party. Let's go out and

get drunk!" And tomorrow, more of the same: "Let's live it up!"
(56:10-12, TM).

Here the roles of pastor and intercessor are fused into one! "Israel's *watchmen* are blind and these are Israel's *shepherds!"* They are one! It is true that the shepherd both leads and feeds the flock, but there is a greater role upon which the functions of guidance and nurture are based – it is the role of 'watching.' And watching is a metaphor for intercessory prayer. No one can be a pastor *without being an intercessor.* It is part and parcel of the job. Here leadership and prayer are linked. Feeding and nurture too rise out of prayer. The problem is clear. A lack of prayer by leaders produces eyes that do not discern, watchmen over the city that do not sound a warning in the night; lazy and undisciplined leaders; and self-centered, self-seeking leaders who use ministry for personal gain. They lack the spiritual understanding gained only in prayer. They are self-promoting graspers, not givers. A party spirit has replaced a culture of prayer and the consequence is that judgment comes. This is a hard word – and one sadly applicable to far too many modern pastors.

In the verses prior to the dismal description of these prayerless leaders, there is an inclusive standard set for the new Temple. Isaiah holds forth the standards of justice and righteousness (56:1). His call for sensitivity to holy days is the reminder that reverence for God must be integrated into the rhythm of our lives. It is the principle of regular worship and spiritual rest (v. 2). Life cannot be lived so that time for the holy is omitted. Out of the principle of justice and and righteousness laced with the practice of worship and rest:

- He calls for *action faith:* "Blessed is the man who does this [salvation and righteousness]."

- He calls for *restraint from evil: "…and keeps his hand from doing any evil"* (v. 2, emphasis added).

Holiness is *behavioral;* it is both *doing* and *not doing.* The mention of the Sabbath (worshipful rest) is between these two – the *doing* of righteousness and the *not doing* evil. Here is the principle:

No keeping of a holy day is successful unless it is coupled with a holy life. No keeping of the Temple, or church, is successful unless it produces a worshipping community that *does* righteousness and justice, and is a *restraining* influence against evil works.

This transformational community is to be open to the nations. It cannot be exclusive for a faithful few. There is to be free admission for all. So the *son of the foreigner,* the immigrant, can come

---

GOD'S DESIRE FOR HIS PEOPLE

- God desires people whose worship is evidenced in their walk and in their ways (Isa 56:7).
- God desires people who are embracing others (the principle of reconciliation) inside and outside Israel (foreigners; immigrants) (vs.3-7)

GOD'S DESIRE FOR HIS HOUSE

- God wants His house to be house of prayer for all people and for people to know him (v. 7).

God Desires His People to Reflect to His Nature

- God is a gatherer (a reconciler). He wants the outcast accepted, the fallen restored, an inclusive harvesting church (v. 8).

These Desires are Not Reflected in Leaders

- God wants leaders to prayfully lead this process. If they don't, the mission will fail and judgment will come (vs. 9-12).

Christ comes and announces – Judgment has Come!

(Isaiah 56:3). Not so in the pre-exilic Temple or in that of the first century. Further, the *eunuch* can come (vv. 3-5) if he keeps the Sabbath, makes godly choices, and holds fast to the covenant. Considered less than whole, any deformed person was barred from the Temple proper. Now the formerly excluded, the less than whole, the outsider, were celebrated insiders. This is the purpose of the church as a worshipping missional community, a house of prayer for the nations.

Isaiah declares a new standard, and Jesus echoes that inclusive "whosoever will" standard. No foreign outsider or excluded insider who now desired to know the true God can be barred from access to the Temple. This is to be a new day for Israel. They are to be a light to the nations – a missionary people to all peoples. It did not happen. Israel shut up the Kingdom (Matthew 23:13) and made the Temple about themselves. And judgment came.

Look at the Structure — What I want! – the prescription!

- **1- 2 *Behavior Matters*** – Keep justice, do righteousness. You are blessed if you do this. Keep the Sabbath and restrain evil. *Worship must affect one's walk and ways.*
  - **3-7d MISSION:** *You* be agents of reconciliation – Give faith away. Don't let anyone say, "The Lord has separated me …"

  - **7e MY HOUSE SHALL BE A HOUSE OF PRAYER FOR THE NATIONS!** What will be! pronouncement!

  - **8 MISSION:** The Lord will be an agent of reconciliation – "The Lord will gather … outcast of Israel and others!"
- **9 - 12 *Behavior Matters*** - God calls for judgment. The reason? The leaders are not godly, praying leaders who will fulfill the vision of Israel as the gathering/uniting and healing nation! They are corrupt and self-indulgent. They are blind, uninformed, and silent. Isa. 56

The movement of the Isaiah passage is simple:

- *Behavior Matters.* Sabbath-keepers must be righteous and restrain from evil ways. Worship must affect one's walk and ways (vv. 1, 2).

- *Evangelism/Mission. You* be inclusive and give this faith away. Don't let anyone say, "The Lord has separated me..." (vv. 3-7). Draw circles, not lines.

- "My house shall be...a house of prayer for all nations" (v. 7).

- *Mission-Evangelism.* The Lord will be inclusive – "The Lord will gather...(the) outcasts of Israel and others" (see v. 8).

- *Behavior Matters.* God calls for judgment because the leaders are not godly, praying leaders who will fulfill the vision! They are corrupt and self-indulgent (vv. 9-12).

The thesis of Isaiah 56: When the behavior of God's people and the condition of His house are contrary to His nature and not being reflected by leaders, then judgement comes!

Andrew Murray wrote:

Christ actually meant prayer to be the great power by which his church should do its work, and that the neglect of prayer is the great reason the church has not greater power over the masses in Christian and heathen countries.[19]

Eugene Peterson levels a stunning challenge in the book *Working the Angles:*

American pastors are abandoning their posts, left and right, and at an alarming rate. They are not leaving their churches and getting other jobs. Congregations still pay their salaries. Their names appear on the church stationery, and they continue to appear in pulpits on Sunday. But they are abandoning their posts, their calling. They have gone a whoring after other gods. What they do with their time under the guise of pastoral ministry hasn't the remotest connection with what the church's pastors have done for most of twenty centuries...The pastors of America have metamorphosed into a company of shopkeepers, and the shops they keep are churches. They are preoccupied with shopkeeper's concerns – how to keep the customers happy, how to lure customers away from competitors down the street, how to package the goods so that the customers will lay out more money. Some of them are very good shopkeepers. They attract a lot of customers, pull in great sums of money, develop splendid reputations. Yet it is still shopkeeping; religious shopkeeping to be sure, but shopkeeping all the same.[20]

1   Peter Wagner and Edwin Orr, both quoted by Alvin J. Vander Griend, *The Praying Church Sourcebook* (Grand Rapids: Church Development Resources, 1997) 13.

2   Richard Thomas, quoted by R. Kent Hughes, *1001 Great Stories and Quotes* (Wheaton, IL: Tyndale, 1998) 56.

3   Quoted by R. Kent Hughes, 216.

4   Vander Griend, 16.

5   As quoted by Dick Eastman, *No Easy Road* (Grand Rapids: Baker, 1971) 44.

6   George Barna, Barna Research Group, "The State of the Church, 2002," June 4, 2004.

7   George Barna, Barna Research Group, "America's Congregations: More Money but Fewer People," Dec. 6, 1999.

8   George Barna, *Inward, Outward and Upward: Ministry That Transforms Lives* (Ventura, CA: Barna Research Group, Ltd., 1999) 5-6.

9   <www.huffingtonpost.com/steve-mcswain/why-nobody-wants-to-go-to_b_4086016.html>. Accessed April 1, 2017.

10   Daniel Henderson, *Fresh Encounters* (Colorado Springs, CO: NavPress, 2004) 46.

11   Henderson, 55.

12   Vander Griend, 14.

13   Henderson, 55.

14   Barna Research Group, "Seven Paradoxes Regarding America's Faith," Dec. 17, 2000.

15   A prayer summit is a three-to-four day, extended, agenda-free prayer encounter. It is often held for pastors of a city using outside facilitators. International Renewal Ministries has conducted more than a thousand of these summits around the world. P. Douglas Small served the movement for more than a decade. For more information on prayer summits, go to www.project-pray.org or www.prayersummits.net.

16   Nancy Pfaff, "Christian Leadership Attributes Dynamic Increase in Effectiveness to the Work of Intercessors," *Church Growth Journal,* 81 (Quoted by Chery Sacks, 125).

17   Barna Research Group, "Seven Paradoxes Regarding America's Faith," Dec. 17, 2000.

18   Andrew Murray, *The Ministry of Intercession* (Springdale, PA: Whitaker House, 1982) 9.

19   Murray, *The Ministry of Intercession,* quoted by Vander Griend, 17.

20   Eugene Peterson, *Working the Angles* (Grand Rapids: Eerdmans, 1987) 1-2.

TWO
Theology of Prayer: Three Aspects of Prayer

Communion with God is the one need of the soul beyond all other needs; prayer is the beginning of that communion.

– George MacDonald

In prayer the soul opens up every avenue to the Holy Spirit. God then gently breathes into it that it may become a living soul. He who has ceased to breathe in prayer is spiritually dead.[1]

– Sadhu Sunder Singh

The great people of the earth today are people who pray. I do not mean those who talk about prayer; nor those who say they believe in prayer; nor yet those who can explain about prayer; but I mean those people who take time and pray.

– S.D. Gordon

Think about all of the terms we use for prayer – adoration, agreement, confession, consecration, calling unto God, crying out to God, intercession, meditation, praise, repentance, supplication, thanksgiving and more. Do you ever get confused?

The terms seem to pull in us in different directions. Upon examination, some of the terms seem to belong to different worlds, requiring different moods. Rather than a congruent pattern, they seem more like a patchwork quilt, a tapestry of different modes of prayer.

How do these terms fit together? Is there something central to prayer, from which all of these terms spring and to which they all flow? I believe there is a central key to understanding prayer. I have come to terms with prayer's diversity by seeing it in three simple categories , plus the fourth that is actually intended to be pervasive, altering the character of the communion, petition and intercession.

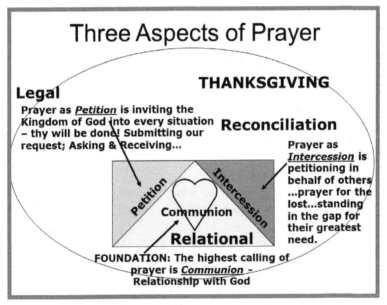

1. Communion with God.
2. Intercession.
3. Petition.

All of these are unwrapped in the context of thanksgiving and praise. Never begin prayer without a grateful, thankful heart of praise (Psa. 50:14; 69:30, 31; 95:2; 100:4; Phil. 4:6; Col.4:2).

Communion with God in prayer should always be the priority of every believer. *Intercession* is concerned about communion between God and others. Whenever that communion is disturbed or broken, an intercessor is needed. It may be unsettled by some pressure or problem in life. Or communion may be nonexistent because the individuals have never invited Christ into their life. Intercession seeks to connect others to the grace of God. Finally, *petition* is the privilege of praying for our own needs. This is Paul's theology of prayer (1 Tim. 2:1).

Communion with God

"God's most exquisite gift to man – the crown jewel of all His gifts – is the ability to converse with Him in prayer."[2] The very heart of prayer is communion with God and enjoying God's Presence. It is the simplicity of spending time with God, just to be with Him because we have found His love so perfect, and unhurried exposure to His holiness is so transforming – and O how we now worship and love Him. Nothing takes the place of this aspect of prayer. This is not prayer as activity. It is not prayer as works or words, language or liturgy. It is deeper than that. The essence of prayer is unbroken and unhindered communion with a holy God. Without this love relationship at the center of our prayer life, the whole aspect of prayer is dark and difficult.

Discipline and Delight

A balanced prayer life must be driven by delight as much as by duty. The greatest motivator is not law, but love! Ultimately, you cannot make people pray. No amount of guilt, no exposure to the pain and problems of the earth can induce a lasting quality prayer life. Crisis praying is too superficial and self-interested to produce lasting depth in prayer. We are pushed into a transformative prayer life; we are pulled into one, wooed there by the love of God. It is the tender call of God Himself, the invitation to be 'with Him,' that makes prayer so precious. It is experiencing His love and peace with joy.

The call to pray is often issued in compulsory terms – "We *must* pray! If we are going to see revival and renewal, it will not come *unless we pray.*" That is true at one level, and false at another. Do we have to frame our understanding of prayer as a necessary evil? While it is a discipline that is utterly essential, it must be embraced with delight. It is as if we were saying, "We wish there were some other way to appropriate these blessings, to call down this mighty revival – without praying. But since this is the only way, well, I suppose we *have to spend time with God.*" What a tragic perception of both God and prayer. There is no love in this kind of prayer life! It is pure duty with no delight that eventually collapses or dries up.

Labor out of Rest

Dutch Sheets says, "We don't wait well. We're into microwaving; God, on the other hand, is usually into marinating."[3] The writer of Hebrews tells us that there is a *'rest'* that belongs to us (4:1, 9-11). He calls us to enter the rest of God. Yes, there is a dimension of prayer that involves labor – even warfare (Ephesians 6:12, 18). It is intense and fierce, battling both the flesh and the devil. But that kind of prayer, though legitimate and essential, is not the heart of prayer. You have not prayed until you have prayed yourself to peace. And you cannot pray until you have peace (Philippians 4:6-8). You must enter *into* the rest of God in prayer in order to then labor *with* God in prayer. And out of that you accomplish mission by working *from* prayer with a clear and certain conviction of success.

We are exhorted to *"be diligent to enter that rest"* (Hebrews 4:11). What a paradox! We labor to rest. What is the labor? The first business of prayer is to make whatever needs I bring, or concerns that I bear, less important than His Presence and rest (see Psalm 27:1-4).

Saint Francis of Assisi said, "When we pray to God we must be seeking nothing – nothing." To experience God, I labor in prayer to push aside the very needs that may have driven me to prayer. How odd? It may seem odd, even contradictory. We have come to see prayer as a means of acquisition. It is and it isn't. Our greatest need is not to leave prayer with an answer in our hands or heads. Wisdom or words of comfort, provision or power, are not our real answers. He is our answer. A pauper leaves prayer with just enough grace to avert his crisis. A wise man leaves with the King himself.

Finding Peace in Communion With God

Philipp Melanchthon, a companion of Luther, noted, "Trouble and perplexity drive me to prayer, and prayer drives away perplexity and trouble." So the first labor in prayer is to get beyond our own needs and lay hold of God himself in perfect communion, realizing that in God and God alone are all the answers and solutions we need. This is the place of rest and peace. Here, a clear certainty rises in our heart: *"We are more than conquerors through Him who loved us"* (Romans 8:37).

This *relational* aspect of prayer is the most important facet of prayer. It is not words or posture – it is wordless. You have not prayed until you have prayed yourself to silence, and in that silence you experience deep levels of peace with God and the peace of God (Psalms 4:4; 46:10). Spurgeon warned that our prayer "should not be a mere leaping out of bed and kneeling down, and saying anything that comes first to mind. On the contrary, may we wait upon the Lord with holy fear and sacred awe."[4]

The highest call of prayer is communion with God! The heart of prayer is worship, and the heart of worship is our love relationship with God, in Christ, by the enabling of the Spirit, out of the understanding of Scripture. The root of the word *communion* or *fellowship* is the Greek word *koinonia*. Prayer is the means by which we find 'common' agreement with God. Here we experience 'oneness,' or peace *with* God. We should not only be at peace *with* God, having submerged our sins in the blood of the Lamb, we should be walking in the peace *of* God.

Communion involves *union* with God – the fusion of life and purpose. This is more than a legal union. It is coherence. Our relationship is marked by a desire to walk in lockstep with the Spirit. We want to live in His shadow, not merely exercise our legal right to pray or call ourselves His children. Communion is not about the positional relationship – the fact of our union with Christ – it is about the quality of the union. We enjoy the Presence of God. We want to pray, to spend time with God.

The aspect of prayer we call *communion with* God is diverse. It is even contradictory. On one hand, it involves casual "chitchat" with God. It is just talking with Him throughout the day as the Companion who never leaves us or forsakes us, the One who is concerned about our every need. Communion with God should be as natural as breathing, as easy as a visit with an old trusted friend. On the other hand, it is anything but casual. It is intense and passionate – as fiery as two lovers wanting desperately to convey to the other the level of their affection and devotion.

Thus, communion with God is personal. God relates to all of us individually. Just as each of our children are all ours, but so different, so each of our prayer lives are unique. Communion is an intimate thing – between us and God. And yet, if we become comfortable in our prayer relationship with God and forget with whom we are relating, we are in trouble. How can we talk to God...and walk with Him?

Abraham said, *"I who am but dust and ashes have taken it upon myself to speak to the Lord"* (Genesis 18:27). Prayer is intensely personal. And yet, there must also be times when all we can do is stand in awe of His glory, overwhelmed by the majesty of who He is.

It is precisely in this tension that we get the healthiest prayer relationship with God.

- I know Him! How could I ever know Him? His ways are *"past finding out!"* (Job 9:10; Romans 11:33, 34).

- I am a friend of God! Jesus has called me *"friend"* (John 15:13-15; James 2:23). And yet, I must never stop standing (or bowing) in worshipful wonder before him (see John 21:20; cf. Revelation 1:17).

- Is there warmth and intimacy in my communion with Him? Yes and no. I feel close to Him, and then I am at times awestruck with the *"otherness"* of God (Isaiah 40:25, 26; 46:5-9).

- Is it possible to know Him? Yes, we can know His voice and sense His Presence (John 10:27; 18:37). Yet, if we develop a style of communion by which we become too familiar with God, our relationship will be out of balance. We will fail to respect God (Psalms 2:11; 19:9; 25:14; 103:13, 17; 111:10). We will forget that we are dealing with the One *"who sits above the circle of the earth,"* and in comparison, we are like grasshoppers (Isaiah 40:22).

- While we can know Him, we must never fail to see that God is Himself an eternal discovery zone. He can be known, but He cannot be fully known. We know Him, in fact, only by His self-disclosures to us (Job 34:29; Isaiah 45:15; Deuteronomy 29:29; Daniel 2:19-22). And one day we turn a corner and see aspects of His character and glory that we had never considered before (Matthew 11:25; 16:17; 1 Corinthians 2:9, 10). *"Great is His faithfulness; His mercies are new every morning"* (see Lamentations 3:22, 23).

Communion with God is back and forth between intimacy and discovery, between knowing God and the unknowable God, between friendship and falling before Him in silent wonder and worship. If you get too close, you become dangerously familiar with holy things. You treat lightly the sacred. You fail to take seriously your frailty and His holiness. If you are too distant, you fail to develop the capacity to snuggle up and rest in the lap of Father God. You never experience the sheer joy of knowing you are loved and accepted in His Presence. You fail to cultivate the capacity to hear His voice and walk in confident assurance not only of His favor on your life, but also of the grace of God flowing from you to others.

Intercession

If the *highest* call of prayer is communion with God, then the *noblest* call of prayer is intercession. Intercession is prayer for others. There are times when we cannot pray for ourselves; we are disoriented or simply out of faith and vision. Perhaps we are sick and exhausted, fighting disease or demons. At such times, we need someone to intercede for us. We need someone to pray as if they were us! As if they were standing in our place, they offer petitions in our behalf to God. What an extraordinary provision. We can pray for others. Others can pray for us.

Standing in the Gap

"So I sought for a man among them who would make a wall, and stand in the gap before Me on behalf of the land, that I should not destroy it; but I found no one" (Ezekiel 22:30).

This is the premier role of the intercessor. Stepping into a gap, we stand before the Lord! And we stand in behalf of the other party – perhaps someone or someplace deserving of and about to receive discipline. The intercessor runs to stand between God and the offending party (Numbers 16:47, 48).

Intercession calls a truce. It pleads for mercy. It builds a wall around the one who is guilty! It seeks to protect the guilty – from God, from His judgment and wrath (1 Samuel 2:25) – and more so, from the ambush of the Evil One, whose role is to steal and kill. Stepping into this gap is precisely what God wants us to do.

The Hebrew word, *paga*, actually means "to meet." Intercession is more than prayer. It is the action that places a pleading Christian between God and others, forcing a meeting of the two. Intercession is not merely a prayer but a spiritual act.[5] Dutch Sheets says, "We bring individuals to God in prayer asking the Father to meet with them...when we're used to create a meeting between God and humans, [the result is] releasing the fruit of Christ's work."[6]

A Place of Battle

The act of intercession is an act of mercy and love. But make no mistake – stepping into the fray, into the line of fire, is no safe thing. The Hebrew term for *intercession (paga)* is often used as a battlefield term (Judges 8:21; 15:12; 1 Samuel 22:17, 18; 2 Samuel 1:15; 1 Kings 2:25-46).[7] Intercessors may shrink back from this place of conflict, if they do not know the heart of God and trust Him. We fear no bullet from His rifle. It is Satan's desire that God proceed with His judgment. He is our accuser (Revelation 12:10), the one who most consistently levels charges against us. When an intercessor stands in front of a sinner, they become a shield of grace. But don't expect the Evil One to hold his fire in such moments. The intercessor may be caught in the crossfire of warfare aimed at the person they are shielding in prayer. This is why persistence and teaming in intercession is so important.

When Israel was in a battle against Amalek, prayer was the determining factor in the outcome. Moses observed the conflict from a mountain, praying all the while. But he became weary in prayer. With his arms raised, he seemed to shield Israel and bend the battle in their direction. When he lowered his arms, Israel began to faint and fail. When he again raised his arms, they prevailed. He became so weary he could not endure. Yet, it was clear that if he failed in prayer, the nation would fail (Exodus 17:8-13).

What a picture of intercession! It is the determining factor in so many battles we fight – for individuals and nations, for families and communities. And it is no easy task. Without the "rest" rooted in the communion aspect of prayer, intercessors burn out quickly. The labor of prayer is too intense. It cannot be accomplished by human strength. And in this passage, we learn another principle. At times, intercession should not be a solo task. Intercessors function best when they are teamed. Aaron and Hur held up the hands of Moses and he rested on a rock (Exodus 17:12). The rock, we are reminded, is Christ. Rest and labor, bound together, turned the battle. At times, we need people to agree with us in prayer – two or three agreeing (Matthew 18:19) – that the will of God would be done.

Intercession is praying for others – praying where there is no quality relationship between God and individuals or families, or between God and cities or nations. The intercessor steps into the gap where a broken or strained relationship exists, and prays for communion to be restored.

A Beachhead for Revival

We should intercede for our friends and fellow believers who need someone to hold up their hands in prayer as they go through a difficult season. The highest call of intercession is prayer for those who have no relationship with the Father, through Christ.

They do not know the Lord! We must pray into that gap, between God and lost souls – families, cities and people groups.

Prayer establishes a spiritual bridge, a kind of beachhead in the hearts of lost people. When we intercede, we make a claim in behalf of the shed blood of Christ for that lost person or family, city or nation. This is a gift of light given to the darkness. It is a deposit of care and love laid at the throne of grace on behalf of the disconnected party. It is a prayer note to God, "Don't forget North Korea, Father!" Or, "Don't forget Jonathan! Or Phillip!" we pray. "I am sending this prayer note, on Your authority, in their behalf, asking You to visit them! Give them a wake-up call. Love them. Grace them. Save them." The Heidelberg Catechism reminds us, "God gives His grace to those who pray continually."[8] Intercession allows us to plead for grace on behalf of others.

We have seen intercession primarily as spiritual warfare, but the heart of intercession is not warfare – it is peacemaking! It is prayer that a world separated from God by sin would be reconciled to Him through the ministry of His Son, Jesus Christ. Christ is praying right now.

At times, the intercessory function is priestly, praying as if we were the distressed or disconnected party, praying for them, from their moccasins. At other times, the intercessory function is prophetic. It represents God and His desires for people, places and things. Praying His will, speaking His word over and into our time-space world.

"He always lives to make intercession for them" (Hebrews 7:25). As we intercede, we agree with him. Indeed, we join him in prayer. We give voice to his voice in the earth that lost people would be found by him. The power of such agreement, such synergy, cannot be measured.

Making War by Making Peace

There is a warfare dimension to intercession, but spiritual warfare is neither the essence of intercessory prayer nor its center. Reconciliation is at the heart of intercession's purpose. It is missional, evangelistic, posturing out of a 'good news' disposition. We will find the Evil One making war with us when we pray for men and women who need to make peace with God. Remember, we stand as victors in warfare, *"having our feet shod with the preparation of the gospel of peace"* (Eph. 6:15). Amazing isn't it? Effective spiritual warfare, paradoxically, stands in peace, the gospel of peace. We will do our greatest damage to the kingdom of darkness not by railing against the darkness, but by pulling men out of the fire, hating the garment spotted with the flesh (Jude 23). The more captives we take captive to grace, the more instruments of peace and reconciliation we deliver to the Kingdom of light, and the more we raid hell's shadows, divesting it of its instruments of unrighteousness (Romans 6:13).

This is warfare by peacemaking – by effecting the gospel of reconciliation. We have been trying to do warfare at the macro, universal, middle-heaven sphere by railing at the darkness. And we have not been effective. Little has changed. But when huge numbers are translated from the kingdom of darkness into the Kingdom of light, that is when and how we see the Enemy of the middle-heaven displaced (Luke 10:18). Paul called for prayer 'everywhere' with hoisted hands, the posture of blessing; without wrath, a desire for God to judge, indeed, quite the contrary, and without doubting that our prayers were heard in heaven (1 Tim 2:8). Paul called for prayer that focused on leaders in authority, and he implied that such prayer might change the very atmosphere of the city, resulting in peace and quiet. He probably meant, as well, that prayer would bring the inner conditions of peace and quiet to the souls of those praying, as well as *"godliness and reverence"* (1 Tim 2:1-2). The end of the passage is stunning. "He [God] wants all people to be saved and learn the truth" (2:4, GNT). The proliferation of prayer in a city, focused on community leaders, changes the atmosphere of the city, the quality and integrity of those praying, and results in conversions of the lost.

Satan is truly an enemy in rebellion against God. His most formidable weapons are deception and accusation (Revelation 12:9, 10). He ministers death. After he has brought his victims under his power, he uses and abuses them, then kills and destroys (John 10:10) not only them, but also others through them. All this is true, but our warfare is most effective when we focus not on Satan's deeds or the darkness, but on the men and women needing liberation. As we see people translated from the kingdom of darkness into the Kingdom of Light, we wage our greatest warfare.

Satan rails and rages at us. He is the roaring lion seeking whom he may devour (1 Peter 5:8), the predator wolf that makes innocents his victims. His ways are warlike, loud and clamorous, noisy and self interested. Jude warns us against bringing a *"railing accusation"* against him (v. 9). We should come in the opposite spirit – the spirit of the Lamb. We should refuse to be baited into an exchange of inflamed spirit-speech. We would be wise, though aware, to ignore, when possible, his intimidating tirades. Rather, as he rages, we should whisper peace into troubled souls. The shackles will fall off. And Satan will lose another victim, an unknowing instrument that he was whittling to nothing in order to exploit them as a tool of death. Our goal is not enemy engagement; it is saving 'Private Ryan.'

Duty and Delight

The *delight* of prayer is found in our communion with God. The *duty* of prayer – though not without delight, but driven by a sense of mission – is found in intercession. You cannot intercede with balance until and unless you spend time in communion. Communion with God is the cause behind intercession.

Having experienced the rest and peace of God (communion), we project that very rest and peace toward people and places where it is absent. We invite the Prince of Peace to assert His rule in that troubled heart or home, that neighborhood or nation. The soul that is saved is first claimed by prayer. Where the Spirit brings liberty to a life, invariably, an intercessor has tracked through the rubble declaring by prayer the power of God's grace in that person or place.

God continues to walk through the earth as He did in Genesis 3. He is the Good Shepherd (John 10) who seeks those who need to be saved (John 12:47; 1 Timothy 1:15; 2:3, 4). He has not changed since Genesis when He called out to Adam (3:9). He moves through the earth, calling those alienated by sin and trapped in a condition of spiritual death. His rescue mission continues. He calls the lost by name – "Fred...John...Lucille...Mary...Edith." All of our names are on His list. "Where are you?" He waits for a response. Adam heard Him calling, but fear prevented him from answering. Is this then the role of the intercessor, to answer for others?

After 4,000 years of Biblical history, God himself came to the earth, and He came as an intercessor. The Word was made flesh (John 1:14). The last Adam, the Christ (1 Corinthians 15:45), walked through earth's garden, now encumbered with weeds and filled with men and women in bondage to sin, blind to God. He prayed over Jerusalem (Luke 19:41-44), the city of light and healing that lay in darkness and was paralyzed by division. He wept at sin's consequences – death – and called Lazarus back to life (John 11:35-44). On the cross, he did His final earthly intercessory work, crying out, *"Father, forgive them, for they do not know what they do"* (Luke 23:34). He prayed in our place. He answered for us. He left the sweat and blood of prayer at Calvary, and the result has been the redemption of billions.

Intercession often involves painful praying in the shadow of the Cross. It is as if the intercessor is crying out as the separated party as Christ did, *"My God, My God, why have You forsaken Me?"* (Matthew 27:46). It was because of sin that Christ was temporarily forsaken by the Father. He was interceding – for you and me, for sinners. Now, we intercede for others who have experienced an exile from God because of sin (Isaiah 59:2; 2 Corinthians 5:20).

Across the earth, the voices of intercessors rise into the heavens, coming into the throne room. At places of sin and on blood-stained turf, they pray. They cry out in moments when God, it seems, is again being nailed to the cross and His messengers crucified. At forsaken places and over seemingly discarded people, intercessors cry out: "Here God! Touch, over here! Redeem this one. Heal that heart. Open these eyes. Save this life! Forgive them, for they do not know what they are doing!" Somehow the substitutionary power of intercession invites God into places at which He has been shut out, into lives where He has been given no open door, into minds closed to the gospel.

In intercession, we give expression to those who are silent. They are hiding, confused, not sure what is right or whom to trust. We give voice to their deepest needs. It is as if we were next to them calling for help, though we may be on the other side of town, or for that matter, the other side of the earth. In intercession, we feel their pain; we weep over their separation from God, and we call God to come and intervene in their behalf. What a powerful privilege and duty is intercession!

While communion is the privilege of prayer, *intercession is the duty* of prayer. We must pray not only for ourselves and those we love, we must also pray for our enemies – those who have not yet made peace with God. We know that we cannot make a decision for people, but prayer opens hearts and minds, eyes and ears, and brings people to a place of decision (see Colossians 4:2; 2 Corinthians 4:4, 6).

Petition

We not only have the *privilege* of spending time with God (communion), and thus the honor of His Presence; we also have "the right" of petition. We can dare to make requests of God Almighty! One might be given an audience with a king; but in the ancient world, to exploit such a moment and transform that event into a hearing for personal advantage – that would have been outrageous. Not so with our King. We come boldly to God. His throne is called 'Grace' (Hebrews 4:16). He longs for us to *"ask of Him"* (see Psalm 2:8; Zechariah 10:1; Matthew 7:7-10).

A *petition* is a request of God offered in prayer. It is actually a legal term. We are presenting a formal plea for provision in the courtroom of heaven.[9] To offer a petition to God is an extraordinary right. As we submit our request to God, we offer to Him our need in a state of dependent faith.

This right comes to us in the covenant we have with God through the blood of His Son, Jesus Christ. Not everyone has the right to pray, at least as a son or daughter of God (Proverbs 15:29; James 5:16; 1 Peter 3:12). Not everyone can lay legitimate claim to the promises of the covenant found in Scripture – only those who have been stained by the blood of the Lamb (Hebrews 8:11, 12) and who therefore pray from within the covenant.

The record of our covenant is the New Testament. But the background, the roots of that New Covenant is the Old Testament, not discarded, but completed in Christ. So we do not make random requests, we make requests out of the covenant provision – grounded in real and certain promises. To ask apart from these promises is to ask amiss (James 4:3). If we make requests that rise out of our own desires, we are wishing. Good praying is over an open Bible, wrestling with the promises of God.

The highest petition was taught by Jesus, *"Your kingdom come. Your will be done on earth as it is in heaven"* (Matthew 6:10). Petitionary prayer has as its first order the invitation for God's kingdom to break into our world, in order for His will to be done and His name glorified. In prayer, we seek His ways and wisdom, and bind our will to His, as Christ, *"not my will, but Thine be done."* As we are aligned with His will, His Kingdom moves forward and His name is glorified. "Come, Lord! Reign. Assert Your rule! Break into my life and into our world to reorder them according to heaven's will. Align things on earth in relationship with Your will Father, as expressed in heaven. Glorify Your name."

We cry out to God, as if we were a pocket of resisters in the midst of a revolution – sending a plea for intervention to foreign powers to assist us in the overthrow of the tyrants who have taken our land and us as hostages. It is not the physical rulers against whom we plead (Ephesians 6:12). It is the invisible nest of rebel angels who rule from the middle heaven and have plans to anoint their own Antichrist as king of the earth, and release the spirit of the False Prophet, his accomplice. Against them we cry out.

After we have wrestled for His will in the earth – *"Your kingdom [rule, reign] come. Your will be done"* – then we are free to pray for our daily bread and other needs (Matthew 6:10, 11). Yet, we should never make this powerful provision of petitioning heaven for real resources about our own self-interests. In fact, never in the prayer that Jesus taught us do you find *I, me or my.* Instead, we are taught to pray *we, our and us. "Our Father, give us our daily bread, forgive us our debts, as we forgive, lead us and deliver us..."* (vv. 6:9-13).

Prayer must be bigger than our narrow slice of pain. We have to learn to pray the cosmic purposes of God, to call down His will into our time-space world – life by life, family by family, congregation by congregation, and city/nation by city/nation.

While the heart of prayer is communion with God, that is not the *all* of prayer. It involves *intercession* – prayer for others. It involves *petition* – prayer for our own needs. It involves *thanksgiving* – a humble gratitude that stimulates faith by a regular review of God's gracious history in our lives. Thanksgiving is sometimes a discipline. It wakes up a cold heart. It systematically surveys the past and looks for traces of God's intervention. It marks the path we have taken and signs of God's hand at work in providing and directing, in protecting.

Creating a Culture of Prayer

It is one thing for the church to begin a series of 'prayer events.' It is another thing for *the entire church to embrace prayer as the norm* – the central spring from which we draw direction and strength for our tasks. If Spirit is breath to the body of Christ, without which we die, then prayer itself is breathing. It is the means by which we inhale the very Spirit of God's life into the body of Christ.

A church without prayer is an absurdity; it does not exist. It may be a warm corpse, but it is dead. Prayer breathes life into the soul of the church. It is the means by which the Spirit guides and empowers the church, by which the Christ-life is infused.

Luther declared, "As a tailor makes a coat and a shoemaker makes a shoe – a Christian prays." Prayer is the defining, distinguishing mark of a believer. John Quam, of the Mission America coalition, says, "When we short-circuit prayer, we give our lives and ministry a secularistic or humanistic framework within which to work."[10]

Prayer is the means by which we consistently surrender to God, inviting Him into our lives and work. Without prayer, we have essentially cut off communication to God. He could talk to us, but He typically won't. Quam argues, "Does God exist to help fulfill our plans, or do we exist to help fulfill the plans of God?"[11] We can participate in the purposes of God only by prayer.

Most of us get the feeling, at least from time to time, that there are more important and effective things to do than pray. We have heard the line, "Two hands working can do more than a thousand clasped in prayer."[12] That is humanistic Christianity at best. We're told frequently that prayer is merely self-reflection, the exercise that allows one to go deep within the self, gather peace and gain perspective, and then release inner power. That is a lie. It is the fusion of New Age principles with Christian practice.

Prayer is about our weakness and His strength. It taps into a very real power – the supremacy of the crucified, now resurrect- ed and exalted Christ. There is nothing like real Christian prayer. Without it, we can do nothing, and what we do will either come to nothing or glorify man. Soren Kierkeguaard reminds us, "Prayer does not change God, but it changes him who prays." E.M. Bounds says bluntly:

> It is better to let the work go by neglect than to let the pray-
> ing go by neglect. Whatever affects the intensity of our pray-
> ing affects the value of our work. Too busy to pray, is not only
> the keynote to backsliding, but it mars even the work done...it
> leaves God out of the account. It is so easy to be seduced by the
> good to neglect the best until both the good and best perish.[13]

1   Quoted by R. Kent Hughes, *1001 Great Stories and Quotes* (Wheaton, IL: Tyndale, 1988) 316-317.

2   Merv Rosell, quoted by Ben Jennings, *The Arena of Prayer* (Orlando, FL: New Life, 1999) 151.

3   Dutch Sheets, *Intercessory Prayer* (Ventura, CA: Regal, 1996) 19.

4   Charles Spurgeon, quoted by Dick Eastman, *No Easy Road,* 39.

5   Sheets, 50.

6   Ibid, 52.

7   Ibid, 55.

8   Quoted by Alvin Vander Griend, *The Praying Church Sourcebook,* 7.

9   P. Douglas Small, *Heaven Is a Courtroom, CD Series* (Kannapolis, NC: Alive Ministries, 2004).

10 Vander Griend, chapter by John Quam, "Seven Ways Prayer Is Changing the Church in America," 33.

11 Quam, 31.

12 Anonymous.

13 E.M. Bounds. *The Complete Works of E M. Bounds on Prayer* (Grand Rapids: Baker, 1990) 371.

THREE
Philosophy of Prayer Ministry: Contrasting the Praying Church and the House of Prayer

Two thousand pastors at a conference responded to a survey in which 95 percent admitted that they spent five minutes or less a day in prayer.

– Al Vander Griend

When the devil sees a man or woman who really believes in prayer, who knows how to pray, and who really does pray, and, above all, when he sees a whole church on its face before God in prayer, "he trembles" as much as he ever did, for he knows that his day in that church or community is at an end.

– R.A. Torrey

I have read many books on prayer, studied prayer and attended seminars on prayer. I have prayed tens of thousands of hours privately, attended church prayer meetings, prayed at church railings, community prayer meetings and while watching

tragedies on the nightly news. I have prayed with thousands
in large groups, with hundreds of friends and strangers in intimate settings and casual conversations: face-to-face, over the
telephone, in restaurants, malls, parking lots, prisons, foreign
countries, on planes, through letters and emails. I have prayed
walking, standing, sitting, rocking babies, kneeling and lying on
my face. I have journaled prayer, spoken prayer, conversed in
prayer, sung prayer, shouted prayer, whispered prayer, groaned
prayer and wept prayer. In all this, I have learned one thing. The
power of prayer is not in the words I pray, the place I pray, the
way I pray, how loud I pray or how long I pray, but in the One
to whom I pray.

– Anne Murchison

Of all the mysteries of the prayer world, the need of persevering
prayer is one of the greatest. That the Lord, who is so loving
and longing to bless, should have to be asked, time after time,
year after year, before the answer comes, we cannot easily understand. When after persevering pleading, our prayer remains
unanswered, it is often easiest for our lazy flesh, and it has all
the appearance of pious submission, to think that we must now
cease praying, because God may have His secret reason for
withholding His answer to our request. It is by faith alone that
the difficulty is overcome.[1]

– Andrew Murray

When Jim Cymbala became pastor of the Brooklyn Tabernacle,
there were only 15 people in attendance the first Sunday, and
a grand total of $85 in the morning offering toward a mortgage pay-
ment of $232 plus utilities and other bills. The building was small.
The walls needed painting. The windows were dingy, and the floor
was bare. It was both "pathetic and laughable."[2] The first two years
were years of testing – meager salaries, funding challenges, constant
struggles. All of that brought him to a place of humility. He learned
a principle: "God is attracted to weakness. He can't resist those who
honestly and desperately admit how bad they need Him."[3]

"The embarrassing truth is that sometimes I did not want to show up for a service," recalled Jim. "That is how bad it was." In that season of holy desperation, God spoke to him,

> If you and your wife will lead My people to pray and call upon My name, you will never lack for something fresh to preach. I will supply all the money that's needed, both for the church and for your family, and you will never have a building large enough to contain the crowds I will send in response.[4]

The Tuesday evening prayer service at Brooklyn Tabernacle is riveting! The house is full. The people are praying – really praying – and the congregation in Brooklyn is no longer little; it is known around the world!

When I arrived in Surabaya, Indonesia, a few years ago, I was told to prepare a brief challenge on prayer for the Wednesday evening service. The church building was packed! I shared; they prayed, and then I was informed that there would be a business leaders' prayer service the next morning at 6 a.m. It would be my assignment to share briefly with those leaders.

When I arrived the next morning, over 500 businessmen sat cross-legged on the floor, praying and crying out to God. Throughout the day, the sanctuary would empty and another group would gather for prayer. At that time, the size of the church was about 70,000 people. In the last decade, it has doubled, and now worships in the largest complex of its kind in the nation. The driving force of the church is 'the Presence' of God related to prayer.

Who has not heard of Dr. David (Paul) Yonggi Cho and his congregation of more than 700,000 members? The very culture of this church (in Seoul, Korea) is bathed in prayer. Prayer-sensitive megachurches are popping up all over the earth. Prayer meetings in majority world nations are drawing tens of thousands. A decade ago, I was at a prayer meeting in Indonesia that drew 100,000 people.[5] Out of such gatherings, the nation is being changed.

A pastor reported that he had...

spent years training for ministry at a strong Evangelical seminary...He learned all he could learn about church renewal
and church growth and applied all he was learning. Nothing
worked. His church was as dead as ever. One day he walked out
of his study and into the sanctuary. Feeling led of the Lord, he
stood at the front of the church in the center aisle and began to
pray for his parishioners one by one. He moved down the aisle,
praying for those who would typically occupy each pew. Day
after day he continued this practice. Soon the renewal he wanted and prayed for began.[6]

What kind of church do you have? Do you have a church that
prays? Or do you have a praying church? Do you have a house of
prayer for *all nations?* What are the differences?

Three Kinds of Churches

1. Pray in Crisis/Casual Prayer

2. A church with a Prayer Ministry

A Pervasive Prayer Ministry: A House of Prayer

3. Prayer is at the HEART of every Ministry ...

Note: In the first illustration, prayer is outside. It is not an organized ministry. In the second, church prayer is an option among many ministries.
In the third, prayer is at the heart of the church and every ministry in the
church.

THREE KINDS OF CHURCHES		
Level 1 Church *The Church that Prays in Crisis*	**Level 2 Church** *The Church with a Prayer Ministry*	**Level 3 Church** *The Praying Church*
Crisis situations are the main prayer focus.	Undergirding ministries with prayer is the focus.	Christ is the center of every activity – especially in prayer.
Prayer is thought of as offering needs to God, not about furthering the Kingdom.	Prayer is only one ministry among other ministries.	Prayer is at the heart of every ministry, the very center of all the church does.
Prayer times are consumed with personal requests.	Prayer time is about praying for other ministries.	Every ministry is encouraged to put prayer at its center.
Prayer meetings are called irregular.	Prayer meetings are regular, but not a primary focus.	Prayer is featured at all church gatherings.
No teaching/training on prayer.	The church offers little training prayer.	Prayer training is featured as part of membership orientation.
Prayer is self-interested.	The church has a 'faithful prayer band.'	The church is determined to raise up a 'prayer army.'
Leaders do not call or model prayer.	A few leaders come to prayer meetings when their schedules allow.	Leaders always attend; they long to pray.
No one meets to pray. Prayer is casual; optional.	Meetings open and close with prayer, as an incidental function.	Members meet just for the purpose of praying.
Prayer meetings are rare.	Prayer meetings are often identical in style and function.	Prayer meetings will vary, along with the style.
No one is tasked to lead the prayer effort.	Typically, there is no prayer staff, or it is treated casually.	Insists on quality and trained staff to direct the many activities.
There is no definitive prayer structure.	There is limited prayer structure.	There is a growing and expanding prayer structure.
Atmosphere is seeded with fear – faithless desperation.	The atmosphere is often stale. Prayer is duty.	There is a deepening and growing humility among leaders.
Given up on prayer.	Prayer is a struggle.	Prayer is becoming a joy.

The Church That Prays in Crisis

When there is an emergency or a great need, a prayer meeting is called, but usually only when there is some sense of urgency! The prayer conducted in this church centers on problems and needs. Prayer is typically a response to a *crisis*.

One way to recognize this kind of church is that the public prayer time is consumed with prayer requests. When its members think about prayer, they do so in terms of offering their needs to God. When they ask another to pray for them, it is rarely about growth in Christ and expanded vision in behalf of His kingdom – it is about some personal or family need.

One survey indicated that 89 percent of our praying was crisis related. Another survey revealed that 92 percent of North American believers are casual (pray as one goes through the day) or crisis pray-ers. Only eight percent were committed pray-ers.

We should pray about needs. Prayer is the means by which we appropriate the grace of God, but that motive alone should never be at the center of our objective in prayer. When we only seek the hand of God, not His face – or yet, His heart – we have defined our relationship with God too narrowly, and often in user terms.

God wants to call us into a loving dialectic – not with a part of Him...not with His hand, heart or face – but with Him! This is a relationship in which we are simultaneously dependent upon Him, and yet enabled by Him to stand strong. His Word says, *"For without Me you can do nothing"* (John 15:5); *"I can do all things through Christ who strengthens me"* (Philippians 4:13).

This tension is resolved only in prayer. I am weak, yet I am strong (2 Corinthians 12:9, 10). I am confused, and then I am blessed with wisdom – having prayed and received from God who gives wisdom liberally (Proverbs 3:4, 5; James 1:5).

Yes, we should pray about needs, but prayer cannot be an exercise associated only with problems and troubles. It must not always be a cry for help. If it is, then the whole dimension of prayer as fellowship with God for the *pleasure of His Presence is lost.*

E.M. Bounds reminds us, "One of the crying evils, maybe of all times [is] – little or no praying. Of these two evils, perhaps little praying is worse than no praying. Little praying is a kind of make-believe, a salve for the conscience, a farce and a delusion."[7]

The Church With a Prayer Ministry

This congregation is intentional about prayer. It refuses to allow its prayer ministry to be characterized by *crisis* praying. This church, aimed at undergirding its ministries with prayer, is determined to be a 'praying church.' This church organizes a prayer ministry by mobilizing intercessors and rallying them to support the ministries of the church with prayer. The teaming and partnering of intercessors with ministries is a decisive improvement over the first kind of church.

This approach, however, makes two critical mistakes. Here, prayer is a ministry among other ministries. It is segregated when it should run through the heart of all ministries in the church. You cannot separate a prayer ministry from other ministries.

In the church with a prayer ministry, those who are musical join the choir or orchestra; those who are gifted to teach or serve join the Christian Education Department; and those who are intercessors sign up to participate in the congregation's prayer ministry. Prayer is one of the many ministries of the church.

In this model, intercessors are mobilized as the *driving engine* of the church and its ministries. It is the ministry that undergirds the other ministries. While churches that adopt this approach place a high value on intercession, they also seem to think that identifying and mobilizing intercessors is the heart of the prayer ministry. Not so. Intercession is a utility in prayer – it is transactional. Although intercession is a driving force, and intercessors *should* be mobilized to pray. Prayer cannot be fully delegated. Intercessors should be worshippers first; and all worshippers should intercede. Prayer *should* never be viewed in a strictly utilitarian manner or for its pragmatic value – even for noble Kingdom causes. The heart of prayer is worshipful communion. It is transformational prayer.

Spurgeon called his intercessors 'the boiler room' of the church. "When I am in the pulpit preaching, 300 people are down here praying."[8] Most revere Spurgeon for his silver tongue. Preachers emulate him to this day. But the shrewd Spurgeon declared on one occasion, "I would rather teach one man to pray than 10 men to preach."[9]

The Praying Church

The life-giving center of every member and every ministry, every activity in the church, is Christ himself – not prayer. But prayer is the means by which we maintain fellowship with Christ, the center, and have access to His grace for both life and ministry. The third kind of church has *prayer at the heart of every ministry,* at the very center of all it does. It refuses to place prayer ministry among other ministries, or to make prayer a mere engine for other ministries. The praying church encourages every ministry to put prayer at the heart of its activities.

The praying church has neither a crisis prayer ministry nor a crisis prayer theology. *The church must be defined by worshipful, transformative prayer.* Jesus declared: *"My house shall be called a house of prayer for all nations."* The activity of His house is prayer, and the focus of that prayer is missional – it is for the nations, for a harvest out of every ethnic stream.

Worshipful, missional prayer not only defines the church, it also defines the believer. John Bunyan said, "The spirit of prayer is more precious than treasures of gold and silver. Pray often, for prayer is a shield to the soul, a sacrifice to God, and a scourge for Satan." Spurgeon said, "The man who lives without prayer, who lives with little prayer, who seldom reads the Word or looks up to heaven for fresh influence from on high – he will be the man whose heart will become dry and barren."

A New Paradigm

The church with *a prayer ministry* (level two, above) and the church that is becoming *a praying church* (level three, above) are significantly different.[10]

A praying church finds ways to involve the *whole* church in prayer activities and experiences.

- In the church with a prayer ministry, *prayer meetings and gatherings are not primary* – they are almost always sidebar meetings held on odd nights and times. In the praying church, *prayer is featured at prime-time gatherings.*

- The church with a prayer ministry offers *little training* in prayer. The praying church offers regular training – it *features prayer training* as a part of its membership or newcomers' orientation.

- The church with a prayer ministry has a *faithful prayer band.* They are to be commended for their faithfulness and tenacity. But the praying church is not content with a prayer band. They are determined to raise up a *prayer army.*

- At the level-two church, *a few leaders come to prayer meetings,* when they can, when their schedule allows. They are, you understand, very busy! And with such demanding ministry schedules, one cannot expect them to attend a mere prayer meeting! Not so at level-three churches. There, *leaders* attend. They come not merely to model prayer participation. They *come because they long to pray,* to spend time with God, to draw on His strength.

- At level-two churches, meetings are opened with prayer, and they are closed with *prayer.* But it *is a polite and almost incidental function* – with very little impact on the meeting. At level-three churches, leaders and members meet just for the purpose of praying. Prayer is at the heart of such meetings. When decision meetings are conducted, participants are likely to stop in the middle of discussions and linger in prayer. *A culture of prayer has been created.* Nothing is done apart from prayer. This changes the environment. It invites humility. It encourages Christlikeness. It diffuses tension and division.

- *Single-dimensional prayer ministries* with few prayer opportunities characterize level-two churches. Often, the prayer meetings that are held are almost identical in style and function, and even focus. Not so at level-three churches, where there are multiple opportunities for prayer. The focus of each of the various prayer meetings may vary, as will the style. The level-three church recognizes that no one style of prayer fits all. The church is enriched by *a buffet of prayer options.* Not only do the prayer groups make use of different styles of prayer, but they may be formed around different passions for prayer.

In the church with a prayer ministry, there is typically *no prayer staff.* If the staff does exist, it is treated casually. But a praying church insists on *a quality and trained staff* to direct the many activities and expand the scope of prayer in the congregation. There is *no definitive prayer structure* in the level-two congregation. In the praying church, there is *a growing and expanding prayer structure.*

- The atmosphere in the level-one and two-churches is sometimes stale and at other times *alive with pride.* In a level-three church, there is *a deepening and growing humility,* particularly among leaders.

- In level-one and level-two churches, *prayer is a struggle.* But in the level-three church, prayer is *becoming a joy!* It is perceived differently there. It is seen as communion with God, not merely the engine that empowers the ministries of the congregation.

Restructuring to Accomplish Mission

Most churches are organized on a hierarchal model. The flow chart typically flows with the senior pastor at the top of the pyramid. Under him is the associate pastor, the director of business affairs and staff supervisors. At the next level are the departmental leaders and volunteers. A hundred of these charts are different and yet the same.

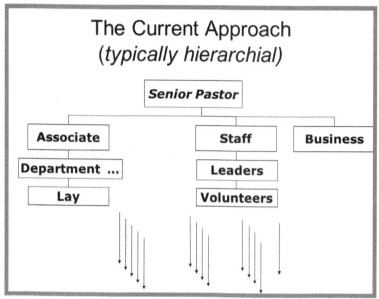

The Current Approach
(typically hierarchial)

This model is not only hierarchal, it is also departmental. The typical church hires as its second full-time person a youth pastor or a worship/music pastor. Additional staff will focus on children's ministries, family development, seniors, singles and more. Somewhere along the line, staff might be hired to supervise discipleship.

Occasionally, a congregation will employ a pastor of evangelism. Almost unheard of, until recent years, was the employment of a full-time director of prayer ministries. Dennis Fuqua, director of Prayer Summits International, says the number of prayer coordinators leading congregational prayer efforts has doubled in the last 10 years, although that number is still small. We rejoice at the number of churches that have hired a prayer coordinator or director of prayer ministries. Our hearts are made glad by the awakening to prayer and the need to be intentional. But there is still something disturbing. The continued use of an old and in-effective hierarcheal and departmental management model will serve to isolate the impact of prayer ministries by segregating it into a department.

Hierarchial And ...
Departmental

Sr. Adult	Trips			→
YOUTH	Group	Activities	Choir	→
LADIES	Tea			→
Children	Musical			→
Singles	Socials			→
Evangelism				→
Prayer	These areas represent the "essence" of the church ... not merely departments!			→
Discipleship				

Supervising Staff

Departments

The Church – A Social Structure or a Spiritual Mission?

Allow me to be argumentative for a moment – to make a point about the character and nature of the New Testament church, contrasted by the cultural models in America today. Where in Scripture are we commanded to hire a youth pastor? Certainly, we recognize the need to focus on the next generation and to support parents in the rearing of their children. So, we hire a youth pastor. But so often, youth ministry degenerates into an odd assortment of youth activities – anything to keep youth busy and out of trouble. And parents, consciously or subconsciously, allow the church to do the discipleship they are called to do (Deuteronomy 6:1-4; Ephesians 6:1-3).

I am concerned that we may become locked into a model of ministry that is not fulfilling the mandate of Christ. We have lost the culture war and a nation that was founded with a godly, Christian heritage has become increasingly pagan. That would appear to make the case for youth and children's ministries. Yet, the statistics are compelling. We are only retaining some five percent of the current generation past high school – despite a half-century in which we have emphasized youth ministry.

Allow me to continue. Where does the Bible tell us to enter into a Senior Adult Ministry by buying a bus for trips? Caring for the seniors who sacrificed to build the church is a good thing. It is, we argue, a part of honoring 'father and mother.' What about Singles Ministry? There is, we insist, a Biblical basis for ministry to wounded people, and so many are divorced, hurt and rejected. We should care; we must minister. What about women's ministries? Or men's ministries? Where are these *departmental ministries* we value so highly in the American church found in Scripture?

The seniors take trips, which is not a bad thing. We do have a mandate to care for widows and the infirm. But the New Testament hardly had in mind the current trend in providing senior entertainment. The singles conduct socials, which are wonderful get-togethers. The women make their annual tea a whopping success. The men have an annual golf tournament that is first-rate in the community. And the children's ministry conducts a great musical every year. All of these are fine things. But they are not *central* to the missional mandate of the church. They are ministries by us and too often for us.

Isn't it time to take a hard look at what we are doing, and why we do things the way we do them? We use sociological categories for staffing and structuring our churches and its programs. The

Biblical model is based on social categories; rather, it rises out of our missional mandate. Christ did not die in order for us to have the best Christmas pageant in town or the best record of any men's softball team in the church league. These things are parallel to godly purposes at best, and completely peripheral in some cases. I fearfully suggest that we are well on our way toward reforming the church into a Christian social club.

If we are not careful, all of our departmental activities will degenerate into wonderful and enriching social activities conducted in an atmosphere of Christian grace. And while we will have a full and demanding schedule in a building that is well utilized, we will not be accomplishing the Biblical mission of the church. We will not be the culture-changing instrument of God that pushes back the darkness and calls men into the light of God, changing communities one person at a time. We are called to be *a house of prayer for all nations!*

- To love God passionately, and our neighbor as ourselves

- To preach the gospel to the ends of the earth, until everyone has heard

- To make disciples of the nations. This is our mandate.

- To that end that we, and the whole earth, worships the God of creation and redemption.

A Matrix Approach

We must not allow good activities to displace the mission, the very purpose for which we were established. Good is always the enemy of best. Does this mean that the various departments and ministries should be abandoned? No, here is what must change. These departments represent ministry to people. What we are missing is mission – or ministry *through* people.

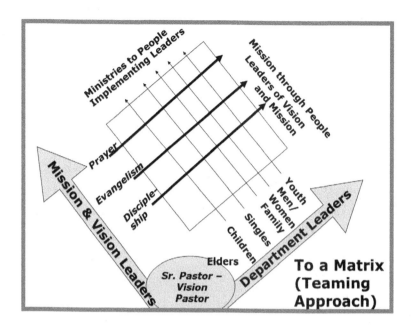

Prayer, evangelism and discipleship cannot be departments. These areas represent our essence, the reason we exist. A new model is required – a matrix model that demands teaming. The model is one in which prayer, evangelism and discipleship are not treated as departments. Prayer, for example, must penetrate every department in the church, as should evangelism training, mobilization and discipleship. The youth must become praying youth, taught to evangelize, mentored in discipling others. So should all the departments.

The pastor must become the servant of all – modeling humility and prayer. He must lead by example. Elders must be chosen on the basis of how they integrate the principles of prayer, evangelism, and discipleship into their lives. Two key leaders must stand with the pastor. One would serve the departmental leaders. The other would be a *pastor (leader) of mission and vision*, who would provide direction to the leaders of prayer, evangelism and discipleship. In a small church, this might be a peer leader among peers. The goal would be for the ministries (departments) to integrate the prayer-evangelism-discipleship mission into their values. In a smaller congregation, this might be the role of one staff member or volunteer. Even so, this is 'the' critical role in the transformation of the congregation into a house of prayer.

The mission and vision leader(s) work with each department leader, creating a team to resource the department goals in the areas of prayer, evangelism and discipleship. Thus, no leader is all things to a particular department. The matrix model demands that no department be isolated from the central purpose of the church. All embrace prayer and evangelism in the spirit of love and care: the Great Commitment (prayer) – 1 Tim. 2:1-4; the Great Commission (evangelism) – Mt. 28:19; Mk. 15:15 and the Great Commandment (love) – Mt. 22:37-39.

Each department has both a leader and also a leadership team. Working with the leader(s) of mission and vision (prayer, evangelism, discipleship), each departmental leader develops a process aimed at fulfilling the mandate of Christ given to the church.

Ministry to People and Through People

Think then, not only about ministry *to* people in various groupings – children, youth, men and women, singles and families – think about ministry through people. We must train and mobilize the church to accomplish the God-given mission of the church. *Prayer drives that mission.*

Prayer cannot be a department or a mere ministry. It should not be competing with other departments for personnel and volunteers. It will need specifically dedicated volunteers, but one of its primary roles will be to mobilize people for mission in every department.

If the church only has ministries *to* people – activities, fellowship, edification events – then the entire focus is on growing the church *inwardly,* which is never healthy. It makes the church about meeting our needs. It creates a self-serving people who look to an imperfect church to do for them what only a perfect Christ can do in a daily prayer and devotional relationship with Him.

The church needs ministry *to* people, but it also must minister *through* people to those outside the church. It is in this middle, between God and hurting people, that we become mature disciples. In this missional aspect, the entire congregation must focus on the community, praying and caring for the lost. This will never happen if prayer and evangelism are isolated as departmental ministries.

A carnal people will stream to ministries designed around them and their needs, and avoid ministries that call for change and sacrifice. Your organizational structure must militate against that trend, mobilizing every member to fulfill the mandate. The purpose for the church – a house of prayer for the nations – must be pervasive. We are to collectively glorify Christ and bring our communities, over which we are praying, face-to-face with the reality of who he is, to the end that they know him. To be a member of the church and not engage in these functions is unthinkable.

The Changing Roles

This demands a change in both the role of the pastor and the members. We have made the church a place of nurture. Our mantra has been, "Come to church, and be fed!" There *is* a feeding dimension to the role of worship. But mature Christians should not live in a state of chronic dependence on the church for their nurture. Neither should they live apart from it.

THIS ... And not abandon the 1st	Include the 2nd .... PLUS THIS
· Nurture	· Mission
· Pastor: Care Giver Shepherd/Relater	· Pastor: Missionary Trainer/Mobilizer
· Pastor – to serve the people	· Pastor – to serve God, to be a holy man of God
· Members	· Ministers
· ID: by profession	· ID: missionary in disguise
· Ecclesia	· Diaspora
· "come to..."	· "go ye ..."
· Temple	· City
· Building	· Redeeming the land

Our thinking must change in these ways. We must become a *missionary church*. The church must be understood to be a *place of mission,* as well as nurture.

The pastor must be seen as a missionary trainer. We have often cast the pastor in the role of caregiver. We expect him to visit the hospital, attend our children's special events, show up for socials, pray at our barbecues. As shepherd, He takes care of us. He is also the preacher-teacher, the administrator of the non-profit enterprise. As a shepherd, he certainly feeds and leads. However, in such an arrangement, we conscript all of the time of the pastor. Around us is an unchurched city filled with people who do not know God. The premier role of the shepherd-pastor is that of watching-guarding, a metaphor for prayer. A good shepherd not only cares for the sheep *in* the fold, but also those who are *not* in the fold, who have been lost from the fold. He must be given time to search for such sheep, to explore, to feed and recover them. We must release our pastor to the city. We must allow his role to be transformed into a missionary trainer, mobilizing the church for community impact.

Prayer – the Highest Call of Pastors

In our current role, the pastor is here to serve the people of our church. We must now give him away – first to God, for prayer. Jesus called His disciples to be *"with him."* The first call of a pastor is to walk with the Lord in prayer, to be a holy man of God! He is not here primarily to serve us; he is here to *serve God,* to *obey Him.*

While there does need to be a scheme of accountability, the pastor cannot be micromanaged by a board. His call is not to be a 'professional' with a broad range of skills. That model failed miserably. The cry across the land now is clear: "Are there any holy men of God?" With all of the scandals abounding, the great need is not for technical efficiency in the area of pastoral expertise; it is to have a man who hides away and hears from God, then speaks clearly with a prophetic message, not only to the church, but also to the city.

Missionary Members

The role of the people in our current model is to simply be church attenders with flexible and minimal levels of commitment. People file in on Sunday, pay dues and pledge convenient loyalty. They are engaged by an energetic praise team and an inspirational message. It is not enough. Eighty percent of the people are not engaged in ministry. Twenty percent do the work of providing for the Sunday-Wednesday experience, which is aimed at enriching the lives of the others who merely attend. The typical member is unchallenged and unengaged.

The church offers limited options for involvement. Almost all are built around the perpetuation of the institution and take place on the campus of the church. A whole new way of thinking must emerge. We have to see *every member* as a *missionary-evangelist*.

Coming to Christ means you volunteer to be a witness that he is alive; that you have met him, and that he has changed your life. The function of the campus activities must be altered so that it is a training facility for community missionaries. It cannot be the place where we merely exchange recipes, gather for a weekly 'hymn sing,' hear a sermon and then live lives largely disconnected from faith during the week.

Everyone Called to Minister – No More "Just a" Layman

We must insist that no one is *just* a layman. The division that encumbers some *with* ministry and releases others *from* ministry must be a thing of the past. All are missionaries. We must insist, You are not merely a doctor or lawyer, a teacher or technician, a banker or beautician, a judge or journalist, an administrator or advertising executive, a politician or police officer. You are a missionary, cleverly disguised as, let's say, a cable installer. It's how God gets you into homes. You are there to do a job and do it professionally; that is your temporal occupation. But you have a mission with eternal implications as well. You are called to spread the love of Christ.

You may be in homes where no passionate and Scriptural prayers have been prayed in years. Now you are on the inside. While you work, you can pray and look for opportunities to show the caring love of God. May it be manifested in your attitude and actions, in your life and language. And if the door opens, may God give the opportunity to move beyond praying and caring, to openly share your faith and encourage those you serve to consider Christ!

You can no longer separate your Monday-through-Saturday

work role from your Sunday worship. You are a missionary. God has ordered your boundaries (Acts 17:26) and sown you into that office as a member of that team. You may be one of only a few in the entire complex who are practicing the disciplines of the Christian faith. Fulfill your mission, missionary!

The Church Sown

We know the church as *ecclesia* – called out from the world and separated unto God. Every Sunday, we exercise this aspect of church. Driving out of our neighborhoods, we pass hundreds of homes with families not connected to a life-giving congregation. We pass places where we work – the supercenters, schools, hospitals and health centers, office buildings and industrial structures. In some of these places, daily life goes on as if there were no God.

At church, we will hear wonderful words, sing inspiring choruses, and listen to a motivating lesson that momentarily challenges us. Within two hours, according to surveys, 80 percent will not be able to recall any significant content from the sermon. We then return to those same godless neighborhoods and workplaces. In some cases, the church and our living or workplace are like two different worlds. Rarely have we wondered, *How could I get the spirit of what I sense on Sunday into this office complex?* Such thinking may not only seem novel, but foreign, perhaps unthinkable and impossible to achieve. Many places in the city have no witness to the life-giving, changing power of Christ. The salt has remained in the salt-shaker. The light has been placed carefully under a cover so as not to offend.

When Moses descended from Mount Sinai after being in God's Presence, he found the people drunk on the spirit of the golden calf. They could not stand the light of God in the face of Moses, so he was veiled (Exodus 34:33). America has been in the process of veiling the church for 70 years, and we have compliantly been fitted with both muzzle and mask. That must change or we will completely lose our nation. We have only a few years to respond to this crisis.

Our mission must be accomplished without intentionally offending. We will gain nothing by insensitivity, but love without truth is only half the gospel. The present arrangement of singing hymns on Sundays, only to make our faith a secret during the week, must be replaced by a more open declaration of our devotion to Christ.

What if we were to take seriously these words of Jesus: *"Where two or three are gathered together in My name, I am there in the midst of them"* (Matthew 18:20)? Is it possible that we, as living stones (1 Peter 2:5), actually give place to His Presence *only* when we are *intentional* by invoking His name prayerfully and in unity (Psalm 133)? Only when we *deliberately* invite His Presence? Only when we are mortared together by *demonstrated* love and aligned by truth?

What if believers all over the city were to recognize that we were in our current vocational positions primarily to offer the life of Christ to those around us? What if we were to envision ourselves as *a new construct of the church mobile,* the church *diaspora* – scattered and sown into the city Monday through Saturday?

Dia means *through; spora* is the Greek term for *seed* or *sowing.* We Christians are sown into every sector of culture. Thus, God seeds a city with His Presence by scattering us throughout the city in schools, hospitals and board rooms to be salt and light.

Tragically, the church is so divided in many different ways – racially, theologically, liturgically, denominationally, educationally, sociologically, as well as in style and substance, in emphasis and ethical theories. Because of these divisions, we experience only a measure of unity on Sunday.

SALTY GROUPS

The purpose of a SALTY GROUP is simply to meet and pray. Prayer builds an invisible altar. It invites God. In prayer you host God in the marketplace, *"Where two or three gather in my name, there am I with them"* (Mt. 18:20). Prayer, that invokes God's name in a worshipful way invites His Presence. You are a temple, for His glory, lively stones fitted together (1 Peter 2:5).

Is it possible that God has called you to your workplace, for the purpose of hosting Him in that place?

A SALTY GROUP is a workplace triad or quad of Christians, praying:

S   Supplicating as a prayer support group, interceding for one another and their workplace peers, sincerely praying to be sweet incense in the marketplace.

A   Asking God for a spiritual awakening at their workplace, for an anointing to carry the Presence of God at work, to be aware of the spiritual environment of their workplace, to hold one another gently accountable to be a godly witness.

L   Loving others, praying for grace to live a Christ-like life, to be a light in what might be a dark place.

T   Truthing, telling the truth, speaking the truth in love, talk (speech) that is seasoned with salt, tempered Christians.

Y   Yielding to the Holy Spirit, yearning for a Great Awakening, the day God comes to work with them, and the workplace becomes alive with His Presence – SALTY!

How can we affect the darkness when the light is so diminished by our separation? How can we overcome intimidation in our fragmented state? On Sundays, our light proudly shines inside the walls of the sanctuary. We sing boldly and declare our faith! What if we could connect the two or three believers at any given workplace during the week and insist, "You are here to give place to Christ by your prayer and unity!"

A small group of dedicated believers – one a Presbyterian, another a Baptist, then a Pentecostal, and yet another a Methodist – could make a difference if they were to believe that God had sown them into their place of work for a witness. What if they quietly prayed together once a week to consider the claims of Christ in the lives of the people who work there?

Is the earth not the Lord's and the fullness thereof (Psalm 24:1)? Does He not own every business enterprise that exists for the good of mankind? Is it not His will to be glorified in all our lives? Would it not please Him for a group of diverse Christian people to work together in godly fellowship? For prayers and praises to be lifted constantly all over the city by people as they labored? For thanksgiving and psalm-like language to be more common, not something strange when it appears in daily life?

Would it not please Him that those in that workplace who did not know God would experience His love and grace in the lives of the believers who testified of Christ by their behavior? Would He not then bless the city and its marketplace? Are we preventing a blessing from the city and the places at which we work by our indifference and secularized lifestyles?

God wants a living temple through which He can manifest Himself and show Himself glorious! The fact that a few Christians work in a given place is not enough. Stones delivered to a site and neatly stacked there but never joined by mortar do not make a building. The church *gathered* is not the church *assembled*. A small group of Christians at the same place does not make a living temple until they come together 'in His name' to invite His Presence into that place.

We should empower, instruct and release our people to create prayer fellowships everywhere in the city! We should say to them,

Join yourself to other Christians whose faith is sound, whose lives are holy, and whose hearts long for Christ to be glorified by the salvation of many.

Become the church *diaspora*. Join together at your place of work or in your neighborhood to give place to the Presence of Christ. Pray together for grace to be a witness in the darkness. Care about the business, the owner, your supervisor, those who work around you, and especially those who do not know Christ.

As you pray, God will begin to love the most unlovable people through you and the other believers. It will not be your love improved, but His love imputed. Be a caring support team one for another, seeking to improve your demonstrated faith and witness. Raise the level of mutual accountability so that it positively affects the quality of your collective witness. Look for opportunities to share Christ. They may not be overt. They may be more indirect like requests for prayer, opportunities to listen, a ready shoulder, the kind response to an unkind word, faithfulness on the job, being a model employee, and more.

Meeting even once a week, just two or three believers together, as lively stones, invites a manifestation of the presence of God into a workplace. This is the reason they are there. God has sovereignly sown believers into worldly environments as vocational missionaries. Once you have established the church *diaspora* in a workplace, keep it going. Add other sites, until you have at least one Salty Group at every worksite in the city. Here are some suggestions:

1. *Make your prayer times, first, about the quality of your own relationship with God* – "God, I want to live in unbroken communion with You, even at this [ungodly] workplace."

2. *Make your prayer time about the credibility of your witness.* Ask God for favor with fellow employees, with the owner and

management. Daniel gained the favor of God even in the administration of Nebuchanezzar. Paul found favor as a Roman prisoner. Esther, the Jew, was favored and chosen as queen of Persia, now modern Iran. God can give you favor for His glory! Pray for that grace upon your group.

3. *Pray for the salvation of those with whom you work.* Pray for their needs. Give them the gift of prayer. After you have solidified your relationships as believers from divergent denominational backgrounds, add a weekly Bible discussion and prayer group over lunch! Make it light and devotional. Avoid theological wrangling. Keep the focus on Jesus. Conclude with prayer. Let it be an entry point for enquirers. Now you have two meetings per week. One is for a believers meeting – for prayer. The second is an open gathering for inquirers.

4. *Consistently ask God to bless the business.* Tell the owner you are praying for the favor of God upon the business. Such testimonies give God the opportunity to show Himself alive to unbelievers. We sometimes attempt to protect God. We fear to say, "I'll pray about that," as if to imply that we had some special relationship with God! Ah! But we do have a special relationship with God, in Christ. Not everyone, according to Hebrews 4:16, can come boldly to the throne of grace. You can give and stand back and see what God might do.

Paul boldly declared in the midst of the storm:

Men, you should have listened to me, and not have...incurred this disaster...I urge you to take heart, for there will be no loss of life among you...For there stood by me this night an angel of the God to whom I belong and whom I serve, saying, 'Do not be afraid...God has granted you all those who sail with you.' Therefore take heart, men, for I believe God (Acts 27:21-25).

The group was astonished! The watchful care of God over Paul's life radiated grace to those with him on that ship. We must believe that we are also highly favored and blessed of the Lord. And we are not to shut up such blessings to ourselves. As vocational missionaries, God blesses us, and through us makes us a blessing to others. By association, others are blessed, just as Lot was blessed by his association with Abraham (Genesis 13:1-6); as

Egypt was blessed by Joseph (41:46-49); as the house of Obed – Edom the Gittite was blessed by the Presence of the Ark of God (2 Samuel 6:11).

We must cease to see ourselves as beleaguered, disempowered people who must keep quiet about our faith or lose our jobs and our retirement. Such thinking is not only faithless, it is the mind-set of orphans who live in fear. We are the sons and daughters of God. We should never act in arrogant ways, but in humility. Yet, we must know whose we are, and that the Presence of God upon our lives carries with it a blessing that flows over even into the businesses that employ us (Acts 3:25, 26). We are missionaries!

A 'Go Ye' Gospel

Our 'come-to' churches cannot be our only strategy for the gospel to go forth. Fifty years ago, conservative Christians spent significantly more time at the church campus. Perfect attendance for a decade or more was not unusual. Sunday school along with morning worship were essentials. The Sunday evening prayer ser-vice flowed into an evangelistic service. Wednesday, the church gathered again. The facility was often busy all week – multiple annual week-long or two-week revivals, vacation Bible schools, men's and women's meetings, gospel singings. Church-all-day with dinner-on-the-grounds was common. Sunday evening ser-vices have virtually disappeared. Wednesday event participation is shrinking. Increasingly, Americans are once-a-week, at best, worship 'celebration' participants.

To average 100 in church attendance today, 200 attenders are needed. Overall, church attendance has fallen from the 50 per-cent level in the 1950's to 17.7 percent of the population today. Many see this as an indication of a lukewarm church plagued by apathy. No doubt that is true. There are noble attempts to reverse the trend – to turn back the clock. The emphasis today is an attractional worship celebration – a magnet approach centered on the church campus. But we are deluded if we think that we can revive the church schedule of 50 years ago. Or even that by reviving it we have achieved renewal.

There is another way! You can never stuff a 'go-ye' gospel into a "come-to" church! We have been capturing all of the free and expendable time of our people to run the church campus operation. We pull all that energy back to the church building for yet another preaching or teaching service with little appreciated impact. To do so, we have attempted to enhance praise and worship and alter the style of services to make them more attractive. It is not working! What if we released personnel resources into the community? What if a team of pastors began to collectively coach the members of their churches toward working together during the week, in their neighborhoods, in the various workplaces, to reveal Christ and promote His kingdom across the city? What if we understood that the church is not about the building, but about Christians, as 'mobile temples,' giving place to His Presence?

The slots for service we offer at our church campuses are far too narrow to gather in all of the talents and abilities of God's people. A neurosurgeon serves as an usher. An investment specialist parks cars and escorts the elderly into the facility. A city councilman works in the Junior Church ministry. Evidence of humility? Yes, and that is commendable. Is it possible, however, that we might find a better use of the status and skills of these people? Broader options for ministry will not be found around the barn, but in the harvest field.

Focusing on the City

We must move from the *temple* to the *city!* When Israel returned from Babylon, provision was made for them to rebuild their Temple, but the rebuilding process stalled. There was a division among the people. They were so poor, so close to starvation, so few in number and facing a formidable task. Consumed by survival needs, God's work was not their priority.

Zechariah prophesied that a mountain would be moved: *"'Not my might nor by power, but by My Spirit,' says the Lord"* (4:6). That mountain was a pile of rubble. It was the debris of what had been the Temple of Solomon. It had to be moved before the new temple rebuilding process could begin. For years, the people gathered at the foot of that rubble for Sabbath celebrations on new moon and feast days!

Haggai, the prophet, stood in the shadow of the rubble where the Temple should have been, and declared, *"Is it not time for the Temple to be rebuilt?"* (see 1:2). And then he added an interesting note, *"You...dwell in your paneled houses"* (v. 4). One translation says *"luxurious houses!"* (NLT).

Where did these poor returning exiles find luxurious houses? How could they afford them? Evidently, as time dragged on and no Temple rebuilding was begun, the people began to take the materials that had been provided by Cyrus to rebuild the Temple to use in rebuilding their own homes. Haggai thundered, *"Go up to the mountains and bring wood and build the temple"* (1:8). Only then, he said would there be grain in the barn (2:15-19).

They did rebuild the Temple – and wept when they remembered how meager it was in comparison to the glory of Solomon's Temple (Haggai 2:3; Ezra 3:12). But there was no great revival. We sometimes feel that we have done all we can do to see revival come. We ask 'why does it linger?' Though the Temple had been rebuilt, the city remained in ruins. They had rightfully restored the *symbol* of God's Presence that they valued, but they had left undone the *substance* of the mission for which the Temple existed.

For another 70 years, the people would make paths through the rubble. When Nehemiah came to the city, he would find places still impassable due to the massive amounts of rubble (Nehemiah 2:14). Revival came only when the community of faith turned their attention to the city.

All over our communities are temples or churches. We make paths through the rubble of the city. Like the exiles, the rubble becomes a part of the unnoticed backdrop. We are accustomed to it, no longer shocked by it. The fresh eyes and ears of Nehemiah were so moved by the sad condition of the city (1:2-5), that he passionately called for a movement to rebuild the walls, clear the city of Babylon's debris, and separate the city itself unto God. Seeing through his eyes, they saw the city as it could be; with his faith, they believed they could do what they had not previously attempted.

Until we shift our focus from the temple to the community, from church buildings to the city itself, we will make little effort at redeeming the land or impacting the city. We have no theology of land and little understanding of the mission of the church in a city. Only three percent of the budget of the typical church is invested back into the community.[11] The psalmist declares, *"The earth is the Lord's, and all its fullness"* (Psalm 24:1). Our cities belong to God. The prophets spoke of the land *"mourning"* and *"trembling"* (Jeremiah 12:4, 11; 23:10; Hosea 4:3; Joel 1:10; Amos 8:8; Zechariah 12:12). Paul declares that *"the whole creation groans"* (Romans 8:22). Genesis reminds us that the earth itself felt the impact of sin (3:17, 18).

Buying into the secularist separation notions, we have not even had the idea of redeeming the land on our radar screen. Our churches are sacred, all else is ignored. Does it make a difference that a city has churches that honor God? Is there a blessing that comes to godly cities (Genesis 18:24-28; Proverbs 11:10, 11; Isaiah 1:21) through godly praying people?

Revival will come with two simultaneous shifts. Our mission in the city is equally important to our task at the temple; and to accomplish both, we must empower lay-leaders – the Nehemiahs – as partners in the process of renewal.

The Levels of Church-Based Prayer Ministry

A crisis or casual approach to prayer ministry is not adequate (level one). Further, a prayer ministry must not be our goal (level two). We want a 'praying church!' (level three). There are various levels of intensity here.

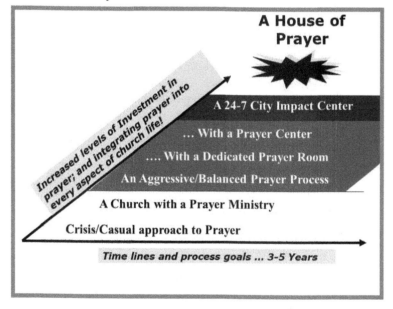

All should launch *an aggressive, balanced prayer process* that seeks to engage the whole church in prayer. This is more than a prayer ministry. And yet, this church may not be able to set aside a room dedicated only to the purpose of prayer.

1. In some cases, a church may add to the aggressive, balanced prayer process *a dedicated prayer room* – a place set aside as a kind of retreat for personal prayer and small prayer groups to

gather. All during the week, people will check in and make use of this prayer room. Intercessors might gather before or even during services to support worship activities in prayer.

2. A few churches will be able to move beyond a prayer room, a kind of personal retreat, to *a prayer center*[12] where prayer is organized and mobilized for both people and ministries. It makes the church a prayed-for church! At the prayer center, prayer support for every ministry is mobilized. Prayer training is offered. Prayer stations (physical displays) inspire prayer. People drop by to pray and for prayer. Needs are emailed or called in to the phone center. Intercessors do the work of prayer – praying over church events, praying into needs from around the world, supporting ministries and missionaries in prayer. The community is bathed in prayer.

3. A smaller number of churches will be able to move beyond a prayer center to a *24/7 prayer impact center.* In such an arrangement, the church is open for ministry and service 24 hours a day, seven days a week. The doors never close. And prayer never stops. Teams are deployed from the church to respond to crises around the city – all hours of the day and night. Wherever there is a need, the church is responding! Wherever there is pain, the church is on-site offering the love of God!

The transformation of the church into a house of prayer for the nations is no small process. Plan on a three-to five-year transition or more. At first, the response will be glowing. Everyone will declare that they want to learn to pray, and they want the church to be a praying church. But when the newness of that idea wears away, sheer determination will be needed by a devout group of intercessory leaders to pursue the process. It is not merely activities that are being added. Prayer is changing both the culture of the church and the daily disciplines of its members. Quite an undertaking!

1   Andrew Murray, *The Power of Persevering Prayer* <www.whatsaiththe-scripture.com/voice/murray.perservingprayer>.

2   Jim Cymbala, *Fresh Wind, Fresh Fire* (Grand Rapids: Zondervan, 1997) 11, 16.

3   Ibid, 19.

4   Ibid, 25.

5   This occurred on May 5, 2005, at the conclusion of the Transform World Conference. At that time, 1 million intercessors had been mobilized across the island nation in 450 prayer networks.

6   Vander Griend, chapter by John Quam, "Seven Ways Prayer Is Changing the Church in America," 15

7   Quoted by Dick Eastman, *No Easy Road* (Grand Rapids: Baker, 1971) 37.

8   Vander Griend, 32.

9   Charles Spurgeon. Quoted in *Turning Point Daily Devotional,* February 17, 2004 (San Diego: Turning Point Ministries).

10 A number of people have contributed to the contrast between a church *with a prayer ministry* and a *praying church,* including: Fred Hartley III, "Best Church Growth Method? Try Prayer!" in Pray! Magazine (no. 7, 1998), 22; Doug Kamstra, *The Praying Church Idea Book: Becoming a House of Prayer* – mobilizing members for prayer ministries; and the late Paul Dozeman of Restoration Ministries.

11 A multi-congregational study on city-impact study by the pastoral leadership team of a Southeastern U.S. city. Is this figure of 3% typical?

12 See Chapter 7.

FOUR
The Four Dimensions of Local Church Prayer Ministry

The church's greatest deficiency today is in power – not in programs, strategies, materials, or ideas. And power for ministry can be released only through prayer.[1]

Alvin Vander Griend

Prayer is the most important work in the kingdom of God. It is a labor for which there is no substitute.[2]

O. Hallesby

Prayer is not merely an occasional impulse to which we respond when we are in trouble: prayer is a life attitude.

Walter Mueller

He that lives in the neglect of secret prayer…that prays only when he prays with others would not pray at all, were it not that the eyes of others are upon him. He that will not pray where none but God sees, does not really pray at all out of respect to God, or regard his all-seeing eye. He therefore casts off the effect of all prayer and of worship, of which prayer is the principal duty.[3]

Jonathan Edwards

Real prayer is communion with God, so that there will be common thoughts between His mind and ours. What is needed is for Him to fill our hearts with His thoughts, and then His desires will become our desires flowing back to Him.

– Arthur Pink

Most churches have a single-dimensional model for prayer. If they have a prayer meeting, and fewer than ten percent of congregations have such a dedicated service for prayer, it is often limited in terms of the prayer formats that are used. The prayer focus too often becomes routine, often too narrow. Intercessors sometimes 'take over' the prayer services with a level of passion too hot for the typical participant unaccustomed to such fervent prayer! Too often, the prayer meetings degenerate into a litany of prayer requests.

What is needed is a multidimensional model. A growing church needs many opportunities for prayer – different times and places. It needs a prayer ministry that is as diverse as the congregation's focus and its mission field.

There are four areas that need to be developed if the church is going to have a balanced prayer process. These are not exercises in prayer or even prayer ministries. These four areas represent the way in which we should measure and balance the prayer ministry.

The Fourfold Focus

1. *A praying people – personal transformation.* At home, daily, personal prayer. A prayer closet. When homes have been dedicated to God and consecrated and fathers bless their children, the act and sound of prayer is not strange.

2. *A praying church.* As a house of prayer, this church is totally dependent on doing the business of God, depending on His strength will serve others beyond themselves. Prayer embedded in every ministry. A church-wide regular prayer meeting; along with multiple opportunities for prayer.

3. *Identified and mobilized intercessors.* The prayer engine of the church is intercession and intercessors. These people are called and gifted to pray. All of us are to be intercessors, but there is a core of people in every congregation whose hearts are focused on prayer. Find them. Affirm them. Disciple them. Mobilize them. Train them. Debrief them. Direct them.

4. *Prayer Evangelism – claiming the harvest by prayer.* We ask for God's Presence to anoint us as we love the lost, opening them to the gospel. Prayerfully, we look for opportunities to share the good news of God's love. Conduct prayer walks and prayer missions. Ask every Christian to begin to pray for unsaved friends and family. Prayer and the harvest must be connected.

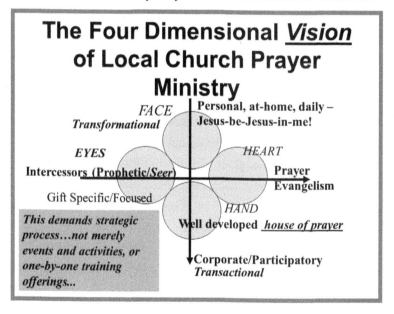

We will consider these four aspects of the congregation's prayer ministry in pairs. First, *personal and family, at-home daily prayer* that nurtures the ongoing transformation of our lives into the image of God is tied to *at-church prayer saturation.* The two are connected. Later (in chs. 5 and 6), we will look at intercession and prayer evangelism as a pair.

A Praying People – The Goal: Personal Transformation

The absence of prayer in the home is more damaging than the absence of prayer at church. Prayer cannot be something that only happens on Sunday in a building, with a ceremony noticeably different than any other experience during the week. If it is, we are teaching our children that prayer is something strange and foreign, unfamiliar to daily life and even irrelevant to real life. That cheapens prayer, making it a kind of plaything that belongs to the imaginary world of make-believe.

We approach discipleship as a program. But God's discipleship program is, and always has been, the home. Ask a leader, "Tell me about discipleship in your church." What you will hear is a litany of programs that have been tried, some more successfully than others. What you will rarely hear is any mention of the family. We see discipleship in institutional terms, not relational terms.

Gigi, the oldest daughter of Billy and Ruth Graham, remembers staying at her maternal grandparents' house, the Bells, who had been missionaries in China, where Ruth was raised. In the early morning, she'd wake up to the savory of bacon, eggs and hot biscuits. On her way downstairs, she'd pass the corner of the living room where she would see Grandfather Bell, Ruth Graham's father, on his knees in front of the big rocking chair.

On her final visit to the Graham farm, her frail, white-haired grandmother, Billy's mother, was radiant with joy. One by one, each grandchild came by her bedside, and she took them into her feeble hands and quoted a Scripture passage, or prayed a prayer, or pronounced a blessing over them. And then she would say, "Pass it on!"[4] That is discipleship.

Tom Bisset, in his book *Why Christian Kids Leave the Faith,* found four primary reasons:

1. They had unanswered questions that troubled them about their faith.

2. Their faith wasn't working; they couldn't see it in "real life" ways.

3. Other things became more important.

4. They never personally owned the faith! They had conformed to faith expectations, but had never had a transforming encounter with God.[5]

Getting families to engage in prayer exercises is not the goal. Transformational prayer that fills the home with the Presence of God, and those in it with genuine Christlike attitudes and relationships, is the goal. Holy moments that are respectful, and yet open, that allow our children to explore, to earnestly question, to sincerely probe – this is the power of faith in the home. Such moments shape perceptions and form the fabric of our habits; they frame our views of God that determine actions – that's discipleship. At home, we have the time to connect the dots between prayer and its effect; between obedience and blessing; between sin and its consequences. Gentle, patient answers to childlike questions – that's discipleship. The early embrace of faith practices – praying, giving, even fasting of food, time, money, etc. – that teaches discipleship. Donald Sloat says, "The way parents treat their children in daily living has more impact…than the family's religious practices, including having a family altar, reading the Bible together or attending church services."[6]

Hugh Hefner was raised in a minister's home. Joseph Stalin studied for the priesthood. Mao Tse-tung was raised under missionary teaching.[7] But they were not discipled. Before you have effective at-home prayer, you'll probably have to get some families strong enough to forgive one another and healthy enough to pray together. Edith Bajema adds:

Children learn about God more through the nuances of family life and parenting than through even the most rigorous daily table devotions. But family worship and prayer is an important element of those nuances. What tone of voice do parents use when they pray or talk about God? Do the words 'God' and 'Jesus' turn up only in prayer and Bible reading, or do they appear naturally in everyday conversations? Is the atmosphere at family devotions one of freedom or control?[8]

What kids hear expressed in family worship needs to be experienced in family relationships. If it isn't, these perceptive little ones may come to believe it was all a lie. Evangeline Booth became head of the Salvation Army after her father. She recalled that her parents "did not have to say a word to me about Christianity. I saw it in action."[9]

Communion with God is the gateway to personal transformation. It is the heart of all our prayer. The success of our efforts must be measured by whether or not we are transformed by our daily prayer times. Praying to be like Jesus – for Christ to live in us and through us. Transformational, intentional, focused time in the Presence of God should change us. The Jewish Council took note of the disciples that they had *"been with Jesus"* (Acts 4:13). His Presence changes us.

If the church is to be a praying church, then our homes must be praying homes. Prayer cannot be something foreign, strange to daily life. Families should have times of prayer. Couples should be learning the power of praying together. Fathers mark their sons and daughters by blessing them, praying with and for them.

If our churches were closed by some tragic action, members who rarely pray at home would find themselves scrambling to sustain faith. Too many Christians live from Sunday to Sunday. Their personal, daily relationship with God is not bathed in prayer and grounded in Scripture. Homes rich with prayer have a faith that cannot be destroyed. As home goes, so goes the church. We need corporate worship, and we need praying homes. No prayer movement is successful that does not wake up prayer in the home.

Don't Forget the Children

When we think about launching a prayer movement, we usually don't think about children or youth. The disciples didn't either, and Jesus rebuked them for their exclusion when he said, *"Let the little children come to Me, and do not forbid them; for of such is the kingdom of heaven"* (Matthew 19:14). *The Praying Church Sourcebook* says, "Children have an intuitive awareness of God; they are quick to respond to God with trust, awe and love."[10]

Dr. Ricky Moore, a professor at Lee University, says of children:

They love surprises. We love schedules. We conspire against being surprised. No news is good news. They live on wonder and delight in things they do not understand. They toss aside toys once they have become predictable. We seek life in knowing things, eliminating the unexplainable and the unpredictable, in knowing things to death. Children know joy. Not just the selfevoked pleasures of stimulation and entertainment, but the deep laughter that bubbles up from their bellies and leaves them feeling weak and good. A joy that can only come forth out of a life that is open to surprises, that trusts and surrenders itself to being surprised. As any child knows, you can't tickle yourself.[11]

Esther Ilnisky[12] is a pioneer in the child intercessors movement. Cheryl Sacks, author of *The Prayer Saturated Church,* tells the story of a service led by Esther at Skyway Church in Phoenix. After only a few moments of sharing, she called for the children. Handing the microphone to a 5-year-old boy, she asked him to pray for all the abused children in the world. With stammering lips and a trembling voice, he prayed simply and powerfully, "God, make the mothers and fathers stop fighting. Tell them it's hurting their kids."[13]

Cheryl writes that he then fell to his knees and wept passionately. He continued to weep until he was driven to a prostrate position by his burden, his face on the floor. Other children moved around him and began to comfort him. This is power of agreement in intercession. How did these children learn such principles?

Prayer is incredibly instinctive. Cultural patterns of proper Christianity have constrained us. Our children may free us. Another young girl prayed, "God, tell the parents to stop killing our brothers and sisters through abortion." By the time for the second service, the platform was full of kids, teens and adults crying out to God. There was nothing to do but let the first service spill over into the second. The simplicity of the prayers of these children arrested the congregation. Tears were the order of the day. The second service didn't end until 2 p.m.[14]

The best models for adults to learn unvarnished, simple and sincere praying may be right in your congregation – your children. They get 'real' when they pray. They don't posture or worry about image. They tend to pray forthright prayers. And they believe. They don't grasp the abstract concepts of prayer; they gravitate to symbols.

Try a candle prayer service with your children. It adds a little flair by creating a lasting memory. Light a candle, darken the room, and pray a model prayer focusing on light and darkness, love and hate, kindness and harshness. Pass the light around. Ask each one to pray that he would 'act' in Christlike, and therefore Christ-light, ways. The kids will get it. And they will pray![15]

Al Vander Griend says, "Praying is not only something we do *for* our children, but also something we do *with* our children. We have much to offer the younger members of Christ's body, and they have much to offer us."[16]

SEVEN LEVELS OF FAMILY PRAYER

The goal is the transformation of the culture of the home to a praying home! Think in terms of seven levels of family prayer.

1. Personal, daily, Jesus-be-Jesus-in-me praying. Focus on transformation in prayer, not merely transaction.

2. Pray as a couple together.

3. Establish and maintain the family altar.

4. Practice informal and spontaneous praying. Prayer moments that are natural, laced into the fabric of life.

5. Plan formal blessing times – birth, puberty, baptism, graduations, etc.

6. The family as an evangelism prayer force – pray for the lost next door and around the world.

7. The family as a missionary prayer force. As a family, adopt a nation for prayer. Adopt an unreached people group. Adopt a missionary for prayer. Join prayer support teams when short-term missionaries are sent from your church. Then, pray for the sending forth of a family member on a missions trip, and finally. Go on mission together as a family.

The Christian Difference

In 2004, George Barna released a report that found no difference in the divorce rate among Christians and non-Christians. Additional research indicates that there is more to that story. For couples who attend church regularly, the divorce rate drops by 35 percent. That's significant.

A University of Chicago survey revealed that 75 percent of the Americans who pray with their spouses reported marriages that were 'very happy.' They were more likely to respect each other. To discuss their marriage goals together. And in a surprising find for the University, they reported higher levels of satisfaction in the area of couple intimacy.

And here is more new data – When a couple has received pre-marital counseling, attends church regularly, and prays together, the probability of divorce is one in 39,000. Church attendance brings a modest drop in divorce. But praying together pulverizes divorce.

A Praying Church – The Goal: Prayer Ministries Mobilized

Daily at-home prayer is the backbone of the at-church prayer efforts. These feed each other. The more people become comfortable with daily prayer the greater the impact of church prayer times. The greater the impact of the at-church prayer times and groups with support materials and encouragement, the more at-home daily prayer should grow.

The Four Dimensional *Vision* of Local Church Prayer Ministry

FACE
Transformational

Personal, at-home, daily – Jesus-be-Jesus-in-me!

You cannot have a praying church without praying homes.

And you will never have a prayerless church with praying homes.

HAND
Well developed *house of prayer*

Corporate/Participatory
Transactional

This corporate dimension is critical. We have perceived prayer as a private matter unaware that our perception has been affected by our culture, one of hyper-individualism. Prayer *is* personal. But it is impossible to have a fully developed prayer life without praying regularly with others. The New Testament church prayed together. Daniel Henderson notes that "more is said in Acts and the Epistles about corporate prayer, corporate learning of Biblical truth, corporate evangelism, and corporate Christian maturity and growth, than about the personal aspects of these Christian disciplines."[17] Sixty-six percent of American Christians are fearful of praying aloud in small groups.[18] That must change.

The at-church prayer movement has two primary goals. First, the movement of prayer, deep and evident dependence on God, to the center of all the church does. The goal is not, however, the development of a prayer ministry. The church is a praying church because the people pray. And such prayer is not primarily pragmatic, it is transformational. It is people who are pursuing the face of God, not merely His hand. The goal of prayer is formation. Yet, it focuses not on us, but on God – on Christ in us, the hope of glory being revealed in us. With that goal in mind, Christ at the center, every effort is made to mobilize prayer support for the ministries and mission of the church. Prayer events test the capacity to mobilize. The number of people who show up for a prayer meeting reveals the depth and breadth of current prayer activity and interest.

A Buffet of Prayer

If the church is to be a *"house of prayer for the nations,"* it must engage its members in prayer. And no one model or style will effectively satisfy the need. Think in terms of a buffet of prayer – prayer groups for every conceivable cause (single moms or dads; prayer for Israel; parents praying for lost children; men's/women's/youth/couples prayer groups; addictions prayer groups, etc.).

Prayer groups should meet at different times and places, providing multiple options. Different styles of prayer should be used among the various prayer groups – silent prayer, prayers of agreement, small-group prayer, quad-praying, the prayer chair, banner prayer, Scripture praying. These multiple prayer events and options – perhaps every day, at different times during the day depending on the size of the congregation – seek to mobilize the whole church in prayer.

A church needs prayer groups that meet weekly, and not less than monthly. The desired ratio is seven prayer groups for every 100 people. These groups should be small and focused. No group should be larger than a dozen participants. Each group should have a specific prayer cause – a focus (fathers praying for lost sons; mothers and daughters praying together; seniors praying for the next generation; prayer for the lost; for missionaries; for the community and its leaders; for unreached people groups). The focus attracts participants, but the real goal, and the purpose for keeping the group small is simple – this is where people learn to pray, as intercessors, aloud. Here they are mentored in sensitivity to the Spirit, the connection of prayer and the Bible, spiritual gifts and prayer. These groups are indispensable.

With the goal of placing prayer at the very center of all the church does, embrace this philosophy: "Every worker in the church should have an intercessor; and every worker in the church should be an intercessor." Adopt the Moravian principle: "No one works unless someone prays." Without prayer, we are simply throwing money and people-power at spiritual needs, and we will see few results.

Every Ministry a Praying Ministry

Every ministry of the church should be backed and bathed in prayer. And yet, every ministry should itself be a praying ministry.

Praying and prayed-for ministries create a pervasive prayer atmosphere in the church. We want to change the culture of the church to be one of dependence upon God, humility, a servant's heart, unity in the place of strife, healthy and loving relationships with a focus on the glory of God – to the end that Christ alone is glorified and many come to faith in Him.

To accomplish the task of being a praying church, we need to nurture prayer. For most churches, this will mean the establishment of a prayer room at the church. Some churches will be able to establish a prayer center. This is discussed in Chapter Seven.

At-home daily prayer and the prayer ministries of the church drive each other. As one rises, the other is affected. When there is more prayer at home, there is a greater impact felt in church prayer gatherings. The greater the impact of the church prayer gatherings, the more people take prayer-fire home with them.

Beginning the Process

Which comes first – at-home daily prayer or congregational prayer events? The only way you can test the level of at-home prayer is to call for corporate prayer. If you call a prayer meeting and no one shows up, it may tell you there is too little daily, at-home activity or interest in prayer. It gives some indication of the level of daily prayer engagement in homes.

What do you do if there is little general interest in prayer? Where do you start? Start with those who have a call to pray – the intercessors. Lace prayer into your corporate prayer gatherings. Calling a sidebar prayer meeting may not be the best tactic. Put prayer in the middle of your Sunday morning worship.

Suggestions for Corporate Prayer Enrichment

1. Make prayer a major feature of your Sunday morning worship event. One pastor uses light control to dim the lights of his sanctuary. He kneels in front of his pulpit and intercedes for his congregation. During this time, the sanctuary is quiet, the people agreeing with his prayer. Some folks slip quietly to the altar and kneel during this time. After he prays, the congregation is encouraged to pray softly, whispering needs to God. Elders and deacons meet people at the altar with prayer needs. The prayer time flows naturally into the next portion of worship.

2. Another pastor makes his 'pastoral prayer' one of the features of the Sunday morning worship. The congregation looks forward to this time of pastoral blessing. Participants are encouraged to move to the front edge of the pew and surrender the back of their pew to the person behind them. This encourages active participation, a time for moving around the sanctuary. This kind of focus and reverence draws the congregation together for prayer.

3. A prayer can be placed on the screen to be prayed by the congregation a section at a time, followed by a pause. Allow for bite-size spontaneous prayer in the context of the planned corporate prayer. Which is the main thing? Reading the prayer on the screen or encouraging heartfelt focused praying?

4. Ask the music director to choose at least one congregational song or hymn that is really a prayer! Cultivate awareness in the congregation that they are singing a prayer. Occasionally, have someone sing a special prayer song. Choir selections should be chosen and offered as prayers. Don't sing words – sing a prayer. In the Revelation, the incense of prayer is translated into a song (5:8-10).

5. Preach a series of sermons on prayer or have the pastor pray his sermon. Teach a section, then model 'praying it.' Let the congregation respond with bite-size prayer responses.

6. After the Sunday message, invite the entire congregation forward for a season of prayer. Have them complete this phrase in prayer: "God, this morning, as our pastor brought the Word, I felt that You were saying to me_____." Encourage the use of a phrase. But don't inhibit divine surprises. Someone might erupt with something exploding in their soul and touch the entire church. Move from the personal to the corporate: "God, I sense You are saying to our church that..." These can be incredibly powerful times in which the congregation is being challenged to discern the word of the Lord, not only to them, but to the church. People observe the preacher and listen to his message asking, "What did you hear from God today?" It creates participants out of passive observers.

7. Reestablish the tradition of the altar. Let people tarry in the Presence of God. Occasionally, bring the entire congregation forward for a season of prayer at the altar. Insist, with as much grace as possible, that all come forward, but be sensitive to the elderly and the infirm.

8. Bring the children into the congregation several times a year, and let them pray. Seat them around the front. Give them the microphone. Their prayers are so direct, so simple: "God, I pray that the mommies and daddies will stay together!" Sensitive subjects are gently mentioned. "God, help the people stop fighting on the television!" You will find wet eyes filling the house when you release the children to pray.

9. Call the men forward and pray a prayer of blessing over them as the priests of their homes. Ask them to form a circle and pray one for another. Charge them with the privilege of leading their family in spiritual matters. Grace them with forgiveness for their failures in this area and for the guilt that keeps them from feeling worthy and spiritually qualified to lead their wife in prayer and bless their children. After prayer, ask their wives to come and join them at the altar. Lead them both in a blessing prayer:

> Men, would you pray with me, 'God, I bless my wife. I thank You for her companionship and partnership. I pray that we will

walk together in greater unity than ever before, honoring You and one another, that I will love her, sacrificially. That together, we can discover Your will for our lives and open the doors of blessing and favor on our home and our children.'

Continuing, say,

Wives, would you pray with me, 'God, I bless my husband. I release him to lead our family in godly ways. I pray that he would be a holy man of God after Your heart. That he would be, by Your grace, an example of strength and humility to our children. I thank You that You have given him to me and that I am his wife.'

Of course, you can word your own pastoral prayer of blessing. As couples stand together and pray one for another, expect tears. Expect some discomfort. For many, such spiritual closeness is not a common thing. You model it at church in order to encourage it at home.

10. Change the way you receive prayer requests. Rather than a long litany of individually called-out needs, have your people offer the needs spontaneously, but prayerfully, "Congregation, as we bow our heads in prayer, mindful that God hears us and cares, would you prayerfully call out the needs of loved ones?" After spontaneous needs are called out, lead the congregation in prayer for those needs.

11. Change the atmosphere of the prayer request time. Daniel Henderson warns that "sharing the trials and traumas of people in the church can easily downgrade to inappropriate chit-chat. Sometimes the devil is in the details." He adds, "A strong worship-based prayer time tends to eliminate loose lips."[19]

12. Some churches have a prayer-request box or chest, and at prayer meetings, members come forward and take the requests out of the box by the handfuls. They go to a quiet place and pray through the needs, returning them to the prayer chest at the end of the prayer session. The prayer meeting usually begins with a general charge and some instructions. The conclusion is one of thanksgiving and praise for answered prayer or an exhortation to *"continue earnestly in prayer"* (Colossians 4:2).

13. Many churches collect the prayer requests beforehand. They are given to the pastor, who will often call many of them out as he prays for the congregation, "Lord, today, we offer these people to you in need: John, recovering from surgery; Ann, needing a job; our youth, and their summer missions trip," and so on.

14. Place prayer requests on a screen during your prayer time. Have each person who will, take home prayer requests and pray for them during the week.

15. Offer a chance for the church to give thanks for answered prayer! Do it in the same way, after you have prayed for those in need. The pastor might continue the prayer time in this way: "Congregation, would you now respond spontaneously to God in thanksgiving for answered prayer? 'God, this week You answered my prayer by_____.'" Have the congregation fill in the blank, encouraging them to use no more than phrases or sentence prayers. Keep the prayer responses moving around the room. Repeat them if necessary, so that all can hear.

16. Keep a record of answered prayer in a book. Sometimes we are so overwhelmed by the sheer number of prayer requests that we fail to see any of the answers. John Hyde (1865–1912), the son of a pastor, is often called the apostle of prayer. Affectionately known as 'Praying Hyde,' he recorded 50,000 specific answers to his prayers.[20]

17. Feature prayer testimonies as a part of the regular service. To control time issues and keep the testimony focused, do them as brief interviews. Choose a different church in the city to pray for each week.

18. Choose a different church in the city to pray for each week. Encourage the members to write that pastor a note (provide note cards in the pew or bulletin) and place their card in the offering. Mail it to that pastor. In the same way, mention a handful of nations each Sunday in prayer, and keep mission praying before the people. Rotate the prayer focus for each Sunday on different ministries in the church needing support by prayer.

19. Show short video clips on answered prayer or prayer inspiration points.

20. Take time for small-group prayer during your services. It encourages 'whole church' participation. Most people do not kneel at an altar at the end of the service – they sit passively during congregation prayer times. Small groups influence people toward participation. The newer your congregational prayer emphasis, the more caution you need to use here. Larger group prayer will ensure that someone in that group will feel comfortable leading the prayer. Smaller circles of prayer – triads, for example – should be reserved for a more prayer-savvy congregation.

21. Encourage some people to pray silently in the congregation while the pastor is preaching, and others to go to a special room for simultaneous intercession[21]

22. Construct a prayer banner service. Even if you do not have colorful banners, you can create posters around various themes: revival, souls, holiness, schools, government, families, drug addiction, purity needs, and more. The list is endless. Place these throughout the congregation, inviting people to pray at them, not to them, but around them with others who share their burden. Encourage them to pray aloud – but not loudly. Encourage them to pray prayers of agreement one with another.[22]

23. Do a concert of prayer. This is an evening in which worship, prayer and thanksgiving are woven together. It can be very simple and almost unstructured. For example, in a 60-minute prayer service, choose six themes, 10 minutes for each theme.

Begin each section with an anchor Scripture. Allow different participants to come forward and read the passage. Say to the congregation, "We are going to pray about each of these themes. One at a time, I am asking you to come to the microphones on each side of the church. Pray about the issue on which we are focusing. Please, limit your prayers to about a minute...no long prayers." Use microphone monitors to hold the microphone. If someone goes too long, a few "amens" from the prayer leader will send a gentle message. Transition each section with music, and move to the next passage. Mix in some small-group time, plus time for silence. If the Holy Spirit descends on one of the segments, stay there all night. Throw the schedule out.

24. Have an evening of "thanksgiving" prayer or a night of missions praying in the same way you organized the concert of prayer. Pray for your church's missionaries. Mention the state of the nation in which they work. Acquire some footage of their work or other challenging missions work. Focus some of the prayer segments on unreached people groups. Stimulate imaginary praying: "God, we do not know what it would be like to be in a culture that had no Bible, no churches...that had never heard the story of the resurrection of Christ." "Church, imagine with me, what that might mean. Let's pray this way...'it would mean_____'!" Have them fill in that blank. Stepping into a situation is largely the role of intercession. Help your congregation begin to step into the needs of people without Bibles, the gospel, missionaries or even the necessities of life.

25. A generation ago, Pentecostals were accustomed to 'concert prayer,' unlike a 'concert of prayer' mentioned above. Concert prayer is when everyone prays together aloud. The Scripture says, *"They raised their voice to God with one accord"* (Acts 4:24). Here is the irony. As Pentecostals give up this

Scriptural practice, Evangelicals are now encouraging it, as one of many ways to pray. Al Vander Griend, from the Reformed Tradition, suggests, "Ask everyone present to pray aloud at the same time, focusing on a specific request or area of prayer."[23]

Many churches are introducing passion into their prayer times by using concert prayer, calling it the "Korean Method of Prayer," Dr. Paul Cho, the pastor of Yoido Full Gospel Church in Seoul, South Korea, is Pentecostal. He says, "When I hear people praying, it sounds like the forceful roar of a mighty waterfall. We know God must hear the sincerity of our prayer because we are praying in unison and unity."[24] If you are a Pentecostal church, don't let this passionate prayer style die. But don't use it exclusively. People will hide in the noise of prayer and may never really learn to pray. If you are Evangelical, encourage out-of-the-box praying.

26. Choose one service a week in which you announce a brief 15 to 30-minute prayer session prior to the service. In Mexico, they fill up the altar before the service begins. Sometimes, after a service begins, they quietly come to the altar and kneel, refusing to be seated in the sanctuary until they have knelt before God. In small churches, a group might gather in the front of the sanctuary for prayer. In larger churches, the entire sanctuary might be given over to prayer. At Brooklyn Tabernacle, when the doors open for their Tuesday evening prayer meeting at 6:00, the early arrivers will find the sanctuary lights dimmed and soft music playing. The movement into the prayer meeting at 7 p.m. is seamless. Suddenly, instrumentalists are present and the congregation is worshiping. That directed prayer service continues for 90 minutes or more.

27. Have different families or intercessors assigned to "pre-service" prayer, though you might open it to all. Rotate the duty to bathe the sanctuary in prayer each Sunday. Be careful that you do not encourage a style of prayer that is not consistent with your worship.

28. Have evenings of conversational, summit-style praying. Ask people to sign up for the special prayer experience. A group of 25 or more is a great beginning to assure a reasonably vigorous prayer event. Put the chairs in a circle. Eliminate empty chairs. Begin with a brief explanation:

> Tonight, we are not going to focus on any specific needs, except our need to know God more fully and be conformed to the image of Christ. Please, no sharing. If you have something to say, 'pray it!' Let's stay vertical. Brief prayers, one after another. I'll coach us along at times. Also, feel free to read a passage from the Bible, because that is the way God speaks to us in prayer. And everyone here is a song leader. So, we pray...and read Scripture... and sing...and pray...and follow our hearts in seeking the face of God. Let's begin with some prayers of thanksgiving.

Move then to prayers of praise, then to worship, until you sense the Presence of God. In the Presence of God, prayer should take on a special dynamic. Focus simultaneously on God's transforming love and His holiness. Don't fear silence, but don't let silence rule the meeting. If necessary, frame the prayers, "Let's imagine Christ came into this room and walked right over to you. What might he say? Could you pray that back to God? 'Jesus, I think You might say_____.'"

29. Have Family Prayer Days, and encourage the families that so often split apart in church activities to be together, at least for part of a service. Lead them in prayer exercises. Have fathers come to a microphone and pray as in a concert of prayer. Have mothers do the same. Then, spend some time having the family pray one for another in a circle of prayer.

30. If you don't have a prayer room, create a collage for pictures of lost loved ones (some churches put it right in the sanctuary and call it their 'wailing wall').

When Daniel Henderson was a pastor in Sacramento, California, he attended a community prayer summit – a four-day, citywide pastoral prayer retreat. The focus of such meetings is to mutually experience the Presence of God with other pastors in a city. Daniel quickly saw the possibilities for this congregation. He announced an all-church prayer summit from Wednesday evening to Saturday afternoon. He had hoped for 30 participants. He had 90. For three days, they prayed, read Scripture to one another, worshiped – all rather spontaneously. They celebrated Communion twice. They spent time praying in small groups. Lives were changed; hearts were healed; marriages were restored. And the personal devotional life of the participants was, he observed, "fanned into a fiery flame."

Dozens were set free in Christ. Suddenly the church was pulsating with new life. Henderson called the experience "a roller coaster ride of congregational change." During the next decade, 30 of these congregational prayer summits were conducted with attendance ranging from 80 to 225. Prayer meetings decorated the weekly calendar of the church – 13 in all. The Thursday evening Fresh Encounter service was patterned on the prayer summit, a circle of relational, transformational prayer. It regularly drew 200 to 400 participants. The church established a World Prayer Center and challenged their people to take a turn at prayer – one hour per week.[25]

You learn to pray by praying. You fan the flames of personal and family prayer with a church-wide prayer meeting. And congregational prayer gatherings are set ablaze by the pray-fire from the hearts of praying people and the hearts of family altars.

1   Vander Griend, chapter by John Quam, "Seven Ways Prayer Is Changing the Church in America," 14.

2   O. Hallesby, *Prayer* (Augsburg, 1975) 68.

3   Quoted by Jonathan Edwards, *The Gospel Herald, Volume 50,* (Oxford University, 1882).

4   Quin M. Sherrer and Ruthanne Garlock, *Grandma, I Need Your Prayers* (Grand Rapids: Zondervan, 2002) 203.

5   Tom Bisset, *Why Christian Kids Leave the Faith* (Grand Rapids: Discovery, 1997) 157-158.

6   Donald Sloat, *The Dangers of Growing Up in a Christian Home* (Grand Rapids: MANDY Press, 1986, 1999)

7   R. Kent Hughes, *1001 Great Stories and Quotes* (Wheaton, IL: Tyndale House, 1998) 416.

8   Edith Bajema, *A Family Affair: Worshiping God With Our Children* (Grand Rapids: CRC Publications, 1990, 1994).

9   R. Kent Hughes, 59.

10 Vander Griend, *The Praying Church Sourcebook,* 60.

11 Rick Moore, "A People Prepared for the Lord" (Message delivered to the Church of God Denominational Leadership meeting, 1994).

12 Find more information about Esther Ilnisky and her ministry at: intercessoryprayerministry.org.

13 Cheryl Sacks. *The Prayer Saturated Church* (Colorado Springs, CO: NavPress, 2004) 29.

14 Sacks, 29.

15 Vander Griend, *The Praying Church Sourcebook,* 62.

16 Ibid, 63.

17 Daniel Henderson, *Fresh Encounters* (Colorado Springs, CO: NavPress, 2004) 97.

18 Lighthouse Leadership Lectures, prepared by Al Vander Griend.

19 Henderson, 39.

20 Philip Graham Ryken, *When You Pray* (Wheaton, IL: Crossway, 2000) 20.

21 For more information on simultaneous intercession, see chapter 5.

22 Prayer banners are available for purchase at www.alivepublications.org.

23 Vander Griend, *The Praying Church Sourcebook,* 50.

24 Paul Yonggi Cho, *Prayer: Key to Revival,* (Waco, TX: Word, 1984) 101-102.

25 Henderson, 25-26.

FIVE
Mobilizing Intercessors

To stand before men on behalf of God is one thing. To stand before God on behalf of men is something entirely different.

Leonard Ravenhill

We must move from asking God to take care of things that are breaking our hearts to praying about the things that are breaking His heart.

Margaret Gibb

The best prayers often have more groans than words.

John Bunyan

Intercession battles poverty-gripped ghettos where people starve for lack of love and food. Intercession engages in conflict with a million evils facing our fellow man. An intercessor must bid farewell to self and welcome the burdens of humanity. In truth, the climax of prayer is intercession.[1]

Dick Eastman

We cannot ask in behalf of Christ what Christ would not ask himself, if he were praying.

A.B. Simpson

What Is Intercession?

Our definition of intercession must not begin with us or with the activity of interceding itself. It must begin with Christ – the ultimate intercessor. Andrew Murray says:

> We have far too little conception of the place that intercession...ought to have in the church and the Christian life. In intercession our King upon the throne finds his highest glory; in it we shall find our highest glory too. Through it he continues his saving work...through it alone we can do all work and nothing avails without it.[2]

Wesley believed, "God does nothing but in answer to prayer."[3]

The dictionary defines *intercession* as "an interceding; mediation, pleading, or prayer in behalf of another or others." A person who does the intercession is called an *intercessor*. Dutch Sheets, in his book *Intercessory Prayer,* gives this definition of intercessory prayer:

> Intercessory prayer is an extension of the ministry of Jesus through his Body, the church, whereby we mediate between God and humanity for the purpose of reconciling the world to him, or between Satan and humanity for the purpose of enforcing the victory of Calvary.[4]

Actually, the Greek term Paul used for intercession (1 Tim. 2:1), *enteuxis* means "to meet with a king." An intercessor is one who enters into the Royal Court of Heaven and dares approach the Throne of God, not for self but for another. This denotes status, premier access. As Chadwick exclaimed, "O, to be known at the Throne." An intercessor may approach the throne, or, they may have been summoned to the Throne, by the Spirit, in the middle of the day or night. Their role is to the middle, between God and His Throne, and some person, place or thing (crisis, decision, a problem, a possibility, etc.). Their role may be priestly – representing the earthly concern to heaven, before God; or, it may be prophetic – representing God's concern for some matter on the earth. Either way, the intercessor is the critical, perhaps, the determining link between God and another; God and a nation or city; God and a breakthrough. The power and value of such a function cannot be underestimated. Intercession is the royal, representative office of prayer. In intercession, we join Christ, the king and redeemer, our bridegroom, in his intercession and we become his intercessor on the earth side of the prayer transaction. We pray from his office, with the authority of his name, in his power, with the certainty of his coming kingdom. We ask that he assert his Lordship now, in some given situation; that he release his power now and demonstrate his authority; that he glorify his name, now. We pray 'his will' into some time-space concern, appealing to his authority in his name. We stand at the cross in the bloody middle and pray certain of resurrection power!

The Focus of Intercession

The highest call of intercession is prayer for the lost – for those not yet reconciled to God through His Son – to come to Christ. By extension, as noted above, the role of intercessor is one standing between God, the Father and Christ, and others in need, especially those in need of salvation. Of course, intercession is not exclusively about prayer evangelism. There are also times when you and I, as Christians, may not be able to pray effectively for ourselves or for those near us. That is when we need an intercessor.

Everyone should do the work of intercession, but there are especially 'graced' people who seem to be called to a ministry of prayer. These people lead the way in prayer for the church – they are the 'prayer engine' of the church. They may be a majority of one. They will usually be the one who both hears and smells the coming rain of revival before anyone else.

The Power of Intercession

A century ago, Norway was no spiritual Eden. Thorlief Holmglad was pastor of a downtown church. His custodian met him as he stepped from the pulpit one depressing morning. "There is going to be a revival in this church!" he declared optimistically. "Does this look like revival?" the pastor asked him, pointing to the nearly empty church. "Come with me," the custodian said, leading the pastor behind the pulpit. "Do you see those watermarks in the carpet? Those are tear stains. I have been praying and weeping here for five years. The Lord has assured me He is going to send revival!"

Two women in a nearby city were also praying for revival in Norway. They prayed, "Lord, if this burden is from You, will You send two more women to pray with us?" The two became four. They asked God to double the number again – to eight. He did. The eight asked for another doubling. The group enlarged to 16.

It was in a restless Sunday evening youth meeting where God chose to interrupt. Those present were not very attentive, and the leader was ineffective in seizing their interest. Suddenly, he saw, in an open vision, something that appeared to him as a white cloud that began to slowly descend from the ceiling. The leader alone saw it. The lower the cloud came, the more restless the young people became, until the cloud touched the top of their heads. "Instantly, without any outward signal, all the youth fell to their knees praying, weeping and confessing their sins."[5]

The youth service carried over into the adult evening service. Adults too descended to their knees in penitent prayer. The next night, with no regular meeting scheduled, most of the people returned, and did so every evening that week. Brokenness of spirit permeated every service. They were in the presence of God, and humility arrested pride and uncovered sin. For 12 years, the revival continued. It spread to other churches, resulting in 20,000 conversions in Oslo alone.

Never underestimate the power of one persistent, humble, faith-filled intercessor. God uses intercessors to resurrect dead churches and change entire cities.

The Characteristics of an Intercessor

An intercessor should enjoy praying. It should not be a bitter burdensome matter at its core. Healthy intercessors pray in the cross-hairs of joy and peace. Pride destroys prayer's effectiveness. God resists pride; he gives grace to the humble (James 4:6). There can be no place for pride or conceit among intercessors. When intercessors see themselves as a spiritually elite group – their effectiveness is ruined. Repentance is in order. When they attempt to direct leaders, rather than humbly share impressions, and yield to pastoral leadership, they overstep their authority. They must be servants to the pastor, submissive to the leadership. They should respect authority and make sure that God alone gets the glory. When they have 'a word' or receive 'an impression' they must learn to share it and then 'let it go.' Self-absorption by intercessors is contradictory to the nature of intercession. No ministry requires more selflessness than intercession. It is the ministry between – the anonymous, but powerful, link between God to the hurting, some need, some person or place. It is essentially 'other-minded.'

Intercessors may wrestle in prayer, but resolution is found in reconciliation – they discover the will of God regarding some person, place or thing – and they agree with God's will and word in the matter. That 'binding' moment, in prayer, may not manifest immediately, but the role of the intercessor is the first step in its manifestation. The intercessor surrenders, in prayer, the person, place or thing – and themselves, as an agent of change – to the will of God. They must be motivated by love. Imprecatory prayers must be the exception, not the rule. God often shares secrets with intercessors. Their spiritual acumen is often developed beyond the average Christian. This can lead to pride. Every intercessor must war against this often unperceived fault. Teachability is critical. The goal of intercession is not warfare, but reconciliation. And the great tool God's grace makes available to us is forgiveness. Intercessors forgive. They stand in grace and peace, drawing circles, not lines. Their gift of discernment, often pronounced among intercessors, can be an enemy to the soul. It can make them critical, caustic, cynical. It has to be bathed in love.[6]

The Qualifying of an Intercessor

Second Chronicles 7:14 is often quoted as a roadmap for national renewal. It lays out three distinct acts on our part: We must *confess* our sin, *humble* ourselves before God, and *turn* from our wicked (warped, twisted, out-of-shape) ways.

Charles Finney, an evangelist in the 19th century, said repentance "implies an intellectual and hearty giving up of all controversy with God upon all and every point...a thorough and hearty abandonment of all excuses and apologies for sin."

When church family felt directed by God to launch a ministry of prayer for the nation, Pastor Jack Hayford said they grappled with the "points for repentance" necessary to prepare hearts for such a prayer undertaking. Hayford cautions that intercessors should not use a list to claim a "now-I've-arrived" attitude of holiness, but they should promote a systematic humility of heart and sincerity before God.

Wise believers come to God with a transparent heart and life for cleansing. They know that the God who summons individuals to *repentance* (Hayford's definition: "a successive transformation of thoughts, attitudes and desires") always offers a *gracious* "summons." God invites us to purity and pardon, not to reproach or rejection.

Moments of self-examination and repentance liberate us. Only those times can unlock our entrance into the chambers of prayer that result in confident, faith-filled, Scripture-rooted, history-changing, nation-impacting intercession. Hayford exhorts, "Take these points in prayerful transparency before the Lord. Let us be rid of every hindrance so that our boldness in prayer will not be limited."

Hayford exhorts intercessors to pray this way:

Father, keep me from any vestige of...

- Religious pride and self-righteousness (Matthew 6:5, 6; Luke 18:10-14)

- Self-will, selfishness, covetousness (Matthew 6:19-21; James 4:3)

- Faithlessness, doubt, unbelief, anxiety (James 1:5-7; Matthew 6:25-34)

- Not loving, respecting, and applying God's Word (Proverbs 1:28, 29; 28:9)

- Spiritual adulteries, having idols in the heart (Ezekiel 14:3-13; 2 Corinthians 6:14)

- Unforgiveness, resentment, having a critical spirit (Mark 11:25; Matthew 5:21-26)

- Family discord, not being a responsible spouse (1 Peter 3:1-7)

- Not being open and honest with the brethren (James 5:16)

- Rebellion, being unwilling to be corrected (Proverbs 1:28-31)

- Not having true concern for the poor and oppressed (Proverbs 21:13; Isaiah 1:15, 17).[7]

The church, it is said, is the only army in the world that marches on its knees. Humility is critical. God resists the proud. He gives grace to the humble (James 4:6).

The Process of Mobilizing Intercessors

Imagine a congregation beginning a music and choir ministry and paying no attention to the gifted and talented musicians in the congregation. If you want a music ministry, you must identify and train your musicians. If you want a praying church, you must identify and train your intercessors.

Some Christians know they are called to intercession. Others may not. Even young Christians may have an intercessory call on their lives and not realize it. In fact, they may be mystified by new experiences that may have been thrust upon them since their conversion. "I cry often," one told me. "It is as if I can feel the pain of others," another confessed. "I wake up in the middle of the night. I know God has awakened me, but I didn't know what to do," still another lamented. "I keep having dreams," one intercessor confided, "and I am always in some strange place, often, a foreign land. At times, in my dreams, I am pleading with someone about their soul. At other times, it is as if I am an unseen observer in some royal hall, listening and overhearing confidential conversations that involve decisions that will affect nations. What is happening to me?" You have just stepped into the gloriously strange world of intercession. You have been called by God to ride the magic carpet of prayer around the world. You have been given keys to unlock the most secure locks and pass through the most protected doors and even the most secure conference rooms on the planet. You are an intercessor. These are the first steps toward launching an intercessory prayer ministry.

Five things need to be done with intercessors:

1. *Identify* intercessors for *mobilization.*
2. *Train* them for *effectiveness.*
3. *Team* them for encouragement, affirmation and *confirmation.*
4. *Debrief* them regularly and consistently for *input and thought.*
5. Direct them for more *focused* prayer.

Step One – Identified and Mobilized Intercessors

Though intercessors are called and gifted to pray, these people are rarely identified, trained, teamed, debriefed or directed. Early in the launch of your prayer ministry, you will want to identify these people who have a passion for prayer. If you are going to move forward in a church-wide ministry of prayer, it cannot be done apart from these people any more than you can develop a music ministry without musicians. If anyone in your church is praying at home, on a daily basis, it is intercessors. And the ones who attend prayer meetings are intercessors. Meet with the intercessors to discuss the ministry of prayer. Typically, they will self-identify. Pray with them; listen to them pray; watch for balance; look for leaders. Assess the degree of wisdom, balance and maturity among them. Use the meeting as a beginning point for their training.

The Four Dimensional _Vision_ of Local Church Prayer Ministry

FACE
Transformational
Personal, at-home, daily – Jesus-be-Jesus-in-me!

EYES
Intercessors (Prophetic/*Seer*)

Gift Specific/Focused

HAND
Well developed *house of prayer*

Corporate/Participatory
Transactional

Apply the passion of your intercessors and their fervor for prayer to help drive the prayer process forward. Don't expect everyone to pray like some of your intercessors pray. Teach your intercessors to learn to pray in ways that model prayer for beginning pray-*ers*. This is part of the training process.

Some scoff at the notion of training people to pray. Yet, the best musicians can benefit from vocal or instrumental training. The best preachers, anointed by God, can benefit from training – learning to interpret Scripture soundly, preaching with tempered passion, constructing a logical and Biblically sound argument for the cause of Christ, and more. Because prayer as a ministry has not even been on our radar screen, we have ignored intercessors. In some places, the term *intercession* is strange and unfamiliar. Yet, intercessors are as naturally drawn to prayer as musicians are to music. Intercessors are graced to pray, but they still need training. We need to recover the prayer-fire of intercessors. We must identify them and train them, team them and direct them, and regularly debrief them.

We should again sound a caution raised earlier. The heart of prayer is communion with God. Most intercessors love to pray. Is that a problem? Yes, in the same way that preachers who love to preach can become imbalanced. More than 60 percent of American pastors read the Bible only in preparation for their sermons. They sometimes fail to value Scripture for its devotional character; they see sermons in every inspiration point. In the same way, intercessors may fail to value prayer for the 'sheer pleasure of God's Presence.' If they always move past 'worshipful prayer' as communion to do the 'work' of intercession, they not only run the risk of imbalance, but the danger of burnout.

Step Two – Training Intercessors

Intercessors must be pastored as well. An intercessor without a teachable spirit is a time bomb waiting to explode. Isolated to

IDENTIFYING INTERCESSORS

In helping intercessors self identify, review with them the characteristics of an intercessor. I have used the 'if you...then you could be an intercessor' test. If you:

- Are awakening regularly, in the wee hours of the morning for prayer.
- Find yourself weeping, burdened, persistently for some person, place or situation.
- Discover yourself in a 'spirit of prayer' beyond yourself, that you did not induce.
- Are mysteriously burdened, though you cannot discern the cause, and yet, the burden to pray continues, perhaps for days.
- Dream or even daydream of people and places in need, perhaps, people you have never known and places to which you have never gone.
- At times, are compelled, almost seized by some invisible hand, to stop, find a place and pray, immediately.
- Are moved to prayer for lost people, regularly, for mission endeavors, for unreached people groups.
- Long and love to give the gift of prayer to others.
- Pray, through the day, seamlessly, almost unconsciously.
- Are consistently aware, at this place or that, about the spiritually lost, or the degree of light and darkness in a place, then moved to pray for the spiritual climate and the people.
- Are often moved to pray over a Bible passage with a missional window, praying scripture, prophetically over some matter.
- Find your first response to be prayer, then and there, in the moment, with a person in need.
- Sense the 'burden of the Lord' for revival and awakening.
- Know the power of 'the watch' and you have been given an assignment from the Lord to some wall.
- Have tasted the tears of lament.
- Have wrestled and toiled in prayer over some city, some congregation or moment in history.
- Have been moved into the mystery of prayer, an Indescribable need, and yet, a compelling urge to pray for that unknown thing.

(Continued on page 133.)

themselves, they will get out of balance. Without direction, they will lock into a single focus and style of prayer that lacks breadth and vision. They will make intercession, not communion, the center of prayer! Finding those who have a passion for prayer is as simple as beginning a music ministry. Make the announcement, "We are beginning a music ministry here at our church. Those interested in participating please show up Wednesday night." You'll get a mixed group of talented and would-be musicians. They will need a director to sort through them, train them, divide them into sections – tenors and altos, sopranos and bass, keyboard and percussion – and quite frankly, to send some of them on their way. When you call for intercessors and those interested in prayer, you'll get genuine intercessors. Some will be veterans; some will be prayer novices. Others will be would-be intercessors. Someone will need to direct the process and sort them out. They will need to be trained and teamed. Section leaders will need to be identified – those who can assist with emergency prayer, lead healing teams, prayer chains, crisis prayer, and all the other various passions you will find among the intercessors.

The training elements might include these elements:

- *Prayer Basics* – Intercessors need to be encouraged to balance their prayer time. Relational prayer time (communion with God for the sheer delight of His Presence) is foundational to people called to do the work of prayer.

- *Prayer Focus* – Keep the focus on the lost, those who have not made a decision to follow Christ. Spiritual warfare sometimes becomes intense when you begin to pray consistently for unbelievers. The Evil One does not want to release those who are captive to sin. As the warfare intensifies, intercessors may shift their focus from prayer for the lost to a preoccupation with the demonic. If they do, they will become the victims of a prayer diversion, unknowingly falling into the trap of the Evil One. He will do anything to redirect our prayer efforts away from the unsaved. Train intercessors to be vigilant in keeping their

IDENTIFYING INTERCESSORS (CONTINUED)

- Have times in which you must pray, and yet, you do not know how to pray, so you grunt and groan, you pray in the Spirit, into the mystery, until the burden lifts.
- Are summoned before God, only to sit in mysterious silence, perhaps for hours, saying virtually nothing, only to then be mysteriously released from the intercession, as if your sentry duty on some wall at some gate or in some tower was suddenly over.
- Love to pray for others and do it, despite the struggle and warfare, with joy.
- Have tasted some victory or defeat, not actually seeing it with your own eyes, yet, you know its certainty.
- Have received, in your heart, a settled word from the Lord, of victory or defeat, of revival or repentance, of renewal or redirection.
- Have experienced a vision or dream, a divine disclosure, a 'secret' about which you have been called to pray.
- Have been given an assignment in the Spirit to pray for some city, some organization or movement – good or evil, some significant person, movement or event.

You could be an intercessor.

prayer focus on the lost! Their warfare is not primarily with the demonic, it is over souls.

- *Prayer Theology* – Bible-based praying is the anchor for experiential, Spirit-led, Bible-fed prayer. It must be persistently focused on the holiness of God, in the context of grace and love.

- *Prayer Resources* – How to pray for the lost, for world missions, for the city, for other believers, for your pastor, for missionaries, and so forth.

- *Listening Prayer* – How to hear God; journaling – recording the experiences of the night watches.

- *Watching Prayer* – The power of 'position' in prayer.

- *Lament* – The role of identifying with brokenness, tearful and passionate prayer, linked through Gethsemane and the cross, to the resurrection and the enthronement of Christ.

Don't assume that intercessors intuitively know how to intercede or what to do with their intercessory experiences. They sometimes do not know what to do or how to handle the burden they feel for prayer, the strange sense of desperation for someone they hardly know, or the drawing to a particular city in a far away nation. They need coaching and training. And all of us need to recognize that, as the prayer movement expands, we are on new turf. We don't have, or even need, neat answers for all God is calling us to experience.

The prayer process will not naturally unwrap. Someone will need to emerge who will serve as the leader of the army of intercessors. And remember, intercessory prayer is only one aspect, only one of the four dimensions of prayer and only one of the seven markers of a praying church. Don't make the mistake of thinking that organizing an intercessory prayer ministry is the same as launching a more holistic ministry of prayer. Only someone with a heart for prayer will inspire prayer and be respected by the intercessors. And only a leader will lead! Don't make the mistake of placing an intercessor without leadership and organizational skills to head your intercessory prayer ministry. And don't make the mistake of choosing a leader who has organization skills but is not a person of prayer.

To reference our earlier analogy, not all singers can direct a choir. On the other hand, it would be rare to find a choir director who was not a singer. Look for a person of prayer, with a call to pray, that also has leadership and organizational skills. Not all intercessors can direct a prayer meeting effectively or lead your intercessory prayer ministry.

> Don't make the mistake of choosing an intercessor without leadership and organizational skills to head your intercessory prayer ministry.

Step Three – Teaming Intercessors

Team your intercessors for encouragement and confirmation. Many intercessors are loners! Teaming is not to create another intercessory prayer group, it is for the purpose of mobilization, for distributing prayer needs and assignments, and harvesting the data out of the seasons of the watch of these intercessors. You want to create a network of communication and encouragement for intercessors.

This can be accomplished in four different ways:

1. *Establish Intercessory Prayer Teams (IPTs).* These should number about five to 10 intercessors, depending on the size of the church. Encourage youth intercessory teams. At least one of the IPTs should be a youth team with a youth prayer leader. The IPTs will not necessarily meet to pray together. They are virtually "partnered intercessors," teamed to jointly share prayer assignments and communication. Appoint a contact person for each team.

2. *If you have a number of IPTs, group them into brigades.* (Use your own terminology.) With each IPT you mobilize three-to-five intercessors. With a brigade, you mobilize and team three-to-five IPTs, and you should be able to call one or several teams to prayer, one more brigades, and do so with the click of an e-mail, group text or facebook site.[8]

   Depending on the size of your church, five prayer teams of five intercessors each would equal one brigade of 25 intercessors. Two brigades of 25 intercessors each would total about 50 intercessors in 10 IPTs. They could be mobilized one team at a time, or one brigade at a time.

   Suppose the number of prayer needs coming into the prayer office are as few as a dozen a day. If you send all prayer needs to every intercessor, the number will be overwhelming. Too many requests will make the prayer alert effort ineffective. Too few will likewise send the wrong message. Teaming intercessors into IPTs and brigades will allow you to rotate the mobilization of your teams, sending one request to the first IPT, the second to another, and so on. An entire brigade could be mobilized for needs with the highest urgency. All prayer needs could also be

PRAYER RATINGS

Develop a rating. All prayer needs are important to the one presenting the need. But all needs don't deserve a midnight prayer alert. Here is a rating system you might consider:

Level 5 – Code Blue – Alert: Life or death. People.

Level 4 – Code Red – Urgent, but not life or death. Emergencies. Major surgeries. Usually involves persons.

Level 3 – Code Orange – Critical. Soul care issues. Medical-minor surgeries, accidents, crises, deprivation of some type, not life threatening.

Level 2 – Code Yellow – Caution. High level uncertainty, not yet known to be critical. More than a routine request. May involve a person or family, a city or nation, a church or company. Often is related to some deadline or threshold.

Level 1 – Code Gray – Care. Typical needs. Direction, protection, aches and pains, guidance, concern for others, etc. These are important, arguably 'critical' to the person making the request. Yet, to keep from overwhelming intercessors, you may find it helpful to filter such needs.

Use either numbers or colors. Also note whether or not the need is time sensitive. It may be a surgery or foreclosure, a judicial date or job interview. Mark each request as appropriate.

Example: TS – time sensitive. Then note the date: January 3; surgery, week of January 3-7. Determine the rating level/color. After some time, update the request at or after the time-sensitive stamp. Change the rating appropriately.

posted to the church's website and viewed by all. And of course, if you have a prayer center, they should be featured there. (See sample rating scale.)

IPTs could be assigned different prayer tasks. They could be deployed team-by-team, or brigade-by-brigade for various assignments. A general call for intercessors will always bring the faithful core, but if that is your model, you may burn them out. This strategy allows you to spread out the intercessory load and involve more people.

3. *Further grouping of these intercessors might be by zip code, precinct or by area of the city.* This is a part of mobilizing the church diaspora, allowing the intercessors to connect and give the gift of prayer to the city, zone by zone, neighborhood-by-neighborhood.

4. *Another way to group them would be in terms of their prayer support for the various ministries of the church.* Here are the priorities:

    •   Priority – prayer for the lost.

    •   Prayer for mission endeavors, missionaries, unreached peoples, closed nations.

    •   Prayer support for the pastor and for every staff member – a Personal Intercessory Team (PIT) crew for every leader and the ministry they lead. One experiment indicated that when leaders were prayed for every day for 15 minutes, 89 percent reported a discernible difference in their effectiveness.

    •   Prayer support for every church ministry (example: interface intercessors with the prayer-evangelism focus, lighthouses and more) and every church event, mission trip, and so forth.

    •   Group intercessors in terms of their heart – their passion and burden for prayer.

Some of these intercessors may lead prayer groups during the week. Some intercessors may function as regular 'prayer mission' teams at various places in the city for change and renewal.

Step Four – Debriefing Intercessors

The Scriptures tell us to *"watch and pray."* The ancient word for *prophet* was 'seer.' There is a connection between the prophetic and prayer. Don't let the word *prophetic* confuse you. This is not meant in a strictly Pentecostal or charismatic sense. Rather, God reveals things to intercessors. For this reason, they need to be teamed (for confirmation), debriefed (for valuable input) and directed (for more effective watching).

A dialectic needs to form between intercessors and elders; prayer leaders and staff. Elders need the helpful eyes and ears of intercessors, and intercessors must learn to offer their report to the elders at the gate and leave it in their hands, trusting their authority.

When intercessors are not trained, they sometimes don't understand the perimeters of their authority. They have nowhere to go with the burning heart given them in prayer, or the clear signal from the Holy Spirit about some issue in the church. Some pastors complain that intercessors in their congregations get out of order. This is confusing to the intercessors, since no order for intercessory prayer ministry has been established. They have no outlet for their insights; no connections for confirmation; no direction and clarity for prayer focus. They have been left to themselves. And without a pastor, they get out of balance.

Pastor the intercessors. From them, pastors may gain valuable 'intelligence' hunches from their night-watch ministry. In their circle, the pastor will feel the strength of their prayer support. Don't forget that the pastor, as a shepherd-watcher, is the chief intercessor among intercessors. Without his intercessory prayer life, he will never effectively relate to intercessors. A business church management style will be rightly seen as a world apart from their spiritually inheritance approach to church life. A pastor can learn much from a healthy relationship with intercessors; as they can from a praying pastor.

Intercessors have to be taught that they are 'watchers on the wall' – not the 'elders at the gate.' They are to submit their night-watch reports to the community of elders. The elders should take their prayer hunches seriously. This will be a new experience for both intercessors and church leaders. If intercessors know that their prayer investment is valued, they can more easily rest in the reality that it is not their calling to 'wake up the city!'

The mobilization and leadership of the church is the calling of pastors and elders, not intercessors. Watchers on the wall who do not respect elders at the gate will never ensure security for the spiritual community. And elders who have little regard for the warning sounds of the watchers will not harvest the wisdom of intuitive and discerning prayers. For intercessors to feel passionately that a warning go forth, and to submit and release that message to the elders through prayer leadership channels, requires maturity.

What if the elders do not share the intuitive deduction of the intercessor? What if the intercessor has translated their intuitive insights into concrete conclusions, without awareness? Can the intercessor submit to the eldership? Can the eldership hear the heart implications of the intercessor and take that into consideration? Can they gently correct and simultaneously affirm? We can all become enamored by our own gifts and fail to see that they are not really our gifts at all, but gifts to the body.

Notice the following example:

Rachel is an intercessor. In a season of prayer, she consistently felt a burden for the young couples in the church. The Lord, she felt, warned her about "trouble" coming. Some very specific things were placed on her heart in prayer. She called the pastor and shared her concerns, respectfully. The pastor listened, thanked her for her concern, and suggested that she continue to pray, but cautioned her about sharing openly the kind of things she raised concerns about. He assured her that her impressions were groundless but that he did not doubt her sincerity. She left confused, yet assured him of her support and commitment to continue in prayer. Within a brief period, the situation exploded, multiple seperations and divorces, creating major relational damage in the church. The pastor was embarrassed. Families left the church. A staff member was exposed in sin. Great confusion ensued. All the ambiguous shadows that Rachel had seen and had shared with the pastor could now be easily interpreted. She had been discerning correctly.

What is her appropriate response?

1. Leave the church and find one that will honor intercessors more readily?

2. Go to the pastor and at least say, "I warned you! I told you so!"

3. Dig in and pray, now more than ever? Go to the pastor and assure him of her prayer support, loyalty and continued commitment to be faithful in her "watch" on the wall?

Of course, the appropriate response is number three. In the first option, Rachel is preoccupied with intercession as if it were her own gift! But that gift, the operation of that grace, is not the "intercessor's gift," it is a gift of grace to the church itself.

The second option is loaded with pride and 'I' language. The seer has gone blind. Myopic, they can only see "self." The third position reveals a true, humble, mature, team pray-*er.* How should the pastor respond if, after a season, this intercessor came again with a prayer burden? Obviously, he should take such a matter under consideration – now with greater appreciation for the insights God has given through intercession and specifically this intercessor. Will that intercessor exploit the past? They must not! Will they "gloat" in any way over being right before? May God forbid! Or will they chide the pastor over not being heard? Not if they are mature!

So often, a church struggle might have been avoided if a communication system had existed between leaders and pray-*ers.* But there is typically no means of debriefing, and the insights of an intercessor are wasted. Any warning given to an intercessor in the night watch is not valued. The congregation has no system, no process by which a spiritual warrior can offer a scouting report to leaders without seeming to be superspiritual.

The *seeing* dimension of prayer is needed to steer the church when things are hidden in the waters, or around some bend that cannot be seen from the captain's wheelhouse. Trust has to be established between intercessors and leaders. The reports, intuitive hunches of intercessors, have to be seriously considered. As leaders trust the intuition of intercessors, and intercessors trust the authority of leaders, the church wins by the use of the whole body and its gifts. It is foolish and prideful for a pastor to take the position that God will reveal all such matters directly to him. The nature of the body is diversity and God favors inferior members, yes, humble intercessors, with His secrets (1 Cor. 12:21-25).

At least once a month, intercessory team leaders should connect with each intercessor on their team and ask, "What is happening in your seasons of prayer?" The answers may not on the surface appear to be revealing. Probing more deeply, several intercessors may report a simultaneous and consistent leading to pray for the same issue. When a trusted intercessor is having a consistent leading in prayer, say, for the youth of the congregation, it might be wise to pass that piece of information on to the staff. If a number of intercessors are focused, by Spirit-led prayer, on the same target, that is a clue that must not be ignored. At the very least, their prayer burden will encourage those who are working in this area. At best, it may heighten sensitivity to the Spirit and avoid a problem or be a prelude to a breakthrough.

Occasionally, teams of intercessors might be gathered to "pray back to God" the rumblings of their hearts. Ask them for reports about their insights, consistent burdens in prayer; about scriptures the Spirit brings forth in seasons of prayer, even visions or dreams; the discerning moments that have come in prayer; words of wisdom or knowledge they have received; prophetic promises or warnings. Every intercessor should be encouraged to keep a journal to document patterns and to seriously record their prayer findings. Gather them to pray, interpret those clues, leadings and prayer burdens. *Overall, keep steering your intercessors toward prayer for the harvest.*

Step Five – Direct Intercessors

Intercessors will usually follow the burden of their tender heart, believing it to be the leading of the Holy Spirit in prayer. This is often after hearing of some significant crisis. Sadly, this can lead to reactionary prayer. Every bit of bad news cannot be owned as a prayer burden and burdens in prayer should be cultivated. Intercessors should follow their heart, but also take on prayer assignments. They should be encouraged to serve as a member of a Personal Intercessory Team (a PIT crew) for a ministry in the church or a missionary or church-planter outside the church.[9] The PIT crews are a prayer support team for key church leaders and ministries. They should also take their place in the congregation's prayer room or center, interceding for various causes and members.

PIT crews function best when they are embedded in the ministry for which they are praying – the youth group (youth and youth workers), men's and women's ministries; singles and children, (children's workers and don't dismiss child intercessors). Each ministry should identify intercessors inside or attached to that ministry. This way, you integrate prayer into every ministry. It can't be alien. The most powerful and effective prayer takes place from the inside out, not the outside in. This is why God became an intercessor, in Christ. He came to the earth to pray, from the earthside, from the inside of a man – this is incarnational praying.

By embedding prayer inside each ministry, and honing and identifying the PIT crew of intercessors for that ministry, you position prayer-fire and dependence on the Holy Spirit at the center of that ministry. This calls for extended teams of prayer – by the chair and the youth group; the children and singles; men and women. This must be more than a quick prayer before and after, more than a moment around some ministry leader before they take to the stage. The inner circle of intercessors – the inner trio like Peter, James and John – should be, at times, exposed to the needs facing each ministry of the church. They should be gently directed in their praying. Informed intercessors pray more effectively. Direct intercessors then harvest their impressions.

1. Team Intercessors. Intercessors that are not willing to be teamed are often loose cannons. They are as helpful to the prayer ministry as a talented musician who resists the direction of the minister of music. Being directed transforms a lone intercessor into a team player – remembering...

> Two are better than one, because they have a good reward for their labor. For if they fall, one will lift up his companion. But woe to him who is alone when he falls, for he has no one to help him up...Though one may be overpowered by another, two can withstand him. And a threefold cord is not quickly broken (Ecclesiastes 4:9, 10, 12).

Here is the power of agreement. Praying together, in the same direction, multiplies strength, prevents burnout, increases the reward and brings breakthrough.

When pastors and intercessors form a partnership, God's grace is released in ways that are exceptional. Protection for the congregation is a natural result because the watchers are systematically deployed to take their place on the wall and their night-watch reports are taken seriously. In addition, their watching should be directed. Pastors can send them messages: "Pray into this!" "Watch with the staff over this issue or that concern." "When you pray, would you focus on these things?"

In directing the prayers of intercessors, the goal is not to control them, it is to include them as part of a broader team. Genuine intercessors will be Spirit-led. Unfortunately, some intercessors operate on a shallow emotional level. They are moved to pray only by emotion or some crisis – often both together. They confuse emotion with spiritual intuition. They have not learned the 'discipline' of being on the intercessory wall when all seems quiet. Spontaneity is the sum total of their prayer experience. They must learn Scripture-based praying, which should be a vital part of your training. Humble intercessors will quickly see that the Holy Spirit works through the leadership of godly pastors and elders who are also watchers on the wall. Spirit-led, Bible-based, pastor-sensitive intercessors – what a combination!

2. Confidential intercessors. Some intercessors will develop as confidential advisers. Sometimes, the issues needing prayer will be of such a nature that they dare not be released on the church's Internet prayer page or through the prayer chain. The requests themselves will need limited exposure and much secret prayer.

The greater number of sensitive issues pastors and elders are dealing with, the more the use of these confidential intercessors will be required. It is important, however, to work at making sure you do not create an elite class of intercessors – the included and excluded. It is also very important that you maintain the principle of plurality. A single intercessor as a confidant-adviser is not wise.

There is also safety in a larger circle of seers (Proverbs 24:6). Many effective intercessors are women – and 95 percent of senior pastors are men. Spiritual connections are among the tightest and most powerful that exist. Tragically, what begins as a noble and pure relationship can become destructive. There is a fine line between the spiritual and the sensual. Pastors would do well to develop a group of trusted intercessors, male and female, and avoid singular bonds, especially with female intercessors. Make the team a mixed-gender group.

3. Convergence moments. When a number of intercessors have prayer experiences that "converge," such collective impressions should not be taken as coincidence. Directed and debriefed intercessors will become a blessing to the pastor and the congregation. The pastor will become a blessing to intercessors by pastoring them and helping them develop their gift. Both share the same vision for prayer and evangelism. The result is a synergy and interdependence when relationships are strengthened and trust is established.

Intercessors must also know their boundaries. They must agree on the lines of authority and communication processes. Gentle pastoral corrections offer intercessors safety from deception and getting off track, keeping them focused and productive. Every pastor should give consistent support and respect to intercessors. Public affirmation of intercessors and other leaders of the prayer ministry gives priority to the work of prayer and honors intercessors for their secret labor. An annual luncheon for intercessors and prayer leaders demonstrates gratitude for those who are praying.

4. Mutuality between intercessors and pastors. Doug Kamstra says pastors and intercessors should do the following:

- Encourage each other.
- Pray for each other and with each other.
- Have regular contact (scheduled and unscheduled, formal and informal).
- Recognize each other's gifts.
- Please God – the basis of the relationship.

Intercessors should recognize…

- Theological differences with the pastor.
- Pastoral authority, because the pastor gives assignments and sets guidelines.
- Different spiritual perspectives, gifts, assignments.
- Different personalities.
- Different expectations.
- Any biases or wounds they have.
- That God alone shapes the lives of others.
- That they (intercessors) need prayer too.[10]

5. *The intercessor's commitment.* Ask the intercessors to make a commitment in the following ways:

By the grace of God, we intercessors seek to serve God, pastors and Christian leaders, fellow intercessors and the leadership team in our community, by daily lifting up intercession and petitions for…

- Lost individuals and families who need Christ
- God's purposes to be established; God's kingdom to be invited
- Pastors and other Christian leaders and their ministry
- Fellow intercessors and their families
- Pastoral servant leaders who give direction to our city vision
- Lighthouses of prayer and their neighborhoods
- Unity in the church of Jesus Christ
- Walls of division to be broken
- Reconciliation to occur
- Strongholds to fall
- A canopy of prayer to cover our community
- A great spiritual awakening in our nation and around the world
- The peace of Jerusalem.

By the grace of God, we seek to serve our community by daily lifting up intercession and petitions for…

- Our mayor and his or her leadership team
- Our civic servants and their protection (police and fire)
- Judges – that justice and righteousness will prevail

- Our schools and hospitals
- Child protective and family services
- Media centers, arts and entertainment – information gateways
- Commerce and business – the favor of God upon our economy and jobs that provide for our families
- The poor and disadvantaged."

6. *Intercessor's agreement.* Each intercessor should consider an agreement. Here is a model:

It is my covenant that I will pray faithfully for the salvation of spiritually lost neighbors, friends and family; for revival in the church to the end of great awakening in the community; to the end of a great harvest with measurable cultural change.

It is my covenant to pray regularly for my pastor – that he would be a holy man of God – and for my church. I will support my pastor's ministry and respect my pastor's leadership. By the grace of God and with the pastor's support, I will be an extension of my church to my community and to the intercessory network.

It is my covenant to pray for my community until there is unity in the church; until all strongholds have fallen; until walls of division are broken; until reconciliation occurs; until a canopy of prayer covers our community; until all the lost hear the gospel; and until God establishes His purposes.

It is my covenant to speak positively, bless and build up my pastor, my church, and other spiritual leaders in my community.[11]

7. *Some intercessor 'Don'ts.'*

- Don't be a 'spiritual bully' or initiate power struggles.
- Don't come on with 'Thus said the Lord...'
- Don't force action after a word from the Lord – let it happen.
- Don't have a critical spirit.

- Don't be judgmental.
- Don't have faulty theology or incorrect applications of Scripture.
- Don't 'stay in the closet' all the time – be involved with other ministries.
- Don't practice gift projection.
- Don't put down others or put pressure on them to pray like you do.
- Don't divide.
- Don't have a 'personal kingdom' (selfish ambitions).
- Don't be so heavenly-minded that you become no earthly good.[12]

8. *Engaging intercessors.* Here are some ways intercessors can be used:

- Adopt a local fire station or police station. Do so especially if you have peace and safety officers in your congregation, or if you have a fire or police station in the neighborhood of the church. Go a step further – adopt police and fire personnel for personal prayer coverings. (adopt-a-cop.org)
- Adopt a local school – one near the church. Bless them. Pray for them. Ask how you can serve them.
- Consider 'prayer ambassador' teams that are sent out to give the "gift of prayer" to the community. These teams of three to five people go in a priestly mode. They go to bless. They bring back needs and allow the church to pray for specific needs in the city and neighborhood around the church. In such times, God shows Himself alive to these people.
- Every classroom should have a PIT crew. Here intercessors occasionally meet with teachers before the Sunday school or discipleship class begins for prayer. Or, as the Sunday school teacher comes into the classroom, the intercessor might be leaving, having spent time in prayer in the classroom, "I'm praying for you. I know you'll have a great day!"
- Every ministry in the church should have an intercessor or intercessory team assigned to it. Every ministry should be a prayed for ministry. The Moravian Principle should be applied: *No one works unless someone prays!*
- Every staff person should have a PIT crew – an intercessory

support team. The rule should be: *An intercessor for every worker – and every worker an intercessor.*

- Pray for neighboring churches. List their names in the bulletin. Have the congregation, or at least intercessors, send them a note of encouragement, "We at Second Church are praying for you!"

- Pray for places where sin abounds – for strongholds of evil in the city of even the neighborhood around the church to be broken. Pray light *into* the area, not merely the darkness *out.* Asking God to remove something only creates a vacuum (Matthew 12:4345). Don't pray evil things *out* without praying holy things *in.*

- Pray for the city, its city leaders and for community needs (1 Timothy 2:1, 2). Have the intercessors take their prayer cues from the community newspaper. Nothing escapes God. Nothing is outside the concern of His kingdom. So many things have spiritual implications.

- Prayer for the lost loved ones of church members should be offered regularly. The names of the friends and family members should be called out in prayer at least once each week, until they come to Christ.

- Prayer for the mission endeavors of the church and for the missionaries supported by the church is the work of intercessors. Sending funds for missions is not enough. We are throwing money at the darkness. We must provide the investment of prayer energy as well.

- Prayer should be offered by intercessors for every member/family of the congregation as often as a reasonable cycle of prayer will allow. In a megachurch, it may only be once or twice a year. In a smaller congregation, every member/family can be covered in prayer weekly or perhaps monthly.

- Prayer should be offered for every business owned by church members. Pray for the blessing and favor of God. Ask God to bless these business owners in order that the Kingdom might be blessed.

- Redeem the land. God wants the *"trees to clap their hands"* (see Isaiah 55:12), the *"seas to roar with praise"* (see Psalm 96:11), for all the earth to acknowledge Him. Look at the places that reflect disorder, darkness, depression, oppression – and send teams to pray in those gaps. Invite God's light. Pray that the land and buildings would be used for godly purposes. Ask that the owner and operator of the building would come to know God. Begin to pastor the community *by prayer* (Ezekiel 22:22-30; Deuteronomy 32:42; Numbers 35:33).

- Sweep the sanctuary – every Saturday night. Do it in teams. Four teams of intercessors would require duty only once a month; twelve, once a quarter.
- Simultaneous intercessory prayer should be offered during the worship service and preaching of the Word.

9. Pastoral prayer support. Develop prayer partners for the pastor. Ask each member to do the work of intercession, whether or not they consider themselves an intercessor. Pastor Dee Duke, of Jefferson City Baptist Church, asks each member to pray for him once a month – they choose the day of the month.

In a larger congregation, this usually guarantees daily prayer support for the pastor. In smaller congregations, every day might not be covered, so improvise. A simple guide for prayer can be provided each week in the bulletin or on the church's Web site.

Pastor Duke says that as folks pray for him, he feels the strength of those prayers. The church, in a 13-year period, grew from less than 200 to over 1,200 regular attenders, an increase of about 1,000 people in a city with only 1,700 residents. Pastor Duke says the grumble factor fell to almost zero. When he steps into the pulpit on Sunday morning, almost a quarter of those present give him a thumbs-up sign, indicating that they prayed for him that week.

- *Build a prayer wall.* It takes just 168 watchmen, each praying an hour, to fill a prayer wall for the week. The wall functions like an old-fashioned prayer chain. Each person prays for a designated hour and calls the next person. Prayer guides can be created. These watches are typically seasonal – once or twice a year. Some churches may be able to recruit enough participants – 600 to 700 – to have a perpetual prayer wall with each person filling a one-hour slot per month. Communities could easily accomplish this goal of a perpetual prayer watch over the city if churches would work together.

Some prayer walls are built around causes – they are issue-driven. They may be built in response to a community crisis, a need, or a call to revival. Others may be seasonal – Lent, or the days between the Resurrection and Pentecost. Some may use Steve Hawthorne's annual *Seek God for the City*[13] prayer exercise as a time to build a prayer wall.

- *Conduct an all-night prayer meeting.* Many of the churches in the Far East conduct all-night prayer meetings, beginning at midnight and concluding at 6 a.m., and they do so on a regular basis. In our culture, such a church-wide gathering might be held once a quarter with one of the intercessors serving as the core of the gathering.

- *Conduct a prayer blitz for special activities, services, and so forth.*

- *Create an e-newsletter for intercessors.* You should have a regular weekly or monthly e-news bulletin, and flash alerts for prayer emergency prayer. The regular e-bulletin would include tips on intercession, journaling, Scripture praying, information and inspiration, and so forth. Offer new web links for prayer growth. Alert them to local, state and national prayer focuses. Keep evangelism and the harvest before them. Share testimonies and breakthroughs.

- *Subscribe to PROJECT PRAY eblast.* This will give updates about prayer events around the world, news for intercessors and tips for local church prayer leaders. It's free. Go to www.projectpray.org or call 855-84-ALIVE.

  Allow for some means of prayer impressions and insights of those in your prayer room or center, and those on intercessory teams to filter back to the prayer leadership team, and on to the pastoral staff and elders, through established channels.

10. Prayer walking. This is organized in different ways.

- *The Church Campus.* Begin by doing a prayer walk of the church campus itself. That is safe but often very powerful. Have the people form small teams of three to five people and move through the complex praying for each room, each hallway, each ministry and activity. Bring them back into the sanctuary for a debriefing.

- *The Church Neighborhood.* Prayer-walk the neighborhood around the church. This provides a broader experience and gets your prayer evangelists together for the shared experience.

Team them in groups of three – no more or they will call attention to themselves. Break up couples for the experience. In the early stages of a prayer ministry, sometimes they find greater freedom when separated. Create routes that can be completed in about an hour. Plan for everyone to return to the church. Again, don't miss the opportunity to debrief them. Have them share their experiences. Make notes.

Make prayer-walking a part of the effort to have the church 're-connect' with the neighborhood. After you have experimentally walked some immediate zone around your church, claim a specific perimeter for influence – a 10-block area, then one mile, then a three-mile zone. Ask the Holy Spirit,

Why is our church on this corner, for this time? Who lives around us and what are their needs? Who is down and out? Who is up and out? How can we be a better neighbor? What difference does our being in this neighborhood make? Would the neighbors feel better off if we moved or closed down? What is the level of the effectiveness of our witness in this neighborhood? Do they know we are here? Do they care? Do they know who we are? How do we find practical, concrete ways to connect the ministries of the church to the needs of our neighbors?

- *The Neighborhoods of the Members.* Now you should be ready to encourage members to prayer-walk their own neighborhoods. There is great support material for these efforts at the National Prayer Committee office.[14] Or get Steve Hawthorne's book, *Prayer-walking.*

- *Mission Walking.* We also want to participate in citywide efforts to cover the whole city with prayer walks. Individuals, usually in groups of two or more, agree to prayer-walk a certain area or receive their assignments for prayer-walking.

- *City Neighbors.* What businesses are around the church that could be 'adopted' for prayer? A firehouse? Schools? Are there businesses owned by your members? What businesses around you need to be 'prayed out?' What land needs to be redeemed? Shouldn't the light drive out the darkness?

- *Our Samaria.* Where is the Samaria near you? Is it a low-end trailer court? Apartment complex? Could prayer make a difference there? Designate prayer mission teams to consistently go and pray in these areas.

- *Mission Teams.* Send teams out to other cities and nations to prayer-walk.

11. Prayer support for the sick. Prayer requests should be passed on to intercessors for prayer. If you have an intercessory family-watch program, pass the prayer request on to the intercessor who prays for that family. If you have a functioning prayer center, one of the assignments of the call center can be to make a periodic outbound calls for prayer support. This helps the pastoral staff in tracking needs. If you have developed healing prayer teams, here is an opportunity for them to shine.

12. Blessing and watching prayer for families. Each intercessor might be given the responsibility of covering certain families in the church in prayer. For example, if you have 100 families and 10 intercessors, each intercessor would be asked to adopt 10 families and pray for them. If each intercessor prayed for one family a week, each family would be covered in prayer four to five times a year.

Let's say that I am an intercessor and a part of an Intercessory Prayer Team with five other intercessors. As a team, we might also share our assignments, serving as a backup for one another. This multiplies the impact of prayer and heightens sensitivity. One family is my primary focus this week, but four others are my secondary focus.

Whenever there is a crisis in those families, the intercessor is alerted for prayer support. The entire team may also be asked to provide prayer support until the crisis abates. Intercessors are not expected to visit the sick unless they choose to do so. The family may not even know they have an intercessor assigned to them or the name of that intercessor. This is can be a silent ministry – a "watching" ministry.

Concerns about families bubbling up in prayer are passed along through the team leader or contact, the prayer center, the prayer coordinator and the pastoral staff.

Using the www.pray4everyhome.com website, intercessors can see a map of their neighborhood. Each day, they receive an email reminder to pray for five of their neighbors. They can amend the list and add others – friends or family. In this way, a church has exponentially multiplied its missional, intercessory reach. The typical county has 100,000 residents. Only twenty-percent are in church on any given Sunday and perhaps, no more than twenty-five percent in any 90-day period. That same county has an average of 35,000 housing units. One hundred intercessors, praying, strategically, for only one household a day, would assure that the entire county had been prayed for, at least once annually.

13. Simultaneous intercession. Many churches provide simultaneous intercession during their services, particularly on Sunday morning. For best results, position your simultaneous intercessors in a soundproof room with mirrored glass so they can hear and observe the service without distracting the worship. Simultaneous intercession can work without a visual link, but only with an experienced group of intercessors. Intercessors should not be passive observers – they actively pray.

Sometimes, you can visibly see the passion of the intercessors affecting the worship. One year at the Church of God General Assembly, I was in the room where I could observe both intercessors and the worship event simultaneously. The intercessors were face-down, almost oblivious to the worship event. As they pressed into prayer with a rising tide of group passion, it was as if the Spirit in the small room overflowed into the convention hall, filled with 15,000 worshipers.

Moving Beyond the Church to the City with Intercession

Dr. Doug Kamstra author and Reformed prayer leader, says that finding and engaging the intercessors at the city level is an important priority in mobilizing a city to pray. Intercessors are present in every church and are willing to step forward when challenged with an intercessory task. Once identified, intercessors should be challenged to pray in one accord for their city. They should be given specific things to pray for, such as...

- The lost to come to Christ – for the gospel to go forth in clarity.
- Unity among pastors and churches based on obedience to Christ.
- Revival in the churches of the city.
- Holiness and righteousness – for pastors to be holy men of God.
- Fruitful evangelism – believers praying for and sharing the gospel with their neighbors and fellow workers.
- Spiritual protection and guidance for public officials, city employees and schools.
- Kingdom solutions to city problems.
- The need for righteousness to prevail and evil to be exposed Intercessors are already praying.

More and more are discovering that they are called and are linking across denominational lines to help establish God's kingdom in a community. Some produce newsletters that link church and city intercessors.

Keep intercessors informed about what is happening as you develop a citywide restoration ministry. Bring them together periodically to renew or reshape your unified vision. Share both prayer requests and answers. Give them a chance to pray together. Listen to intercessors. They hear from God. They frequently sense God's will before others do.[15]

Intercessory Prayer for My City

City intercessors should also meet for prayer. Houston, at one point, mobilized intercessors across the city for monthly prayer, gathering as many as 1,000 intercessors in the rallies.Such intercessors might also meet for prayer coverage of special city events.

At the city level, intercessors might take on the task of...

- Praying systematically for leaders and those in authority.
- The mayor, city council – its issues and even its agenda.
- Pastors and churches in the city – everyone covered by prayer.
- Law enforcement – police and sheriff.
- Fire departments.
- Crime blotters – concentration on high crime areas.
- Praying over the local newspaper for city events, revival, restoration needs, reconciliation, families, spiritual strongholds, the destiny of the city.[16]

E.M. Bounds says, "Praying, true praying, costs an outlay of serious attention and time, which flesh and blood do not relish."[17]

Not only must we overcome flesh, but we also must overcome Satan, who is a great enemy to prayer. C.S. Lewis, in *The Screwtape Letters,* gives us a view on how Satan might coach his demonic assistants in their warfare against believers. Listen in: "Interfere at any price in any fashion when people start to pray, for real prayer is lethal to our cause."[18]

1   Dick Eastman, *No Easy Road* (Grand Rapids: Baker, 1971) 57.

2   Andrew Murray, *The Ministry of Intercession,* quoted by Vander Griend, 17.

3   Quoted by Vander Griend, 17.

4   Dutch Sheets, *Intercessory Prayer* (Ventura, CA: Regal, 1996) 37, 42.

5   Ben Jennings, *The Arena of Prayer* (Orlando, FL: NewLIfe Publications, 1999) 171-172.

6   Doug Kamstra, *The Praying Church Idea Book: Becoming a House of Prayer – mobilizing members from prayer ministries* (Grand Rapids: Church Resource Publications, 2001). Note: This book is the best resource for prayer ideas available anywhere, bar-none. No prayer leader should be without this book. It is filled with different ways to group your prayer ministry. Prayer organizations from around the world are listed that offer all kinds of help.

7   This section adapted from Jack Hayford: "Qualifying as an Intercessor" <www.livingway.org/articles>.

8   Keep checking on the development of the Virtual Prayer Room – a ministry concept of Project Pray: www.projectpray.org.

9   Cheryl Sacks may have been the first to apply NASCAR language to this term – PIT crew: Personal Intercessory Team member is a part of a PIT crew for some ministry, staff member or missionary.

10   Kamstra (Grand Rapids: Church Resource Publications, 2001). 1-800-333-8300 < www.FaithAliveResources.org>.

11   Ibid.

12   Ibid.

13   The annual 40-day prayer – *Seek God for the City* – is available for use in the traditional season of Lent. They can be ordered from www.waymakers.org. Sample guides from previous years are available. The prayers are well-scripted and the entire book is rewritten each year. The book is an extraordinary resource – taking participants on a 40-day prayer tour of their city, and around the world at the same time.

14   <www.pray4everyhome.org>

15   Adapted from Doug Kamstra, *The Praying Church Idea Book: Becoming a House of Prayer – mobilizing members for prayer ministries.* Chapter 8: "Intercession for Our City."

16   Kamstra.

17   Dick Eastman, *No Easy Road* (Grand Rapids: Baker, 1971) 12.

18   <www.jessaminechristianchurch.com/prayer.htm>.

SIX
Prayer Evangelism

Some want to live within the sound of church or chapel bell. I want to run a rescue shop within a yard of hell.

– C.T. Studd

James Calvert, a missionary to the cannibals of the Fiji Islands, was urged to abandon his mission by the captain of the ship offering him and his team transport, "You will lose your life and the lives of those with you if you go among such savages!" Calvert replied, "We died before we came here."[1]

The fourth dimension of the prayer process is *prayer evangelism.* The *edge* of prayer is turned by exposure to the heart of God for the lost. Nothing drives that process more consistently than the mobilization of intercessors. But intercession must be intentionally turned outward. The whole congregation must be regularly nudged to see beyond themselves. Without an intentional prayer-evangelism interface, prayer becomes narcissistic and unhealthy. Intercessors must lead the way in prayer for the lost. Andrew Murray predicted that "the man who mobilizes the

Christian church to prayer will make the greatest contribution to world evangelization in history."[2]

Jesus: Go Pray!

When Jesus left the earth, he sent his disciples to a prayer meeting and gave them a stiff order: *"Don't leave until you receive the promise of the Father"* (see Acts 1:4). The promise was not a thing, but a Person. The disciples were not to begin evangelizing until the Holy Ghost showed up, and then with him, they would begin their mission. The prayer meeting was about a mission so huge, so daring, they could not do it alone. Their mission was to announce that God had come to Earth, but he had been brutally and wrongfully crucified. The Messiah had been assassinated, and man was guilty. We, humanity, had killed God – but we had not destroyed him. He is alive. And Jesus is going to return – not as a suffering lamb, but as a conquering King. Everyone must prepare to meet him.

It was a terrifying and impossible undertaking. They were not to be fooled into believing they could accomplish this formidable, extreme task by themselves as we seem to be today. They waited on the Spirit. Their praying was inflamed by the four "alls" of the Great Commission:[3]

- All AUTHORITY – access to *sweeping power* necessary for the mission, through prayer; going with confidence.
- All NATIONS – *a global, nation-changing assignment.* Prayer for every nation on the earth so the gospel could be planted there; making disciples, bringing people groups under the discipline of grace.
- All COMMANDS – operating in a *spirit of obedience* to Christ, they were to reach back into the strategic training of the last three years for perspective.
- All TIME – an eternal perspective; a multigenerational task; a timeless message.

Prayer evangelism should include a focus on unreached people groups; prayer support for the missionaries of the church; the neighborhood around the church and that of each member; minorities nearby and those across town; loved ones who have not come to faith in Christ. It takes a team to move this kind of prayer process forward in a local church.

Intercessors cannot be mobilized without leadership. In the same way, prayer will not take on harvest eyes without someone stewarding regular prayer exercises for the lost – abroad and at home.

The Four Greats of the New Testament

In the four "Greats" of the New Testament, four things stand together:

- The Great Commitment (pray for people everywhere, 1 Tim. 2:1).
- The Great Commandment (love God, and your neighbor, even enemies, as yourself, Matthew 22:37-40).
- The Great Commission (sharing the gospel, Matthew 28:19, 20; Mark 16:15).
- The Great Consummation (worship, Psalm 66:4; I Chron. 16:23-31; Rev. 5:13).

We know the Great Commission – *"Go into all the world and preach the gospel"* (Mark 16:15). We have not adequately connected the Great Commission to the Great Commandment – *"Love God with all your heart, mind and might, and your neighbor as yourself."* A people who are not passionate about God, not deeply in love with Him, will never convince their neighbors to follow Christ. They themselves are too much in love with the world. They may reproduce lukewarm Christians, but not radically saved converts willing to lay down their lives. Why is the church so compromised? Why have we lost our first love?

Beyond the Great Commission and the Great Commandment is the Great Commitment, given to us by Paul: *"Pray for people everywhere."* These three stand together – the Great

Commission cannot be fulfilled apart from the Great Commandment. In the Great Commission we have the words of the gospel; but in the Great Commandment, we have the music. O what a difference it makes when you add music to the words! Jesus told us, *"By this all will know that you are My disciples, if you have love for one another"* (John 13:35). Of the early church it was said, "My, how those Christians love one another!"

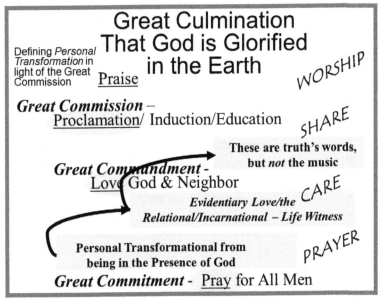

Where do we find a passion to love God and one another? To love our neighbor as we love ourselves and to love our enemies? Only in prayer. It is not our love *improved*. It is His love *imputed*. It is *"the love of God...shed abroad in our hearts"* (Romans 5:5, KJV). Christianity does not begin with me loving God. It begins with His love, first to me, and then through me (1 John 4:10).

As we spend time with a holy, loving God, He changes our character. And when we move beyond communion to intercession, we find God loving through us those for whom we pray. Prayer changes us. It changes our disposition, even toward those who have harmed us. You cannot pray for people, genuinely and sincerely, without eventually loving and caring about them. Daily time with God, the Great Commitment (prayer), fuels our capacity to fulfill the Great Commandment (care). And the more we pray for others, the more God will love people through us, fueling the Great Commission (share). All of this, to the end, that the rebellion on the earth comes to an end, and the whole earth, creation with its creatures, worships God! This is finale - not missions. Worship is the end goal.

We need a love affair with Christ, coupled with an *agape* love for our neighbor. That Godlike love will open their hearts and minds to the gospel. They will ask about the "hope within us." This is the evidentiary, incarnational aspect of prayer. The Great Commission involves the *proclamation,* the declaration of the gospel. But the Great Commandment necessitates the *incarnational,* the transformational, testimonial aspect of the gospel.

The more we pray – sincerely and passionately – the more God transforms us into His likeness and the result of the love of God is revealed through us. Intercession leads to a transformational witness in the life of the church. God's power becomes evidently visible in and around our lives. He shows Himself glorious.

The late Joe Aldrich, founder of the pastor's prayer summit movement often said, "We do not *have* the message, we *are* the message. It rides on the back of the beauty of a transformed church." And that requires people who live transformed lives.

David Brainerd was a powerful missionary whose short life of 29 years cast a long shadow. Heading to the forks of the Delaware to share Christ with a fierce Indian tribe, he camped on the edge of their settlement. His every step was being monitored with eyes he could not see. A small detachment of braves intended to take his life that night before he could enter the tribe's camp the next day. As they came near the missionary's tent, they saw Brainerd on his knees. His eyes were closed fast in prayer. He was oblivious to anything around him – the murderous braves and the poisonous snake that had quietly slipped into his tent.

At first, the detail of braves was certain that the 'great spirit' had sent the viper to do their work for them. The rattlesnake coiled, lifted its head to strike, flicked its forked tongue almost touching the face of Brainerd. Then suddenly, the serpent slithered away into the nearby brush. In the space of seconds, Brainerd's status changed in the minds of the Indians, from a man certainly marked for death, to one with special spiritual status – "The Great Spirit is with the paleface!"

The next day he was given the welcome of a holy man, never knowing that he had squeezed through a narrow passage the evening before, with certain death lurking on both sides of him. Intercession crowned him with the obvious favor of God. Intercession transformed enemies into admirers. Intercession opened the closed hearts of an entire tribe.[4]

Prayer – the Starting Place

Thomas Jefferson edited the Bible. He reduced it to the moral teachings of Jesus and left out everything else. Influenced by the French Revolution and rationalism, he had a particular disdain for the supernatural. His Bible ends with the words, *"There they laid Jesus, and rolled a great stone to the mouth of the sepulcher and departed."*[5] Paul declared boldly, *"If Christ has not been raised, your faith is worthless; you are still in your sins"* (1 Corinthians 15:17, NASB).

If there was no Resurrection, the Cross can mean no more than the sad truth that a noble man died. It is the Resurrection that gives us new life. But behind both the torture of the cross and the triumph of the empty tomb is the agony of Gethsemane.

That night of prayer made all the difference. In the Garden, Christ gained both the power to endure the cross and provision to embrace its victory.

Often God calls us into a closet of prayer because He knows that we are about to face a cross of testing. Prayer stands at the beginning of every victory. Out of it we gain the power to stand (Ephesians 6:18), the persistence to endure and the provision to overcome. Every evangelism undertaking should be preceded by prayer. Don't make prayer a mere prelude to an evangelism undertaking; that trivializes prayer. It invites God to tag along with us on *our* noble mission for His purpose. Go first, in and by the extended power of prayer. Then go as the Lord leads. Here is an example.

Arthur Mouw was a missionary to Borneo, the big island of Indonesia. He arrived there and experienced a great harvest along the coast. Presumptuously, after significant mission success, he planned to take the gospel inland to the head-hunting Dyaks. The team with him loaded their canoes and headed up the river. Three days later, when they beached their boats, they were overcome with a dark and foreboding presence that almost manifested itself and strangled them. They cried out to God as they retreated to their canoes.

Pushing the boats back into the water, they felt immediate relief. Such a phenomenon might be explained away as a mere anxiety attack if it happened to one or even two of the team. But when such a thing happens to an entire group, it should offer to us some evidence of the very real power of our Enemy. The group aborted their mission – dazed, confused, uncertain of what had just happened.

Mouw said later, "I believe we met the Prince of the Dyak tribe that day." In the days that followed, their mistake became clear. The Borneo mission had been bathed in prayer. The Dyak trip had not. They went to prayer. They mobilized intercessors back home to intercede. And when they sensed God's timing, they went to the Dyak tribe again and found the same kind of harvest among the head-hunters that they had found earlier along the coast.[6]

In a South African refugee camp a missionary team set up equipment for the showing of the *Jesus* film. An eerie atmosphere developed as witch doctors began to gather, chant and throw their bones on the ground in ritual praying. Howling and offering incantations, they were calling up the spirits of their ancestors. The *Jesus* film team was in spiritual warfare. They began to pray. For three hours they desperately implored God to send favor and bind the power of the Evil One. At the end of their season of prayer, they joined hands to symbolize their unity, and then began to march victoriously in a circle around the entire camp, praying. Such symbolic action has about it a power – not in the symbolic act itself. The power is in the obedient alignment with God.

Symbolic action is that action which, when prompted by the Spirit and offered by us in cooperative obedience, completes a transaction in the spiritual dimension that will manifest itself in the natural.[7]

As darkness came, a thousand refugees crowded into the circle to watch the video. The witch doctors ceased their chants. Silence came.

Those who show the Jesus video in new fields for evangelism say the Crucifixion scene often brings tears. But no one was prepared for the 'mournful wailing' that rose with an increasing crescendo from this group. Everyone was crying. Paul Eshleman tells what happened next:

> Rivers of tears poured down dirty cheeks. Young men, old men, and women beat their breasts and cried out, "Oh, God! Oh, God!" Some were on their knees, some stood with eyes closed and arms raised, others lay prostrate on the ground. The interpreter lay on his back in the dirt, praying, thanking God, crying, worshiping, confessing. Everywhere people were confessing

their sins. The film was forgotten. These people were in the Presence of a holy God, and they were overwhelmed. They ignored all the ropes, and huge clouds of dust filled the air as people watching from both sides of the screen rushed to the front.[8]

Even the members of the team were overwhelmed with God's Presence. They couldn't speak. They couldn't pray with those who approached them. It was a God-moment. They fell to their knees confessing their own sins. For 30 minutes, weeping and travail were the order of the evening. Then the film was continued – the burial, the Resurrection.

When the interpreter explained that death could not hold Christ in the tomb, a spiritual explosion took place. Now there was clapping, cheering, dancing, hugging. Jesus was alive. And he was alive in that circle around which the team had prayerfully and victoriously walked a few hours earlier. They never finished showing the film. Every person in the audience wanted to receive Christ. The next Sunday, 500 new believers showed up at the local 40-person Christian church. Prayer had won a victory.

This prayer-evangelism process must be led. A director of prayer evangelism must be appointed to serve as a member of the prayer leadership team in the church.

Every Member Praying for the Lost

The most important feature of prayer evangelism is a consistent and strategic plan to pray for the lost. Every member should be challenged to pray for his neighbors. C.S. Lewis offers a forceful charge, "Next to the blessed sacrament, your neighbor is the holiest object presented to your senses."[9]

The Scripture makes it clear – God has ordered our boundaries. He moved the family in next door to us (Acts 17:26). He parked the pagan at the desk next to us. Why? He wants those people exposed to the salt and light He has placed in our lives. We, on the other hand, are constantly on a mission to escape the darkness, to fellowship with nice Christians, to avoid profanity and cigar smoke, to surround ourselves with pleasant and polite people.

God is on a different mission. He wants to press us up against the corruption around us and plunge us, as light, into the darkness. He has more confidence in the power He has placed within us than do we. We often see ourselves as besieged Christians in a culture increasingly hostile to Biblical faith. God sees us as His missionary force. We are looking for a Christian haven. He is looking for a Christian to park at some gate to hell. His ways are not our ways.

The process can be started in a simple way. The essence of prayer evangelism is a commitment to first pray and then, to be "a light" to the lost people around us, to be intentional with regard to the lost in these ways:

- Identify at least five people who are not Christians. This may require some relational work, since the average American knows fewer than three neighbors.

- Make a list of these people and place the list in a place where you will see it regularly – the sun visor on your car, your computer screen, the bathroom mirror, the flyleaf of your Bible. Your prayer for them fulfills the 'Great Commitment.'

- Pray for them at least *five minutes* a day for five days a week.

- Ask God to help you find ways to care for them (the Great Commandment).

- Respond to the open doors God gives you to *share Christ* with them (the Great Commission).

The prayer that is prayed for these people is one of blessing. Use the word *bless* as an acronym for prayer:

- **B**ody – pray for things physical, housing, health, healing, and so forth.

- **L**abor – pray for work needs, job issues, employment-related concerns.

- **E**motional – pray for peace of mind, fulfillment, joy, happiness.

- **S**ocial – pray for relationships, family needs, children, marriages.

- **S**piritual – pray for their salvation, for them to come to know Christ, an awakening for them as a family, as individuals, for their hearts and their home to be open to Christ.

It should be a most basic requirement for all new members to pray for their neighbors to come to know Christ! Love them, care for them, and as God opens the doors of their hearts, share the gospel with them.

Prayer Evangelism engages:

- A person, family or small group committed to pray for, care for, and share Christ with family members, friends, classmates, co-workers and neighbors, especially those who do not know him.

- A congregation whose leaders pray for, care for, and share Christ with unsaved persons. Such congregations usually experience both renewal and growth – *renewal* as members grow strong in prayer, become channels of Christ's love to those around them and articulate their faith more confidently.

There are six characteristics of effective prayer evangelism:

1. It is a lifestyle of prayer that leads to evangelism.

2. It is relational.

3. It demands that we care *before* and *as* we share.

4. It elevates 'loving our neighbor' as a critical piece of our call in following Christ, as being the primary horizontal expression of our love for God.

5. It emphasizes the incarnational as being as important as the *proclamation.*

6. Its breakthrough points are often *kairos* moments.

All of us have five types of neighbors:

1. The unchurched people who *live* next door.

2. The unchurched /non-Christian people who *work* next to us.

3. Our unsaved/unchurched *family* and family-like friends. They may not live next to us or work with us, but these are the people we are closest to. This is the relational network that the New

Testament refers to by the term *oikos,* family or family-like friends. When the gospel comes into such a relational network, it sometimes wins whole families or groups (Acts 11:14; 16:15, 31-34; 18:8).

4.   There are dark *places* in the city *that need light.* Few Christians are in these areas. For example, we would not typically expect Christians to frequent the bars of the city, to hang out with drug dealers, work at the local tattoo parlor, frequent the nightclub or the pornographic bookstore. The people who work in these places need to be 'adopted' for prayer. They often lack a Christian friend or neighbor. This is *intentional* missional neighboring.

5.   As we pray daily for lost loved ones, we will become more sensitive to hurting people around us. Expect spontaneous 'Samaritan' moments (Luke 10:33-37). In our pathway, we will suddenly find hurting people whom God himself has put there. These neighbor moments are sometimes our finest witnessing opportunities. *Pray* for these people! *Care* and look for readiness in their hearts to *share* Christ.

BECOMING A LIGHT

Identify **five people** around you, not practicing their faith.
- Physical Neighbors
- Workplace Associates
- Relational Friends/Family

Pray for them **five minutes** a day. Do this **five days** a week. *Pray.* Ask God to love them through you; to show you ways to *care;* to give the courage to respond to opportunities to *share* Christ.

Joseph Bayly says praying for others encourages him. He and his wife do it regularly:

A flight attendant on my flight reminds me of a woman whose husband has died. I pray for that woman and her children. The pilot makes me remember to pray for friends who are also airline pilots, and for JAARS (Jungle Aviation and Radio Service) and MAF (Mission Aviation Fellowship).

Driving the car, I see a street name, a billboard advertisement, a real estate sign, a church: each leads to an association that results in prayer...if your mind wanders to something else when you're praying...pray for that something else.[10]

As the prayer evangelism ministry unwraps in the church, think about this ministry in four phases.

PHASE ONE: Inside the Church – Nudge the Neighbor in the Next Pew

You might begin the prayer evangelism process in a nonthreatening way, inside the church itself. It might be surprising how many people attend church with some frequency and yet without a vital connection to life in Christ. Here are the preparation steps:

1. Choose a prayer evangelism leader and team.
2. Train a core group to coach others and enthusiastically lead the process.
3. As a rule, you want to train a number of catalyst cheerleaders in the pews for your effort.
4. Choose a time for the five-week experience and collect support materials.
5. Mobilize intercessors to provide prayer support.
6. Launch a 'light up your pew!' experience.
7. Provide brief, focused training with tools.
8. Use the Sunday service to introduce the concept.
9. Include the five-blessing prayer as a bulletin insert and walk your congregation through it.
10. In the bulletin, provide a place for members to make a prayer. Pause in the service and allow them to gather the names of members around them for whom they will pray daily for the next five weeks.
11. Keep encouraging the exercise. You may want to ask them on the first Sunday to pray for only one family near them in the pew, and then add another the next week. By week five, they are praying for five families. By revisiting the experience

each week, you pick up folks who were not present when you launched the program. By adding a new family each week, you keep the experience fresh.

12. Follow up with encouragement for the exercise.
13. Showcase the stories as they begin to emerge.
14. Assess the results. Did it bring people together? Did it assure people that God hears and answers prayer?
15. Cast vision for a neighborhood launch of the lighthouse process.

PRAY 4 EVERY HOME

'Pray 4 Every Home' is an effort that began when a group of pastors – overwhelmed by the growing number of people who don't know Jesus and aware that the status quo of church work was not having a great enough impact – simply asked the question: "What if we prayed for every household by name?"

'Pray 4 Every Home' creates a personalized prayer list for your own neighborhood. After a simple, one-page sign-up, a real-time list is immediately created with names of some 100 nearby neighbors along with a map of your neighborhood.

You can then choose to receive a daily email with five neighbor names and a prayer prompt to use in your prayer time. Add names of other individuals or families for whom you are praying to further customize your prayer list. In 20 days, each participating Christian will have prayed for 100 families!

Learn more at: pray4everyhome.org.

PHASE TWO: Take It to the Streets – Neighborhood Prayer Evangelism

After your launch of the 'nudge your pew neighbor' inside the church, train catalysts for the 'Pray 4 Every Home' project. Take them through a five-week experience focused on their neighbors. After the first experience in which they have prayed for their neighbors, ask them to pray a second round, looking for opportunities to care and share Christ. Assess the results. Make your adaptations and plan to launch the process as a church-wide experience.

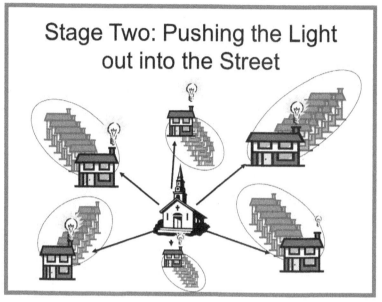

Stage Two: Pushing the Light out into the Street

The participants in your pilot project should make great leaders for the church-wide effort. Nurture these leaders and allow them to mentor others. Follow the same general process you used inside the church. The desired ratio is 1:10.

At some point, you may want to consider a workplace initiative. That simply means that believers are also praying for work associates who do not know Christ. These need to be tracked and encouraged as well.

After a year of concentrated prayer, Al Vander Griend tells the story of a neighbor in Grand Rapids, Michigan that reported the following:

- Neighbors were friendlier to each other.
- People on the block had gotten out of drugs.

- Two unemployed women had found jobs.
- A father had stopped drinking.
- A Bible study had started.
- A father was healed after a heart attack.
- A woman was miraculously healed from an illness.
- A person was delivered from an evil spirit.
- Five persons came to know Christ.[11]

I challenged people to pray for their neighbors in one church in North Carolina. One evening, Jack reported to me his experience.[12] Coming home from work one night, he remembers the heaviness of the Lord – an overwhelming and inescapable burden to pray for his neighbors that night and in a specific way. After parking his car, he began to prayer-walk the circle on which he lived. None of his neighbors who shared the cul-de-sac went to church.

> I felt that I should pause in front of each of the five houses and raise my hand toward each house. It was a tough assignment for me. I was so afraid of what someone might think if they saw me. But, there was such a solemn sense of obligation from the Spirit. I knew I had to obey.

When he finished, he returned to his house with an 'I'm glad that's over!' feeling about the experience. He continued to pray for each neighbor, but nothing happened for almost six months.

Then Larry, the neighbor to his left, commented one day,

> I notice that you never wash your car or mow your yard on Sunday. The rest of us are out here – but we all see you dressed up, and leaving on Sunday morning. Everyone in this neighborhood has had some kind of bad family disruption except you. You go to church every Sunday, don't you? What's it like?

He shared Christ with Larry and Wanda, provided materials, talked with them at their kitchen table – and then watched them begin the regular habit of attending church every Sunday.

Fred lived on the other side of him in the third house. They sometimes washed their trucks together. Fred was a good man, but not a believer. Facing some uncertain challenges, he and his wife opened up to faith and began to attend church with Jack and his wife, Fran. Two houses over, the fourth house, another couple found their marriage in trouble. They had watched the changes in Larry and Wanda, the couple in the first house, so they began to talk with them and attend church with them.

The sixth house on the circle was owned by Jerry and Sue, who had moved to Texas. Their nephew lived in the house with a 'for sale' sign outside. But the night Jack had been so driven by the Spirit to prayerwalk the circle, he had not prayed for the nephew, but for Jerry and Sue. Why? He didn't know. They weren't planning to move back. But they did. And in the year they were gone, in the six months following that nighttime prayer-walk, Sue had come to faith in Christ. Jerry was another story. But prayers are still ascending for him.

The only house into which salvation has not come was the fifth house. Linda lives there. She is a single girl who shared that house with her elderly mother, who died during this same period. Jack and his wife reached out to Linda, but she put up a rather thick wall of disinterest. They keep quietly praying for her as she now watches five cars, not one, drive out of that circle every Sunday to make their way to some place of worship in the city.

PHASE THREE: Connecting the Neighborhood Lights

The prayer evangelism director should have a list of participating members in the love your neighbor effort. You may want to distinguish between neighborhood and workplace lighthouses, noting both on your map. You might discover that your workplace prayer evangelism focus is as intense as the neighborhood effort.

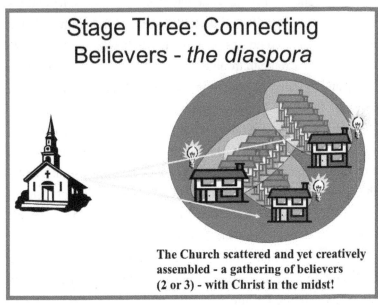

Stage Three: Connecting Believers - *the diaspora*

The Church scattered and yet creatively assembled - a gathering of believers (2 or 3) - with Christ in the midst!

The prayer evangelism leader will want to connect these lights – in neighborhoods and workplaces. Three or more love-your-neighbor participants could be linked together for regular communication and support. They should talk regularly about their challenges and their successes, encourage one another in the task of being a good and effective Christ-like neighbor, pray together for one another.

The purpose of this teaming is collaboration. Convergence takes place when intercessors pray for neighborhood businesses in which your people live and work; and members are also praying for neighbors and associates to come to Christ. By moving out of isolation and into collaboration, we create a new level of synergy for the prayer evangelism effort. Think in these terms:

- Single Member Prayer Evangelism
- Neighborhood prayer-evangelism teaming
- Workplace prayer-evangelism teaming
- Zip zones with members identified and connected
- City quadrants

A university professor told of a colleague who abruptly dropped out of his new teaching position after only three weeks. With his unexpected resignation, the dean bluntly informed him that he would not teach again at that institution or anywhere else.

> I found my friend Charlie living in an attic apartment in Hamilton Square, New Jersey. I must admit that his apartment had style: travel posters pasted all over the walls, a good assortment of books...a stereo playing a Wagnerian opera. I sat down on a bean-bag chair that swallowed me up. After we had exchanged niceties, I came to the point.
> "What have you done?" I asked.
> "I quit," said Charlie. "I walked out. I don't want to teach anymore. Every time I walked into that classroom, I died a little bit."
> It wasn't long before I realized Charlie was not about to go back into the classroom, so I asked him what he was doing with himself these days. He said, "I'm a mailman."...I said to him, "Charlie, if you're going to be a mailman, be the best mailman in the world."
> He said, "I'm a lousy mailman. Everybody else who delivers mail gets back to the post office by about two o'clock. I never get back until six."
> "What takes you so long?" I asked.
> "I visit," said Charlie. "You'd never believe how many lonely people there are on my route who had never been visited until I became a mailman. What's more, now I can't sleep at night...15 cups of coffee a day!"[13]

On first glance, it appeared as though Charlie had slipped from the professional sector into the blue-collar crowd. A bad move – a loss of status. But Charlie had really found his calling – visiting the *"orphans and widows in their distress"* (James 1:27, NIV). If every mail carrier were a believer, and they prayer-walked their route, instead of just delivering mail, the entire nation would be covered in prayer almost daily.

PHASE FOUR: Prayer-Evangelism Clusters

Do you remember the little Sunday school chorus "This little light of mine, I'm gonna let it shine?" As the darkness has gathered in our nation, the "little lights" are needed more than ever. No one wants to live in a city where night falls and all the streetlights are out. And yet, that is the spiritual nature of certain areas of our cities. The night has fallen, and there are little lights scattered here and there. Whole sections of our cities have been given over to the darkness and virtually abandoned by the church. We must do better. We need a city with a network of connected and powered streetlights.

A little light here and there is not effective in pushing back the darkness. We must have a citywide, systematic and empowered prayer evangelism movement – one that is well-coordinated and effectively maintained.

What if the congregations of a community were to begin to work together? What if they encouraged and supported their members in connecting with Christians of other congregations? All for the cause of concentrating the gospel in sections of the city, neighborhood by neighborhood. Most congregations will note when they map their prayer evangelism party that their concentration is too sparse to make a difference in the whole. Other Christians live around us, but we do not know them. The denominational/congregational division of the church of the city works to our disadvantage. To create critical mass, we need unity.

A collaborative, multi-congregational prayer evangelism movement is needed across the city, section by section, should be aimed at connecting the praying Christians of many congregations in the same area to increase light density. By collaborating, these praying Christians will find more creative ways to impact their neighborhood. They could also collaborate with regard to specific neighbors. Imagine a Baptist neighbor teaming with a Pentecostal two blocks away: "I can't seem to reach my neighbor, Charlie. But you are a fisherman and so is he. Maybe you can help me reach him!"

Imagine a concern for the lost around us that transcended our denominational/congregational concerns. Would it matter if our neighbors came to Christ in a Presbyterian congregation? Or an independent fundamentalist congregation? Our goal must become selfless – to see this neighbor won to Christ, even if I do not win them, and they attend another church.

Simultaneous Citywide Lighthouse Impact

The combination of many small lights turning on during the same time periods – synergistic efforts, the power of unity – could make a greater impact than our small lights functioning independently.

Here is what we could do if we partnered in prayer evangelism:

- Collaborative training could be offered, cost-effectively and more frequently.

- A love-your-neighbor forum could be created on the Internet for each church and for the city effort.

- The synergistic collaborative efforts of multiple congregations simultaneously engaging the city, neighborhood-by-neighborhood, would have greater impact.

Examples of Prayer Making a Difference

A California church rented an apartment in a low-income complex with 200 units. They provided for a couple to move in and start a love-your-neighbor project. The couple, along with a team from the church, spent their first month praying. They then began calling systematically on each unit in the complex, offering the gift of prayer. Residents in 198 out of 199 units responded positively. Many gave prayer requests right on the spot.[14]

For several years, members of the Georgian Hills Baptist Church in Memphis would ask members to submit the names of friends, relatives and acquaintances who did not know Christ so that the church's evangelism team could pray for them. The prayer team received training in intercession and then met weekly to intercede earnestly for the persons whose names had been submitted. In one year, the intercession team began by praying for 95 persons. By the year's end, 88 had heard the good news and had come to Christ.[15]

Getting Started – Become a Bean Collector

Many people will forever prayer-walk their neighborhoods, but never knock on a neighbor's door to share Christ or offer prayer. How do we bridge this gap? A recent study revealing that the estimated percentage of U.S. households that were food insecure was 12.7 percent of U.S. households. Almost 50,000 agencies are working to solve the problem.

Delivery is not the issue – the inadequate food supply is the culprit. Even with corporate donations by the food industry, the problem cannot be solved. What is needed is a new source of food which is right next door. Canning Hunger (www.canninghunger. org), an organization in Southern California, has discovered "that people who have food are willing to share it with people who need food, if you make it convenient enough for them." When people were asked if they would help fight hunger by giving a can of food to a neighbor, who would get it to a distribution center, over 95 percent of the people said they would help.

Here is how it works. You volunteer to collect food in your neighborhood for the city food bank or a collaborative project between churches in the city. Send a simple note to your neighbors, sharing your concern for the disadvantaged and tell them you are willing to be the designated 'bean collector' on the block to allow your neighborhood to contribute to the community food bank. This creates a 'relationship portal' between you and other neighbors. You are fulfilling your obligation to the Great Commandment to love others. Your compassion calls a caring, loving spirit out of your neighbors. They'll feel better about you and themselves. It wakes up their desire and need to be more caring and considerate of others. That's conviction.

Relationships begin to form in the neighborhood. As the bean collector, you share stories with neighbors about how their efforts have made a difference in families. "What a great feeling to know we're a part of making a significant difference!" And of course, as the neighborhood bean collector, you get a chance to grow closer to your neighbors, discover their needs, network the neighborhood and spread a little bit of the love of God around.

One bean collector told his story:

> The first Saturday we called 20 people in the neighborhood telling them that the next Saturday we would collect for the food bank. I spent three hours collecting food and I learned more from and about my neighbors in that brief morning than I had in seven years of living next to them.
>
> One neighbor asked: "John, you are doing this for your church?"
>
> John replied, "Well, yes, in a way – our church is a part of the city food bank and that is where the food goes!"
>
> The neighbor then said: "That means you know how to pray, right?...My son has leukemia. Could you come in and pray for him?"

Suddenly, John was no longer a bean collector. His compassion for others revealed him as a believer. And out of the time invested, he not only mobilized his neighbors to care for others, but he has been able to care for his neighbors.

Plan a collection about every 60 to 90 days. Let your neighbors know that you won't be by every week, just four to five times a year. The first collection will be an introduction. On the second collection, you can thank your neighbors for the previous collective effort.

By the time of the third collection, there is sometimes an opportunity to offer prayer for a donating family. Don't force a spiritual moment, let it begin naturally. Let them open the door. When the strategy is being utilized, 50 percent of the neighbors, by the third or fourth collection connection, evidence prayer needs. And 50 percent of those prayer requests are meaningful and personal.

If only 3 million Christians became bean collectors, we would close the hunger gap in the nation. That's only five of church attenders, about a thousand people in the typical county of 100,000 residents. This bridge to neighbors would not only bless disadvantaged families in the city, but more importantly, we might spark a revival.

Hold a Christmas Party

Norm and Becky Wretlind did a simple thing. They threw a creative Christmas party and invited their neighbors – the very neighbors for whom they had been praying. It was a perfect bridge. The neighbors met each other, and for some it was their only opportunity to consider the true meaning of Christmas. A lot of friendships started that day. Redemptive grace flowed in the neighborhood.

Over the next few years, Norm and Becky repeated the Christmas party. Soon it was not a seasonal thing. A home Bible study began. That led to the conversion of more than 60 neighbors. Extraordinary! Whole families came to embrace Christ as Savior. Norm says he was living in the "Book of Acts." Out of that neighborhood experience, a church was born. Today over 1,200 neighbors gather weekly to worship the Lord.

Prayer Evangelism – The Goal: A Focus on the Harvest

Expect prayer levels to rise in the church as intercessors are trained and teamed, mobilized and debriefed, focused and featured for their work. Others, unaware of their call to intercession, will join this effort. The work with intercessors will impact at-home daily prayer and at church attempts to mobilize prayer. Intercessors are truly the engine that drives prayer in the church. They are already motivated to pray.

These intercessors will occasionally see into the spiritual night things discerned by no other means than prayer. They will offer intuitive insight that warns and averts crisis. This may not happen often. Someone has observed that a large portion of the watchman's duty cycle is boring. Intercessors who constantly see large, dark demons over the church are wearying, to say the least.

The more common occurrence will be an intensifying passion for the lost, especially if you are intentional in linking intercession and the harvest. The whole church should learn the value of prayer for the lost. Left to themselves, intercessors are not as effective as they will be when teamed and focused outward. Prayer must be missional. Paul asked the Colossians to *"pray, that a door might be opened for me to preach the gospel"* (see Colossians 4:2, 3). Prayer opens doors, penetrating the hearts and minds closed to the gospel.

"Out of the Box" Intercessors

- One church does a 'wash 'n pray' servant evangelism ministry. They wash the car for free, actually for the pleasure of gaining access to the inside of a car where they pray as they clean. Those outside "lay hands on the car" as they wash the car. Be sure to bless the driver.

- One Northern youth group offers a servant evangelism deicing treatment in the winter.

- Offer free coffee on a cold day at shopping centers. Pray for the people. Or just say, "Have a blessed day, today!"

- Do a bus tour of the city with intercessors. Miami pastors began to do this once a month. What happened was eye-opening. They were confronted with the struggles of pastors, the pleas of mayors, the depth of the evil practices in the Greater Miami area.

Spiritual mapping revealed a ring of occult churches and shops around Dade County.

- Put up a 'prayer tent.' On the campus of the University of Tennessee, one pastor puts up a prayer tent weekly during the months and weeks that weather permits. He offers to simply pray for students who pass by the free speech mall. On some days a hundred students may receive prayer at the prayer tent.

- Experiment with a 'free prayer' booth at the county fair, your local college campus, or even at your church on Sunday. In a large church, many people may long for a personal touch, for personal prayer that is not always offered in the service.

- Conduct a "20 Hours With God!" prayer experience for youth. Have them spend Friday evening in transformational, conversational prayer. Focus on Christlikeness. Lead them to repentance and self-examination. Let them pray one for another. Take them to the streets to pray on Saturday. Debrief them afterward. Record your experiences. Consult with Project Pray about how to organize such an event.

- Conduct prayer missions into the city as a specialized function of the intercessory teams in collaboration with the intercessory prayer division leader. These teams should function within the framework of the intercessory prayer division. Special teams of intercessors who feel called to pray for the city should be organized and deployed, debriefed and celebrated.

Think of the four dimensions in yet another way:

1. Daily prayer must focus on the *face* of God.
2. Intercessors connect with the *eyes* of God – they are the seers, the watchers on the wall.
3. The ministries of the church need the *hand* of God, His touch and anointing upon them if they are to be effective.
4. In prayer evangelism, we connect with the *heart* of God – always focused on the lost.

This is not about dissecting God – quite the opposite. It is about grasping the whole of God with the whole of prayer. To move a congregation to the four-dimensional model is a process. Prayer events will not accomplish this alone.

Persistence Is Required

An atheist in London was married to a believer who constantly prayed for him. She had a Bible, which she read consistently. One day, in a fit of rage, he threw her Bible in the fireplace and stormed out of the room. When he returned to watch the book burn, he was surprised to see one small section in the midst of the fire that remained unburned. He retrieved it from the fire. The words were still legible. Trembling he read, *"Heaven and earth shall pass away, but my Word shall not pass away"* (Matthew 24:35).

He fell to his knees before the fire, seeking God for forgiveness. The story does not end there. The man's sister was a believer, as was his wife, and she was also an intercessor. The very night of this explosion of anger followed by a dramatic conversion, she had been engaged in persistent prayer for him.[16] O, the wonder of prevailing prayer.

1   Story told by David Augusber, *Sticking My Neck Out* (March 1979) 154; quoted R. Kent Hughes, *1001 Great Stories and Quotes,* 65.

2   Quoted by Ivan French, *The IFCA Voice,* Sept. 2, 2003.

3   Ben Jennings, *The Arena of Prayer* (Orlando, FL: New Life, 1999) 26.

4   Fred Barlow, *Profiles in Evangelism* (Murfreesboro, TN: Sword of the Lord, 1976), 34.

5   R. Kent Hughes, 353.

6   Jennings, 123-124.

7   Doug Small, *The Mysterious Ways of God – The Power of Symbolic Action* (Kannapolis, NC: Alive, 1995).

8   Paul Eshleman, *The Touch of Jesus* (Orlando, FL: New Life, 1995) 15-21.

9   R. Kent Hughes, 349.

10 Joseph Bayly, *Out of My Mind* (Grand Rapids: Zondervan, 1993) 140-143.

11 As told by Alvin J. Vander Griend in *Lighthouses of Prayer Training.*

12 As told to Doug Small.

13 R. Kent Hughes, 338, 339.

14 Doug Kamstra, *The Praying Church Idea Book: Becoming a House of Prayer – mobilizing members from prayer ministries* (Grand Rapids: Church Resource Publications, 2001), 17-20.

15 Phone interview with Greg Frizzel while pastor of the Georgian Hills Baptist Church in Memphis, TN.

16 Eastman, *No Easy Road,* 99.

SEVEN
The Prayer Center

I care not what black spiritual crisis we may come through or what delightful spiritual Canaan we may enter, no blessing of the Christian life becomes continually possessed unless we are men and women of regular, daily, unhurried secret lingerings in prayer.

– J. Sidlow Baxter

I saw something today which affected me more than anything I ever saw or read on religion. While the battle was raging and the bullets were flying, General [Stonewall] Jackson rode by, calm as if he were at home, but his head was raised toward heaven, and his lips were moving evidently in prayer.[1]

In order to encourage a flourishing prayer ministry, you need a physical space to nurture, practice and train in the area of prayer. The choir needs a practice room. The youth need a center for their activities. Christian education and discipleship ministries need education space. No one disagrees.

The prayer ministry also needs a space from which they can work. A prayer office needs to be established out of which the leadership team functions. If possible, a church should consider establishing a prayer center. A prayer room is a good beginning, but a city-impact center is the optimum. Of all the options we will discuss in this chapter and the next, the prayer center is my preference for a local church. Size does dictate the intensity of the prayer room/center and the number of prayer volunteers. A congregation of 350 or less is probably best served with a prayer room. Congregations above 350 might be able to sustain a prayer center. Congregations above a thousand should consider a prayer impact center. All along the continuum, pastors and prayer themes can mix the various components that match their mission.

In the Pentagon war room, there are maps, computers, charts and information systems full of descriptive data. Every conceivable military situation is rehearsed and studied there.[2]

One component of a prayer center is a situation room, where strategies and tactics are rehearsed. Here prayer-evangelism scenarios are scripted. Here we calculate the cost of the mission, the personnel needed, the timing – all the elements. Remember, prayer and mission are irrevocably linked. So the prayer center is not only a place of prayer, but the center to launch evangelism strategies.

Sound research should inform and inspire the prayer process at the center. The church should know the beachheads that must be taken for immediate and generational impact. What and where are strongholds? Where, and by what means, are the most people being taken into captivity? How and why do they remain enslaved? Prayer should be constantly offered for these people and places, along with pleas for wisdom and clarity for outreach strategies. Without clear research, we don't know how to effectively pray. Without intentional and Spirit-informed strategies, we offer a hodgepodge of evangelism efforts that lack either a long-term or cohesive design. Without a situation room, prayer and evangelism mobilization remain disconnected with discouraging results.

LEARNING FOCUS

- Are the *people* of the church *praying* – at home, daily? For personal transformation?
- Have the *intercessors been identified?* Are they being trained? Growing?
- Is there an interface between *prayer and evangelism?* Does the church have harvest eyes?
- Do you have a *pervasive prayer movement* in the church or simply prayer programs?

The prayer center becomes the hub of support to unwrap the four dimensional model for prayer:

1. *Praying people: personal/family/at-home* – transformational daily prayer
2. *A praying church* – The ministries of the church must become praying and prayed-for ministries. Implement the Moravian principle: "No one works unless someone prays! An intercessor for every worker, and every worker an intercessor." There should be multiple prayer options available at this church – a buffet of prayer ministries.
3. *Identified, trained and mobilized intercessors.*
4. *A prayer and evangelism interface* – prayer that connects the church with the harvest field, the lost.

To feed these four dimensions, the church *needs* a prayer center (room/office), focused on all four tracks. It should be designed to support and encourage:

- *Development* of a personal prayer life in church members
- *Provision* of models and resources for daily, at-home, personal and family prayer
- *Mentoring* of people in prayer
- *Mobilizing* of prayer that supports the ministries of the church
- *Harnessing* of the energy of prayer by directing prayer, and giving prayer assignments to intercessors and prayer center volunteers

- *Identifying and gathering* intercessors. The prayer center is the place where they connect, are informed and mobilized.
- *Nurturing* of the whole prayer ministry – children, youth, families, singles, men and women, believers and unbelievers
- *Connection and coordination* of prayer and evangelism – keeping a window open on the world and the needs of the lost
- Information on unreached people groups and their adoption.
- The missionaries of the congregation and the nations in which they work.
- Information about the mission field near, around the church, its degrees of need and lostness.
- City leaders, those in authority, community influencers, for whom we are charged to pray.
- Community service agencies for whom the church might pray – schools, fire, police and safety personnel.

The role of the prayer center is also to balance the vision of God's face, hands, eyes and heart; to both mobilize intercessors (veteran prayers) and mentor brand-new believers; to support personal prayer development and corporate prayer gatherings; to undergird the ministries of the congregation in prayer, and at the same time develop harvest eyes for missional praying. This is the hub, the center, for the prayer efforts of the church.

This four-dimensional process moves forward on two legs – learning and doing. Ben Jennings, the great prayer leader for Campus Crusade, says, "Prayer is both taught and caught. Without its Biblical principles being taught, prayer is unstable. Without our catching the principles by applying them to our lives, it is sterile."[3]

LEARNING

Prayer training[4] should be offered in all four dimensions. Imagine seminars like this in each of the four areas.

1. Personal At-Home Prayer

- Spending an hour with God
- Scripture in personal prayer
- Setting up your own prayer closet
- Family devotions
- Teaching your children to pray
- Praying couples
- Praying for your wife/husband
- Models for personal prayer time
- House dedication
- Blessing ceremonies
- Prayer and the stages of life

2. Congregational Prayer Training[5]

- Relational prayer experiences
- Leading small prayer groups
- Praying Scripture as a congregation
- The power of agreement in prayer
- Prayer groups that work
- Pastor's Prayer Partners
- Partnering in prayer
- Nursery training: blessing babies

3. Intercessors Training

- Training intercessors
- Debriefing intercessors
- Praying for missionaries
- Reconciliation in intercession
- Warfare and intercession
- Teaming intercessors
- Intercessors and pastors
- Watchers on the wall and the elders at the gate
- Correcting intercessors without killing passion
- The use of confirmation for "prayer hunches"

4. Prayer Evangelism Training

- Praying for unchurched neighbors
- Praying for lost friends and family
- Ways to care for a neighbor
- Models: The "HEARTS" prayer; "BLESS" prayer; five-finger prayer
- The gospel as story
- The power of *Oikos* – loving your circle of unsaved friends
- Prayer-walking
- Prayer mission training
- Giving the gift of prayer

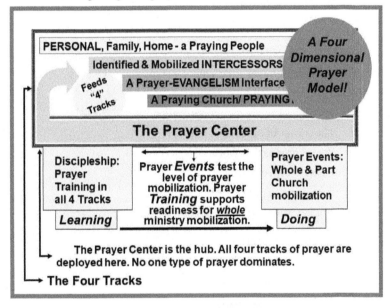

DOING

Testing Your Capacity to Mobilize

Prayer training (teaching) must be balanced by prayer events (doing). The power is not in the learning, but in the obedient doing. Prayer events test your capacity to mobilize a part of the congregation – or at times the whole congregation – for prayer. So you *learn,* and then you *do!* Train, then test the power of that learning by doing what you have taught. Without being intentional, without testing your prayer training, you are only deceiving yourself into believing that you are making progress. These are the two legs on which you advance: learning and doing; doing and learning.

When you call for prayer events, you discover the degree to which you can effectively mobilize the church. How many show up when you call a prayer meeting? If they do not come, why not? Have they learned the value of prayer by the experience of answered prayer? Prayer events allow "learning by experiencing." Prayer training applies the learning and mobilizes to do prayer. No training should stand apart from implementation. Every teaching/training event should be applied.

Assessing Your Effectiveness

After you both *teach* (prayer training) and then *do* (prayer events), you must *assess* the doing (a prayer leadership function). How well did your people integrate the teaching? Are they comfortable in the practice of the principle? Do they understand? How effective are they? In many cases, you will be able to see the 'learning gaps,' and that will tell you where you need additional training. It may take some courage, but the prayer trainer will have to speak to the *learning gaps.* Avoiding training and teaching in the 'gap' areas will guarantee the failure of the prayer ministry.

The Process
Cycle One

- Teach (prayer training).
- Do (prayer events).
- Assess (a leadership function). Discover the learning gaps.

Cycle Two

- Then teach (specific training, or coaching) into the learning gaps.
- Then do – test the learning again.[6]
- Assess – the learning gaps are closed. "We've got it."

Cycle Three

- Teach successive principles, going to the next level.
- Then put those principles into practice.
- Assess.

Cycle Four

- Teach into any learning gap.
- Assess by application.
- Address the learning gap, if necessary.

Cycle Five

- Move to another chapter of training.
- Learning and doing, then assessing – that is how the process advances.

When you launch your prayer training in any area, here are some tips for effective training:

- Make time in the training to practice prayer!
- Give 'doing' assignments on the principles about which you are 'learning.'
- Offer churchwide training in prayer at least once each year.

Emphasize the positive, but don't ignore the struggles people are having as they attempt to bring prayer both to the center of their lives and experience prayer as couples and families at home.

Don't try to fit everyone into the same box! Not everyone will be comfortable praying in the same way. Nor will they be passionate about the same causes. Vary your formats. Offer a variety of models for prayer. Help people find a prayer style that fits them.

Allow for 'individual, informal learning.' Buy a trainload of prayer books. Pass them around, first to your prayer leaders and then to the congregation generally. Get them reading about prayer, watching videos.

Tell stories about other prayer ministries, prayer break-throughs, even about prayer struggles. Feature them in your prayer bulletin, churchwide newsletter, or even on occasion in your Sunday service.

Focus your training evenly on the four dimensions:

(1) Learning to Pray at Home; (2) What's an Intercessor? – Come and Find Out If You're One; (3) The Power of a Praying Church; (4) Secret Missions – Stealth Praying (Prayer Evangelism).

The prayer center will eventually become the heart of ongoing teaching and doing. It becomes the functional prayer and training center, the nerve center for the whole prayer process in the local congregation.

The Models

There are three distinct models that are appearing across the nation and around the world: the prayer room model, the prayer center model, and the Davidic house of prayer model.

Let's distinguish between these three models. The *prayer room* is a kind of prayer retreat. The *prayer center* should be designed to serve as the nerve center of the church. It both trains and mobilizes prayer. The *Davidic house of prayer* is characterized by combining the 'harp and bowl,' or 'worship and intercession.'

The prayer center would be the model for the smaller church. The mood is passive. Individuals drop-in and enjoy prayer alone or with others. Prayer resources should be available. Prayer groups should be formed and encouraged to use the room. The room may contain maps of the world, the city, the mission areas upon which the congregation focuses, near and far, and pictures of missionaries. It might contain a visual of church staff, particularly the prayer and evangelism team for prayer. It might include a prayer list as well as community missions prayer list. Even a small prayer room could make use of media with a laptop and a small display. Consider playing videos available from Shoutcast or a Power Point with scrolling prayer needs. Don't leave out mission and evangelism images.

The prayer center, for the larger church, is not passive. It can serve as a retreat. However, at the prayer center, individuals are recentered for prayers. The goal is to staff the prayer center with rejoicing prayer. The larger the church, the easier this task becomes and the more the center interfaces with the needs of the city.

One of the primary purposes of both the prayer center and the Davidic house of prayer is 'to invite God' regularly to come into our midst – as individuals, families, a church, a city, state and nation. He comes where He is invited.

The prayer center speaks to...

- Our *hearts*...developing a relationship with God, loving Him.
- Our *homes*...do I live in my home so that it is marked by the Presence of Christ?
- Our church as a *house of prayer*...reclaiming the sanctuary for Him!
- Our city as a *harvest field* of unreached people!
- Our *hope*...the reality that we are pilgrim people.

Here are the *personal,* the *corporate* and the *kingdom* elements of prayer.

Three Intensive Local-Church Prayer Models

As your prayer movement develops, you will need to choose a congregational prayer model. Each church must find its place on the continuum. The intensity and use will determine the various levels of staffing and planning. Let's distinguish between these three models:

- The 'Harp and Bowl'
- The Prayer Room
- The Prayer Center

The harp-and-bowl model was introduced in Kansas City as a collaborative 24/7 prayer process of the churches in the city to be an expression of city-wide prayer partnership. It is the most widely known house of prayer in the world.[7] In some cities, this model is being introduced as a 'house of prayer for the city' – typically apart from any particular congregation.

The Differences

The harp and bowl is ongoing, worshipful, corporate prayer. The prayer *room,* by contrast, is typically private. It is a place for personal prayer, intercession for others and edification for self. It may be used by individuals or small groups, or by intercessors.

The prayer *center* is bigger in size and also broader in focus than either the harp-and-bowl model or the prayer room. It is missional. It should be used by both individuals and small groups. It harnesses the ministry of intercession. It is about mission. Prayer for the lost and needs of the city are a key focus of the prayer center. The prayer center and the prayer room are often confused as one. They represent significantly different approaches. Let's take a closer look at each of these three models.

Harp and Bowl

The harp-and-bowl model emphasizes 24/7 prayer and worship – 24 hours a day, seven days a week. This follows the model of the Tabernacle of David – a constant stream of worship, prayer and praise, offered to God from Mount Zion (2 Samuel 6:17, 18; 1 Chronicles 6:32). This bold vision longs for the day when, in some part of the city, there will never be a time when someone or some group is not in prayer and communion with God in behalf of the city and the purposes of God. For most churches, this is an impossibility. As a component of unity, begin the church of the city, this could easily be a reality, given the identification of intercessors across a city/county and the unified support of pastors.

The term *harp and bowl* is from Revelation 5:8, where we get a glimpse of heavenly worship. The *harp* is a symbol of praise and worship. The *bowl* is filled with incense, a symbol of prayer. So here are the images of worship and prayer mingled together. This has led to a relatively new emphasis in prayer which insists that joyful praise and worship be connected with intercession.

In the harp-and-bowl model, the prayerful incense of praise mixed with worship is offered to God. This connection of prayer with praise may be unique to some intercessors. Yet, in the Old Testament, *feasting* was more often connected with prayer and worship than was *fasting*. There, the high and holy days of prayer and worship were feast days. The exception was the Day of Atonement. The Sabbath was also a weekly day of prayer; and it was associated with rest and peace.

What are the characteristics of the harp-and-bowl model?

- The focus is vertical – the worship and prayer experience is directed to God. It is offered to Him as a gift – from worshipers who represent the church, or even the city.
- Worship is interspersed with prayer and praise. It is by nature more corporate than private. Worship teams lead the experience. They do this in two-hour shifts.
- Music is vertical. It is more than a background and atmosphere for prayer. It is more than Christian entertainment. In a typical worship service, the activity of worship, and the music of worship, is more horizontal – the choir and musicians sing with a focus on the audience. The preacher preaches with a focus

on the participants. In the harp-and-bowl model, the activity of prayer and praise is vertical. God is the audience. Others listen in as music is offered to God, as prayers are prayed to Him, as praise is offered through Biblical and fresh prophetic psalms. It is almost unimportant as to how many people are present in the room, since God is the audience. Participants sometimes join in the singing and praying. Others may be prostrate before God in worship and prayer. Some stand. Some sit. Some kneel.

- Psalmists and prophets flow together. Intercessors and worshipers become one.

- As the incense of praise and prayer ascends to God, heaven reaps the harvest of sweet incense. And the descending dew of the Holy Spirit often results in the prophetic – insights are gained, revelations are given, admonitions come, as do new psalms of praise, words of encouragement or warning.

- The goal of the harp-and-bowl model is to offer praise to God – a never-ceasing stream of worship.

- Here, the church is open for worship 24/7 – 24 hours a day, seven days a week. Worship leaders and participants slip in and out, but the prayer and worship continue.

These harp-and-bowl centers have appeared everywhere – in large cities and small towns and hamlets. Some identify with the International House of Prayer (IHOP). But this is not the only model. There is ZHOP, the 'Furnace' and Boiler Rooms. The movement is spontaneous and youthful. It represents a very different wineskin for the church, perhaps, the wave of the future.

There is such a prayer movement in North America – but it is largely outside the traditional church. Rejoice. God is raising up sons and daughters of prayer.

Prayer Room

The prayer room is a physical place dedicated to use for prayer by believers. It may be small or large. Typically it is a smaller space – 200 to 300-square feet, the typical size of a large Sunday school classroom.

- The emphasis in the prayer room is on prayer, more often private than corporate.

- Literature may be present to enrich the prayer experience, but the use of that literature is optional.

- Prayer stations may be established with thematic banners or information on people in need of prayer, issues for prayer, missions, and so forth. Because of the size of the room, these may be wall displays.[8]

- People slip into the prayer room, typically unscheduled. They pray according to their own heart, following the direction of the Spirit. They leave when they have satisfied the prayer call on their heart. Small groups may use the room during the week for prayer meetings.

- The room may also become a place for prayer counseling and prayer ministry to someone in need.

- The room is often used before and after corporate worship experiences for prayer.

- It may or may not be staffed; most often it is not.

- It provides a retreat, a place to find quiet.

- Music is optional. If it is used at all, it is in form of a CD player with worship tapes. This can become a problem. Some 'prayers' are used to bringing their own music as an accompaniment to prayer – this was a custom of the prophets and kings (1 Samuel 10:5; 18:10; 1 Chronicles 25:1; Luke 7:32; 1 Corinthians 14:7). However, one person's music can be another's distraction.

Prayer Center

While the prayer room is a bit of a retreat for personal or small group prayer, the prayer center is a noisy window on the needs of the church, the city and the world.

Physically, the prayer center is a much larger place than a prayer room. It is recommended that a prayer center be at least 1,000 square feet, twice that if possible. Ten times that amount may be needed in a larger church. A city prayer-impact center will require significant space. While the prayer room may have a desk for sign-in and sign-out registering people coming and going from the room, the prayer center has an office. It may be small and should be secluded to avoid distractions – but it is often very busy. In the office...

- Prayer requests are harvested and distributed.
- Prayer needs around the city and the world are collected and formatted for prayer.
- Prayer assignments are suggested to prayer workers.
- Prayer alerts are prepared and flashed on the screens for prayer participants.

The music and video are controlled for the prayer center. (In the prayer room, people often bring their own music, but in the prayer center, the atmosphere is more protected.)

Characteristics of the Prayer Center

The prayer center should have carpet, at least in certain areas, to invite kneeling or even lying prostrate before the Lord. Cushions can provide an aid for kneeling, inviting humility before the Lord. Lighting should be designed for incremental levels and adjusted as deemed appropriate. Lower levels of light are recommended, though varying levels are desired. More light should be available on the information displays and perhaps at the altar, and on reflective symbols such as crosses. The point is to create a meditative atmosphere.

Every center should have cubicle capacity – small soundproof spaces for individuals to have a 'prayer-room' experience. This gives the prayer center a 'retreat' capacity. This is an important balance, since the prayer center insists on being connected with the problems of culture around it. It exists to pray about those conditions and should be interfaced with a prayer-counseling station for phone and Internet-interactive prayer.

The prayer center is intentionally missional. It programs the prayer focus to be missional. It assigns missional praying to its volunteers. It stewards its obligation to the Great Commission. The prayer room, by contrast, has no such consistent and intentional missional prayer program. The purpose of the prayer room exists so believers can have a place for prayer, whereas the prayer center is not only for believers but also for unbelievers. The prayer center has a stream of information coming in concerning the lost, the world, the harvest; and it has a stream of people called to prayerful ministry flowing out of it to touch their community, nation and world.

The heart of the prayer center is a constant exposure to the pain of the world and its response to that pain in prayer in the context of 'the rest' of God. Staffed by believers, it is open to unbelievers who need prayer. It should be the place where hurting people can come in times of need for prayer ministry. It should be a place that can receive prayer requests and needs from people in the church, the city and the world.

While the prayer room is a 'retreat' for personal and small-group prayer, the center is a 'window.' Using technology, it is positioned electronically, as a nerve center for happenings in the church, the city and the world. The prayer center should have a media interface – a place where prayer requests are constantly harvested and prayers are sown in the heavens in response. World news and events may be flashed on monitors, and intercessors/people of prayer respond. Needs are rolled on screens or video monitors listing the needs of people, church ministries, city/social/spiritual concerns and the world.

As the function of the prayer center engages the needs of the congregation and city, it also interacts with them. Notes of support are sent out; cards and letters are mailed; prayer mission teams may be deployed systematically or spontaneously.

The personnel of prayer center should be trained to assist others in prayer and to do the work of prayer. They pray with both believers and unbelievers who come to the prayer center for prayer. They respond to email and phone calls for prayer. The prayer center director oversees the operation of the center, which is hopefully open seven days a week.

The city impact center is open 24 hours a day. Start by opening your prayer center and having staff present during the "high use" hours (mornings: 6:30-9:30; evenings: 3:30-7:30).

For 24-hour impact, without the personnel to have the center open, use an ongoing prayer chain. Each day, have a different person serve as the 'day watch-leader' to coordinate prayer for that day so the whole burden does not fall on the center director. The watch-leaders might also take responsibility for setting up and keeping current the prayer station displays and for leading a prayer group..

Prayer center volunteers serve the center in two-to-four hour shifts. They are trained. They are present to pray for people who drop by the center. They are there to do the 'work of prayer – to fulfill assignments in prayer.' They are present to harvest needs that come in by phone or email and post them for prayer and direct them on to the intercessors.

The Style and Emphasis

Unlike the Davidic house of prayer model (harp and bowl), the focus of the prayer center is not on unceasing, *corporate* worship/praise and prayer, but on the *corporate work* of prayer to support the ministries of the church and pray in the harvest.

In the prayer room, people come and go as they fulfill the call of the Holy Spirit for prayer. While the prayer center provides the opportunity for people to do the same, it also frames an agenda for prayer. And it harnesses the energy of prayer to do the work of prayer. Thus, some individuals come to the prayer center to take their shift as watchmen on the wall, to own responsibility for prayer support of various church ministries, city needs and world concerns.

The prayer center works vigorously to balance these areas:

- Transformational prayer (personal growth through prayer).
- Transactional prayer (doing business with God; and the business of prayer support for every ministry effort of the church).
- Intercessory prayer (watching before God, hearing from God – the prophetic and seer dimension of prayer).
- Prayer that encourages the development of harvest eyes (this is a critical component, without which the prayer room or prayer center is too narrow and narcissistic).

The prayer center harnesses prayer for the seven circles of care and concern:

1. Ministry to God for the sheer pleasure of His Presence.
2. Personal renewal through prayer; praying that corporate worship will be especially laden with a heavy sense of God's Presence.
3. Family prayer and support for family needs by prayer.
4. Congregational ministries and missions, undergirded by prayer. (This is prayer to invite the power of God into the life of the congregation to the end that we fulfill our mission.)
5. City prayer – praying for the pain of city around us; calling down the blessing and favor of God on the neighborhoods in which we live. (A concerted effort to bear the burdens of the hurting.)
6. The nation – prayer for government leaders, the needs of the nation and community, moral/spiritual issues, current events, for great awakening.
7. The world – for mission endeavors, for the 10/40 Window and the missionaries of the church, unreached peoples and nations.

We are reminded that when *"Zion travails, she brings forth"* (see Isaiah 66:8; Micah 4:10). All of us want to see the birthing of a mighty great awakening, an ingathering of the last-day harvest (Joel 3:13-16; Matthew 9:37, 38; John 4:35; Acts 2:16-21). We stand on our tiptoes in anticipation. The child has been promised. The reports have come to us from the far corners of the world – *"God is doing a new thing in the earth,"* (Isaiah 43:19). We long for it here in North America.

A strange phenomenon sometimes occurs among women in majority world settings. Barren wives simulate the condition of pregnancy. It is not clear whether it is a conscious phenomenon on the part of these women or whether they are the victims of their own overwrought desires. The physiological indicators of pregnancy are present. The abdomens of these women swell. They eventually experience labor pains, but they never deliver a child. They can't because they were never pregnant. Perhaps the driving force behind this phenomenon is the high value placed on children and childbearing in these countries. Perhaps it is some other deeply personal need. Whichever, it is still a sad affair of deception, illusion and disappointment.

Sometimes the same phenomenon occurs among intercessors. There is swelling anticipation of prophecies, promises and travail. But Zion never delivers. There is no child called "revival" or "renewal." No city breakthrough comes. We must learn a simple principle and apply it to all intercession. Travail delivers the child, but it never produces it. Intimacy produces the child.

Intimacy cannot do the work of travail, nor can travail overcome for a lack of intimacy. Intercessors too, must root their prayer lives in simple intimacy with God. Out of such moments, the Lord plants His purposes in our hearts and brings them to maturity. And in the very real labor of passionate prayer, we give birth to those purposes.

We cannot make the mistake of thinking we are in some new dispensation that erases or makes illegitimate painful, travailing prayer. Nor can we omit moments of pure pleasure in the Presence of God, moments of refreshing from the Holy Spirit. A prayer life that does not know both of these elements will become fanatical, or stale and unfruitful. A prayer life that embraces one without the other will be imbalanced and prone to burnout or blowup.

1   William Federer, *America's God and Country* (recounted to Chaplain William W. Bennett regarding General Stonewall Jackson) 27.

2   Robert Waymire, a Christian strategist for global evangelism and former U.S. naval officer, quoted by Ben Jennings, 185.

3   Ben Jennings, *The Arena of Prayer* (Orlando, FL: New Life, 1999) 17.

4   PROJECT PRAY offers a comprehensive training program with 15 training modules. It is designed for use by multiple congregations. The serial guides contain teaching resources with discussion guides and video briefs, tools (plug-n-pray resources) and an opportunity to talk-it-over and take-it-home. Principles, practical tools and application in a series of one evening training events. The ministry trains facilitators to lead the training. <www.project-pray.org>.

6   The purpose of Prayer Leader's Continuing Education process is to bring together prayer leaders and intercessors four times annually for ongoing training and resources.

6   It may not be necessary to repeat training or convene a meeting to address learning gaps. If it is – be positive. In some cases, it might be a matter of doing some personal coaching with one or more persons struggling to implement some aspect of prayer.

7   <www.propheticroundtable.org/Harp-Bowl/Network.html>.

8   Prayer banners in different sizes and themes are available at www.alivepublications.org.

EIGHT
Understanding Mission, Vision and Values

The devil is not terribly frightened of our human efforts and credentials. But he knows his kingdom will be damaged when we begin to lift up our hearts to God.[1]

– Jim Cymbala

Prayer does not equip us for the greater work, prayer is the greater work.

– Oswald Chambers

The greatest need of the present-day church is prayer. Prayer should be the vital breath of the church, but right now it is gasping for air. A great leader said the church goes forward on its knees. Maybe one of the reasons the church is not going forward today is because it's not in a position to go forward – we are not on our knees in prayer.

– J. Vernon McGee

Satan will not mind how we labor in prayer for a few days, weeks or even months, if he can at last discourage us so that we cease praying, as though it were of no use.

– George Mueller

The transformation of the church into a house of prayer needs a plan. In this chapter, we will talk about drawing the future by developing vision, mission and values.

This may seem a bit far from your heart of prayer. "Let's just pray!" I have heard it a thousand times. But, if someone does not think ahead – not to the next prayer meeting, but through the next three-to five years – your prayer ministry will struggle and probably fail. You will simply move from one good prayer idea and activity to another. You will lack a clear sense of mission, vision and long-term strategy.

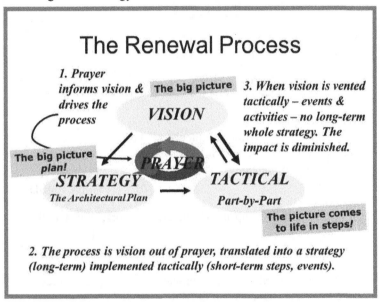

The Renewal Process

1. Prayer informs vision & drives the process

The big picture

VISION

3. When vision is vented tactically – events & activities – no long-term whole strategy. The impact is diminished.

The big picture plan!

PRAYER

STRATEGY
The Architectural Plan

TACTICAL
Part-by-Part

The picture comes to life in steps!

2. The process is vision out of prayer, translated into a strategy (long-term) implemented tactically (short-term steps, events).

In Aubrey Malphurs' book, *Developing a Vision for Ministry in the 21st Century*,[2] he begins with *values*. Then we move to *mission, vision and strategy*. Mission and vision are, in a sense, the same. Mission is a concise statement; vision is an expanded and intuitive view of what the house of prayer will eventually look like. Strategy is the plan to get you there.

Once you have hammered out your values, articulated a mission statement and expanded that into a vision declaration of the future of your prayer ministry, then you need a strategy. That strategy will need to be broken down into tactical parts. The vision is the big picture. Strategy is the big-picture plan. The tactics are the steps – the component parts of the big-picture plan.

Developing a mission, vision and values statement can help you determine direction for the prayer ministry at your church. What do these terms mean? How are they different? Values dictate why a ministry does what it does.[3] Values are determined not by what we say is important, but by what we are actually doing. A congregation that has no regular prayer gathering, no identified intercessors, no prayer training, but prayer only for a few minutes for personal needs and requests on Sunday morning is a church that does not value prayer. They may value singing, giving 30 minutes or more to it in the Sunday worship event and holding special gospel concerts, but they don't value prayer. They may value teaching and preaching, by insisting that the pastor deliver a sermon each week. What we *do* is the indication of what we *value*. Little or no prayer, *no prayer meeting* reveals that prayer is not valued.

Notice these prayer values, each has a behavioral (doing) expression.

Ten Prayer Values
What We Believe and How We Behave

Values are constituted not by what we articulate as important, but by what we demonstrate as important by our behavior. Prayer is not a value until it impacts behavior. Things articulated are not values; things practiced are values.

- **We value prayer;** *therefore, we will feature prayer in our worship and make prayer a central element of all ministry.*
- **We are a praying people;** *therefore, we will nurture at-home daily prayer,* family prayer, husband-wife, parent-child prayer connections,

providing resources, training and nudging new and old Christians to deepen their prayer lives.

- **We believe that we are a kingdom of priests** and that prayer and worship is our highest calling, and that as priests, we are not only recipients of blessing, but the conveyors of blessing; *therefore, in prayer, we commit to pray for the favor and blessing of God upon others;* for protective care, upon our pastor, the church staff, the church family, our city and our nation. *We bless,* we do not curse. We ask God not for what we deserve, but for blessing – for continued grace and mercy!

- **We value holiness and righteousness** as the mark of God upon a people, and we recognize that the church desperately needs revival and our nation needs a great awakening; *therefore, we regularly and consistently cry out to God for revival in the church and a great awakening* for our nation.

- **We believe in the power of petition,** that God answers when people pray rightly; *therefore, we faithfully take the needs of the church, one another, the city and the world before the throne of God and ask for grace!* We provide a means whereby requests for prayer are taken seriously and held up in prayer persistently, beseeching God expectantly for an answer.

- **We believe in the power of God through intercession;** *therefore, we identify, train, team and mobilize intercessors* for the undergirding of the ministries of the Church, and for the support of the various mission endeavors of the congregation.

- **We believe that prayer is essential to the success of every endeavor,** that without Him we can do nothing, and whatever we do in His behalf without dependence upon Him is less than it might have been, given dependence in prayer; *therefore, our rule is no one works unless someone prays!*

- **We believe that the reception of the gospel unto salvation is a spiritual issue;** *therefore, we pray for the harvest,* that blind eyes will be open to the gospel, ears will be enabled to hear and receive the truth of Christ: hearts may be receptive to the good news that goes forth in power out of prayer.

- **We believe that there is a definitive connection between prayer and the harvest;** *therefore, we insist that prayer must have a missional dimension,* that we must pray for lost loved ones, for the unreached in our city and the world.

- **We believe, "God governs the world by the prayers of His people;"**

therefore, we pray for our city, state and national leaders. We pray about world conditions and various global crises. We invite God's intervening reign. We pray, *"Thy Kingdom come, thy will be done."*

Values to Mission and Beyond

- **Values**, by definition, are not things you *declare* as important, but things *you now do* and thereby *demonstrate* as important.

- **Mission** is a concise declaration that describes the reason your prayer ministry exists. The statement will be at the core of all your activities. It is a consensus of what God is calling you to in prayer, rising out of informed research and reasonable values.

- **Vision** is an expanded version of your mission statement, a picture of where you are going and what it will look like when you finish. It is one with the mission but more expansive, more descriptive.

- **Strategy** is the vision in detail, the big picture plan. Like a set of architectural drawings, it is the design for the prayer effort, the plan from which you will develop the sequence and process for transforming your congregation into a house of prayer.

- **Tactics** are the piece-by-piece unwrapping of your effort. One program alone is not a strategy. Tactics are the multiple elements, the moving parts of something larger, of a strategic process. Tactics are the simple steps.

Values determine the mission.[4] Is our mission to honor the prophetic cry of Jesus in the Temple, echoing the prophet Isaiah, *"My house shall be called a house of prayer for all nations?"* (Isa. 56:7). If that is truly our mission, we will demonstrate the value of prayer by actually praying for the nations. Simply put, values are behavioral. They involve doing the things that move us toward the fulfillment of our Biblical mission. The mission is what the ministry is "supposed" to be doing. Three elements that must be included in our mission are very clear:

- The Great Commitment: Pray for people everywhere, beginning with kings and those in authority, that they might be saved. *"My house shall be a house of prayer for the nations"* (1 Tim. 2:1-4).

- The Great Commandment: Love God! Be a passionate Christian – having given your heart to the Lord and committed yourself to things eternal, laying up treasures in heaven. And let your love relationship with Christ be an evidentiary witness to your neighbor. Love God; love others. This is the incarnational gospel. (Mt. 22:37-39)
- The Great Commission: Preach the gospel; share the good news. Tell everyone. Get the message to those near (the neighborhood around the church, the city) and those far away (the ends of the earth); baptize them, inducting them into the kingdom of God and His church; disciple them, teaching them to obey the precepts of the Word of God. (Mt. 28:19, Mk. 16:15)

Mission of the Church

A house of prayer and worship that catches people up in the love of God, making them passionate for Him and His causes; infecting them with a vision beyond themselves and a caring love for others – especially the unsaved and our neighbors near to us – as they look for opportunities to demonstrate the light and life of Christ; to share his transforming love; to lead into a saving relationship with Jesus; to disciple others until they have been transformed by the power of the Spirit and principles of the Word.

This mission statement builds on the Great Commitment – prayer; the Great Commandment – *love;* and the Great Commission – *sharing the gospel.* Do you recognize these elements in the mission statement above? It is quite lengthy for a good mission statement. A more concise version might be:

A house of prayer and worship that leads us to love God and care for others, living beyond themselves and looking for opportunities to share light in a way that brings others into a saving relationship with Christ, until His life breaks forth through them.

Here again, do you see the three elements – prayer, care, share? Here are two additional mission statements provided by Cheryl Sacks in her book, *The Prayer Saturated Church:*

Our purpose is to encourage and support believers at Grace Chapel to communicate confidently and joyfully with God through all areas of prayer.

The mission of the prayer ministry at First Church is to pray, motivate and teach others to pray, and to provide prayer opportunities for our church's members, inspired by the Holy Spirit.[5]

The power of a mission statement is not merely in word-crafting. It is in the agreed meaning of the statement. The statement is a forecast of the future of your prayer ministry, a reference point to which you will return often for perspective. It will become a guardian that will keep you from darting down wrong courses, and chasing the vision and mission of others. The mission should be your authoritative mandate. It is what God has called you to do, to build. You can do no other.

The mission statement sets the trajectory. It includes some values and excludes others, purposely. You can change it or amend it, but you must always take it and its implications seriously. So, laboring over your sense of what God is calling you to do will force fresh, clear thinking for the future. It will fuse the many minds into one; it will unify and catalyze.

Writing Your Mission Statement

Here is a more technical approach to writing your mission statement. Fill in each phrase with a substitute phrase. "Your enterprise" will be the name of your church or prayer ministry, and so on. Below is an example:

Your enterprise...verb/action...adjective and noun/descriptives #1 and #2..."resulting in" benefit..."for"...someone..."and"... others...Underlying value #1 and #2...or more.

Here is how you might use the above framework to write your mission statement:

The Lakeview Church mobilizes its people to pray, and freely share the gospel of Christ, resulting in a prayed and cared-for community for the glory of God and the salvation of the lost out of obedience to the Great Commitment, the Great Commandment and the Great Commission.

Distinguishing Between Mission and Vision

Mission and vision are not the same. The vision is an expanded statement, a *picture* of the mission. Mission *feels;* it has passion. Vision *sees;* it paints a picture. Vision answers the question, "What does a house of prayer look like?" It is descriptive of the end result. "When we get there, we'll know because..." Both the mission and vision statements are directional. Without direction we wander. We noted earlier that George Barna's research indicates that only two percent of pastors can identify a vision for their church.[6] "Where are we now, and where does God want us to go?" is a directional question that should be visited at least once a year.[7]

As you translate your mission statement into a vision statement, here are the elements of clear vision:

- Provides direction
- Unifies (We're moving toward the same goal – the same vision/ picture of the future.)
- Facilitates function (each sees his part in the whole)
- Enhances leadership
- Fuels passion
- Encourages risk-taking
- Sustains the process
- Creates energy, synergy
- Explains our purpose
- Motivates sacrifice and giving[8]

How do you distinguish between mission and vision? Here is a contrast between the two in seven different areas.[9]

CONTRASTED AREA	MISSION	VISION
Definition	Statement	Snapshot
Application	Plans	Communicates
Length	Short	Long
Purpose	Informs	Inspires
Activity	Doing	Seeing
Source	Head	Heart
Development	Science (taught)	Art (caught)

While the mission statement is concise enough for people to remember, the vision statement may be a document.[10] It contains a ministry purpose with these elements:

- the mission
- the values
- the strategy
- people needed for deployment
- location[11]

The vision statement is inclusive. It is a comprehensive statement.

Here is an example of a Biblical vision statement:

For the Lord your God is bringing you into a good land, a land of brooks of water, of fountains and springs, that flow out of valleys and hills; a land of wheat and barley, of vines and fig trees and pomegranates, a land of olive oil and honey; a land in which you will eat bread without scarcity, in which you will lack nothing; a land whose stones are iron and out of whose hills you can dig copper. When you have eaten and are full, then you shall bless the Lord your God for the good land which He has given you. Beware that you do not forget the Lord your God by not keeping His commandments, His judgments, and His statutes which I command you today (Deuteronomy 8:7-11).

Notice how visual and descriptive this prophetic declaration is. You can see it! That is what a vision statement does – it paints a vivid picture of the mission. In chapter 7, we offered a bit of a vision statement in our description of the prayer center. Begin your vision-writing process in this way.

- *Imagine*...a church in which everyone was prayed for by name, at least once a month.
- *Imagine*...every ministry a praying ministry.
- *Imagine*...a center for prayer with creative displays that inspire prayer, inform us regarding what to pray for and how to pray.
- *Imagine*...a church with an eye for the neighborhood and the world – praying consistently for those around us to come to Christ.
- *Imagine*...a phone-bank that connects people across the city to caring intercessors available to pray for and with them 24 hours a day.
- *Imagine*...prayer teams mobilized to leave the incense of prayer throughout the city.
- *Imagine*...prayer seminars and workshops that teach us to pray.
- *Imagine*...a place where I could take my family to spend an unstructured hour with God – a prayer room designed for kids; prayer closets for personal quiet times; prayer stations to inspire prayer beyond myself; an intercessor's chamber to join in prayer for everything from the current world crisis to crying out for an unreached people group or a missionary in trouble.
- *Imagine*...

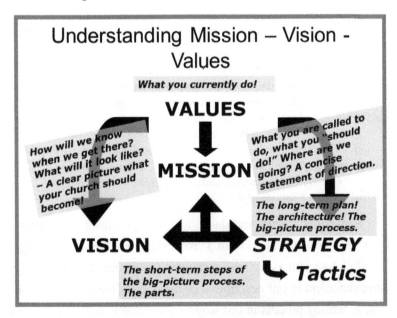

Moving Beyond Vision to Strategy and Tactics

Vision is not enough to begin the building process. You may be able to envision your new house on the hill with a walk-out basement, a backyard patio, a pool, and a wide inviting front porch with a swing. But chances are you will need to hire someone to draw the plans.

The *strategy* is the architectural drawing of the vision. It is an involved process. It is the structural plan for completing the mission. *Tactics* are the part-by-part, stage-by-stage unwrapping of the vision and plan.

- VALUES – what you currently do
- MISSION – what you are called to do, what you "should do." A concise statement of direction is needed.
- VISION – a clear picture of what your church should become. How will we know when we get there? What will it look like?
- STRATEGY – the long-term plan (the architecture, the big-picture process)
- TACTICS – the short-term steps of the big-picture process (the parts)

At the end of this book, you will find a strategic process for transforming the church into a house of prayer. A longer and more complete version can be found in the book, *Milestones – Markers on Your Journey Toward Becoming a House of Prayer.* You might also want to consider the book, *The Praying Church Made Simple.*

Remember, vision is the *big picture.* Strategy is the *big-picture plan.* Tactics are the *pieces,* the small *action steps.*

The mission is, for example, to build the house of prayer. The vision is represented in the illustration and sketches of the finished house. The strategy is found in the architectural plan and drawings. The tactics are the subcontractor illustrations and drawings.

The strategic process has a number of elements necessary to make it whole:

1. *Research* – an assessment of current prayer ministries and their effectiveness, and prayer ministry needs.

2. *Discovery* – the learning process by leaders about where to find the best materials, the cutting-edge models, the better practices for prayer ministries from which we can learn.

3. *Envisioning* – How can we best tell the story of the call of God to make our church a house of prayer? What pictures do we need to offer? Whose testimony can we give? What plan do we need to systematically inform and inspire the congregation with the love call of Christ to spend time with him, personally and corporately?

4. *Teaching* – What teaching and training needs to be offered, and in what order? In what venue? How do we get teaching and training to the people, and not merely try to bring them to the training? How do we both organize and deploy our training for effectiveness?

5. *Doing* – How do we mobilize the entire church for prayer? In what parts? In what sequence? What is our critical-mass point – how many people do we need to mobilize before we change the culture of the church? What different training components do we need in place – individual devotions, family prayer, intercessors training, lighthouses, prayer-walking, a prayer room, and more – and what is our timeline for initiating each of these prayer ministries?

6. *Leadership* – How will we structure the mission? Who carries the vision on the prayer leadership team? Who clarifies our focus when we lose perspective? Who can draw maps to help us get to our destination? Who has not only a passion for some component of the process but also the leadership gifting to organize and lead that part of the prayer ministry?

7. *Assessment* – How will we measure success? How will we achieve balance in our prayer process – in all four dimensions – so that it is not exclusively an intercessor's venture, or all about church prayer, for example, with little at-home prayer? Or bent toward transactional evangelism praying with too little emphasis upon transformational prayer? How will we determine when learning is integrated and when we should go to the next level? The prayer leadership team should probably conduct an annual retreat to plan and assess. They should invite members of the diverse prayer ministries, particularly those that are playing a key role in implementation or needing encouragement in the development of the ministry they are leading.

Strategy (the big-picture plan) is unwrapped in sequential and interdependent pieces, one after another. These smaller steps are called *tactics*. They are only strategic as they are related one to another and to the big plan. Here are some initial tactical steps you might consider for the first year.

- Start a church-wide prayer meeting.
- Look for teachable prayer leaders and begin to meet with them at least monthly.
- Develop them into a leadership-learning team.
- Encourage daily at-home prayer.

These three things – a church-wide prayer meeting, developing leaders and establishing the pattern of daily, personal prayer – constitute the first three of the fifteen milestones in the transformation journey. You will be greatly helped if your church and a handful of other congregations have launched a Prayer Leader Continuing Education process which brings prayer leaders from multiple congregations together quarterly to consider their prayer process. Subsequent steps in the process are:

- Enter into a discovery process.
- Conduct a prayer ministry planning retreat.
- Chart the course – values, mission, vision, strategy, tactics
- Project a strategic plan and empower leaders to implement the plan.
- Hold a prayer envisioning event.
- Engage the congregation in prayer activites. Go wide. Go public with your effort.
- Begin to build out all four dimensions of the prayer ministry.

Persevere.

Break your strategic plan down into steps forward – create a timetable. These are the sequential action steps for this year. Keep prayer stories in front of the congregation in this way. Move your long-term process forward.

- *Keep the Big Picture in mind*. In the early stages, you will never visit your values, mission and vision statement, or your strategic plan too often.
- *Constantly Assess*. Are we doing what we have learned? If so, we really learned it! If not, teach and train into the learning gaps.
- *Celebrate small victories!* See the challenges, but don't see them alone.
- *Be guided by your strategic plan* – don't be tempted to chase a new rabbit that crosses your path! Don't substitute small programs for large purposes.
- *Be sequential*. Exploit the power of sequence. This is the difference between the tactical (one small piece/program/activity) and the strategic (linking those pieces together). Assess readiness to move to the next step in your strategic plan. You are building a house of prayer. Be flexible, but be strategic. (Don't pour the concrete floor if the plumbers and electricians haven't put in their subterranean pipes no matter what the building schedule calls for.) Teach before you do. Practice with small groups before you take the process to the whole congregation. The parts must fit together.

Sequential Planning

Here is an example of sequential planning:

You conduct:

(1) a prayer evangelism training event   [learning and doing]
in order to

(2) create prayer evangelism teams, [leaders – trained leadership]
which must be subsequently   *(duly authorized)*
carefully appointed and   [doing – applied learning]
functioning for

(3) the coming church-wide emphasis
on prayer and mission,   [a wider learning/event]

(4) after which you will plan to
expand your teams and choose   [leadership: assessment]
your wisest and most intuitive   (restructuring)
people as leaders of prayer evangelism
teams as preparation for the

(5) community evangelism festival,
at which your church will provide
leadership in modeling prayer   [doing *out of learning* – you
evangelism for other churches,   want a proven team here]
                                      [others can learn by
                                      observation – junior
                                      team leaders]

(6) after which you will
regroup to assess,   [leadership function]

(7) teach into the training gaps and [re-learning]

(8) launch another level of
recruiting and training   [learning]
not only in your church,
but now for the city,
all for the purpose of

(9) putting together a training team for
                                      [leadership broadened]

(10) ongoing ministry in your church [broadened doing]
and as a service to other churches
in your area.   [broadened teaching and
                                      training]

One weak link threatens the integrity of the whole chain. The
power of your prayer ministry will not be in one single area – but
in how you link the strength of each area together.

Also, notice the growing breadth. You move from training a team to congregational engagement, and then to serving other churches, and to teaching a city.

Satan considers prayer an act of aggression. Retaliation in spiritual warfare is common. Spurgeon reminds us, "By perseverance the snail reached the ark."[12]

Strategic.

The prayer team should meet monthly, first as a learning team; then to provide evaluation and vision for becoming a house of prayer.

Your goal is to mobilize an entire church to pray. At first, everyone will say, "Yes, let's make our church a house of prayer!" Then the reality of what prayer will cost will become clear, and your initial enthusiasm will fade. Don't be discouraged. Persevere without being punitive toward those who pull back – you'll have some surprises in this area. Refuse to allow a "they don't want to pray" pessimism to develop among your leaders. It is a subtle form of pride that will paralyze your movement. It leads to a division that immobilizes you.

There can be no 'them' and 'us' mentality allowed to take root. Your prayer journey is much like a long interstate trip. There are many entrances and exits along the way. Some people will leave you and later rejoin the movement. Others will not initially come into the stream of prayer. They may choose another entrance point. For example, not all will respond to a three-day prayer summit. The idea may be too intimidating for them. Some intercessors will not want to be a part of an intercessory prayer team.

Not everyone will attend the churchwide prayer gatherings. No single prayer slice, program or event will capture everyone. Some will join the parade through the entrance of prayer evangelism. Others will join when you announce prayer training for lost family members. Still others will join when you form prayer ministry teams. Some will see a need for family prayer – for learning to bless their children – and that will be the key to their response. A few will join you in support of national concerns and moral issues. Some may have a specific passion to pray daily for Jerusalem.

If you expect everyone to come through one door, one event, or one training model, your prayer process will fail. It must be broad and long term. Keep offering different entry points into the journey by creating side doors into prayer. As the prayer leaders work with department leaders to help them integrate prayer into every aspect of life to the church, the members will inevitably be exposed to new prayer styles and models, literature and language. Don't expect the members to come to your prayer training or events. Take prayer to them. Push it into every seam of church life.

This will happen as the leaders of Sunday school classes, small groups, men's and women's ministries, children and youth, couples and singles are trained as prayer leaders. Insist on this principle: To be a leader of any ministry in this church, you must be a prayer leader.

CELEBRATING PRAYER

- Celebrating seeing God's answers to prayer reinforces our sense of God's faithfulness.
- Have people write answers to prayer on a "prayers answered" banner.
- Construct a visual prayer chain – petitions are one color, answers are another. Every time a prayer is answered, the "petition link" is taken down and replaced with an "answered link."
- Share answers to prayer as well as requests for prayer during worship.
- Place a "prayer-answer box" next to your "prayer-request box."
- Hold a special worship service periodically to celebrate "God sightings."
- When people return after an illness, welcome them and thank those who prayed for their recovery.
- Hold an annual appreciation dinner (or breakfast) for those who have been involved in the church's prayer ministries.

1 Quotation taken from *Fresh Wind, Fresh Fire.*
2 Aubrey Malphurs, *Developing a Vision for Ministry in the 21st Century* (Grand Rapids: Baker, 1999) 14. Note: Slide adapted from Malphurs.
3 Malphurs, 14.
4 Ibid, 14.
5 Cheryl Sacks, *The Prayer Saturated Church,* 110-111.
6 Barna Research Group, "Seven Paradoxes Regarding America's Faith," Dec. 17, 2000.
7 Malphurs, 18.
8 Ibid, 28.
9 Ibid, 32.
10 Ibid, 31.
11 Ibid, 75.
12 Craig Brian Larson, *Illustrations for Preaching and Teaching* (Grand Rapids: Baker, 1993) 59.

NINE
Building a Prayer Leadership Team for Impact

Time spent in prayer will yield more than that given to work. Prayer alone gives work its worth and its success. Prayer opens the way for God himself to do His work in us and through us. Let our chief work as God's messengers be intercession; in it we secure the Presence and power of God to go with us.

– Andrew Murray

The secret of failure is that we see men rather than God. Romanism trembled when Martin Luther saw God. The "great awakening" sprang into being when Jonathan Edwards saw God. The world became the parish of one man when John Wesley saw God. Multitudes were saved when Whitefield saw God. Thousands of orphans were fed when George Mueller saw God. And He is *"the same yesterday, today, and forever."*

– Unknown

In the year that King Uzziah died, I saw the Lord sitting on a throne, high and lifted up, and the train of His robe filled the temple.

– Isaiah 6:1

Launching a prayer ministry is a team effort. First, it is too large an undertaking for one person. Second, George Barna reminds us that leadership always works best when it is provided by teams of gifted leaders serving together in the pursuit of a clear and compelling vision.[1]

Members of the team should *eventually* include:

- Prayer ministries coordinator
- Personal and family prayer coach
- Prayer resource leader/departmental consultant
- Intercessors coordinator
- Prayer evangelism coordinator
- Marketplace prayer mobilization
- Prayer Training director/discipleship pastor
- Prayer room/center director
- Members-at-large

As you begin your process, you want to keep this larger leadership vision in view, but filling these roles is not your immediate concern. The first year, the team should be a learning team.

At first, open your monthly learning-leader teams to those you hand select and those who sense a calling to be involved in leading change toward the integration of prayer into all you do. For the first year, meet and pray and learn. Become one. Exchange your fixed, tired ideas for fresh notions of what it means to be a house of prayer for the nations.

In the second year, expand your learning. Enter into a discovery phase. Explore models. Project a multi-year plan. Solidify your leadership team. Begin the process of associating your learning-leaders with the team roles you have in view.

Keep these three things in mind as you progress:

1. *Vision* – Keep going back to the big picture of where you are going (vision and mission). Redraw the vision; rewrite the mission statement.
2. *Strategy* – Keep refining the big-picture plan, the long-term

process, step-by-step diagram. This big-picture plan must include all four dimensions for the house of prayer.

3. *Tactics* – Keep implementing the single pieces, in sequence, event-by-event, step-by-step. Remember, you train in prayer to do prayer. You conduct one event as a preparation for another event. You keep working your sequential big-picture plan.

It is easy to move from 'vision' to 'tactics,' and skip strategy or the hard work of developing a strategic plan, but that is a mistake. The energy of vision must not be vented on a single or even a series of multiple short-term events apart from a larger, long-term strategy. No one piece of training or deployment will accomplish the whole mission. Translating vision into strategic process is much more difficult than releasing it though a single or series of tactical events. Drawing and redrawing the map is tedious work, but it will pay off in the end. It is a wise stewardship investment.

Not everyone will appreciate this, nor will everyone have the patience to endure the details of drawing and redrawing the architectural plan. You will have your share of buckaroos who will declare, "We don't need all this thinking and planning. I know how to do this – Let's go; the Lord will lead us." In some instances, they may prevail. But the process they implement will almost always lack the breadth and scope of strategic planning.

Keep the strategic planning team lean. Don't overwhelm the full implementation team with all the details – just the next steps.

How does all of this work functionally?

Out of his prayer times, God gives a pastor vision and direction for the local congregation. He is called to assist Christ as the Lord builds His church. The overall vision for the church is used by the prayer team to develop a prayer vision. All the goals of the prayer team must be consistent with the values, the mission, and the overall purpose and vision of the congregation as a whole. And yet, in a sense, the prayer effort is the context that shapes and feeds the larger vision.

Within that framework, there are three critical roles for developing a prayer ministry:

1. *The vision keeper* – This person carries the burden and vision as one who dreams with the pastor about what a "house of prayer" looks like. This is prayer for the congregation. In choosing this person, it is not enough to look for a person of prayer, it is also a question of leadership and perspective. Who can see the big picture and articulate it along with the pastor? Who can provide leadership, as an extension of the pastor's ministry, in the area of building the church into a house of prayer?

2. *The architect/strategic planner* – This is someone who, by the description of the vision, develops a plan to construct a prayer process, step-by-step. The strategic planner is good at organizing ideas, at translating vision into steps one, two and three – a detail person. It is not a matter of just planning an event, but of strategically putting together the pieces for three-to-five year growth and development process for prayer ministries in the local church. Neither the pastor nor prayer coordinator may be good at drawing maps. Find someone who is a detail person – a long-term thinker and planner. The role of this person will be intense early in the process. Later, they will serve as a consultant to the pastor and prayer coordinator.

3. *Implementers* – These are the people who are willing to run with the vision. They must, however, be willing to work within the plan. They gather resources to accomplish their assigned job – both people and materials – and they get the job done. They are the subcontractors. These hands-on individuals do the work of building the prayer ministry.

If you are building a large house, the strategic, architectural plan may be thick. Such blueprints are rarely compelling in terms of beauty. They are not meant to inspire, but they are critical to building a sound structure. One page will provide a profile of the entire project. Another will reveal the floor plan. Yet another, the structural details. Page after page will show various components of the building particulars – the schematic for the electrical, plumbing, heating/air conditioning, framing and more.

Each subcontractor will be concerned only with the portion of the plan that details his job. The general contractor needs a grasp of the whole project. He calls for each subcontractor as needed, collaborating between them, encouraging dialogue, minimizing conflict and maximizing a seamless process.

If you are building a large house of prayer, you need an architect and a general contractor. In most cases, the prayer coordinator will serve both as the vision keeper, with the pastor, and the general contractor. Even if they have the capability to be the architect, for objective and healthy interpersonal dynamics, it is probably best to involve another person. In any case, the prayer coordinator should be on the strategic planning (architectural) team. Your plans and ideas might be as thick as a book when the architect finishes his work. The pastor (the visionary), the prayer coordinator (general contractor of your project) and the architect (who translates the big picture into the big-picture plan) now need to be a team.

The job of the prayer coordinator is to build the house of prayer according to the plans (strategy) which are guided by the vision (the picture). Each of the various prayer-team leaders (subcontractors) will feel passionate about their area of prayer. The prayer coordinator, like a general contractor will call for various teams as needed. For example, before prayer evangelism efforts are launched, intercessors should be identified and mobilized. Before you form prayer groups, you must train prayer group leaders. Each prayer group and ministry must complement the other, but that will not be without some tension.

Once a plan is on the table, the pastor and prayer leader affirm the plan of the map-drawer/architect, "Yes, this is what we want!" Now, the fun begins and so does tension. The visionary is like a compass – he leads intuitively. The architect is like a map-drawer – he leads methodically. The general contractor is a director – he leads practically. He is able to see the vision, read the plan, and direct subcontractors. Now we move to another level of conflict, the tension that often develops between contractors and architects over the sensibility, the reading of the plans. Communication and teaming skills are critical elements now.

Contractors working on the ground look for simpler ways to do things. Architects seek to protect the structural integrity of the plan. The subcontractors (prayer ministry leaders) are builders – implementers – but they are not always strategic. The architects are not always practical. Have fun. Keep your feet shod with 'peace.'

STRUCTURE
Functional and Dynamic Structure

This describes how the process moves forward. It begins with vision, and that lies with the senior pastor, amplified by the prayer coordinator. It proceeds through the strategic planning process, and that involves the architect or a prayer consultant. It unwraps as it is led by the church prayer coordinator (contractor) and the prayer ministry team leaders (subcontractors).

Strategic Planning Team (SPT)

While the Strategic Leadership Team provides direction to the whole prayer ministry, it does so out of a comprehensive plan, a strategic plan developed by the Strategic Planning Team, composed of the following:

- The senior pastor (or whomever he appoints)
- The prayer coordinator
- The architect or prayer consultant

Others can be added as needed. However, you should keep this team small, no more than five members. Adding people to this team who have a passion for a favorite slice of the prayer ministry may not be wise. Using them as consultants, as you build the plan, is indispensable. Overall, strategic, big-picture people are needed here along with a good dose of practical wisdom.

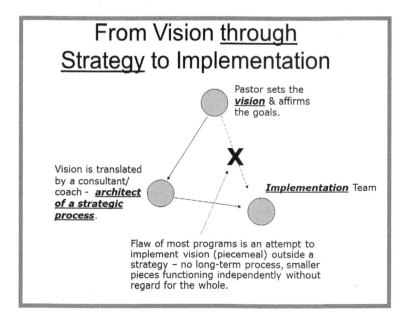

From Vision <u>through</u> <u>Strategy</u> to Implementation

Pastor sets the *vision* & affirms the goals.

X

Vision is translated by a consultant/coach - *architect of a strategic process*.

Implementation Team

Flaw of most programs is an attempt to implement vision (piecemeal) outside a strategy – no long-term process, smaller pieces functioning independently without regard for the whole.

Strategic Leadership Team (SLT)

This model is composed of eight task-and-team coordinators, listed below with their focus areas.

1. *Prayer ministries coordinator* – the coordinator of prayer ministries is the critical and most important function of the prayer ministry: a praying people.

2. *Personal and family prayer coach* – nurtures personal daily prayer, encourages prayer closets, the practice of couples praying and the family altar.

3. *Department support coordinator* – nurtures the role of prayer as a central component of every ministry in the church; works under the prayer coordinator and the pastor of mission and vision, and with the department leaders in the matrix model to help them integrate prayer into their departments. This is the person who interfaces with each ministry department – seniors, family/couples, men, women, college and career, singles, youth, children, etc.

4. *Intercessory prayer coordinator* – recruits and structures intercessory prayer; helps build PIT crews; and mobilizes, trains, deploys and debriefs intercessors.

5. *Prayer evangelism coordinator* – builds the 'great commission' dimension of prayer ministry.

6. *Marketplace coordinator* – the team leader identifies members in the workplace for prayer and evangelism mobilization. With less than twenty-percent of the population in church on any given Sunday, we must develop a more intentional 'go' strategy. The first step is to encourage members to take prayer to work with them – and pray for those who work around them. Every city needs a workplace prayer and evangelism, 'salt-and-light' strategy.

7. *Training coordinator* – builds a curriculum, recruits and trains trainers for prayer ministry; an ongoing training process in all four areas. This task is often the role of the discipleship pastor.

8. *Prayer room/center coordinator* – the prayer center will become the nerve center of the church.

The prayer coordinator serves as the team leader, collaborating with the pastor. This team should meet frequently and regularly, particularly during the first years of the prayer ministry launch. This team directs the prayer ministries of the church.

Implementation Team

The Strategic Leadership Team (SLT) is the static core of the dynamic implementation team. The implementation teams will expand and contract for your forthcoming special projects. For example, let's say that your tactical plan calls for the prayer-walking of a one-mile radius around the church in preparation of the distribution of the Jesus video in that same area. In that season, the strategic prayer leadership team will need to approve and support that event or project. Each implementation team will reflect on new aspects and activities of the prayer process. As they are implemented, they will move the process forward. Examples of leaders who may serve on implementation teams include the following:

- Children's intercessory leader – in anticipation of a conference on child intercessors
- The youth pastor – in preparation for a special citywide youth prayer celebration following the See You at the Pole annual prayer event
- Healing teams prayer leader as that ministry is launched
- Missions team coordinator – as teams are sent out to prayer-walk countries, for example, in the 10/40 Window.
- The coordinator of prayer for an upcoming citywide crusade.

Typically, with the launch of any new prayer ministry or the coordination of one of the key tactical pieces in the annual church prayer process – the leader of the initiative should be invited to meet with the Strategic Leadership Team, if not the entire implementation team.

Prayer Ministries Council

The Strategic Leadership Team cannot lead the prayer ministry alone. Each of the focus areas are actually a cluster of various prayer ministries, each needing a leader, and in many cases, a team. In some models each member of the SLT team would develop a team of prayer leaders to assist in their area of responsibility. For example, a member of the SLT might serve as the prayer evangelism coordinator on that team, he recruits a coordinator for neighborhood prayer evangelism; then zip-zone network leaders. His team is actually a collage of leaders of microteams. Another area needing specific leadership might be prayer mission teams, and so forth.

All the leaders of the various prayer ministries and microteams should serve as a part of the congregational prayer council. Every prayer ministry would be integrated into one of the eight areas that are stewarded by the prayer ministries SLT. The SLT guides the operation of the total prayer process, and the prayer council allows for all the component parts – the tactical, microteam leaders and implementers to come together.

This group should be convened at least annually for prayer, dialogue, envisioning and teaming, or perhaps at an annual prayer leadership retreat, or as a sidebar meeting at an annual prayer training conference.

The kind of prayer ministries these people might lead include the following:

- Adopt-a-cop or a fireman in prayer (shield-a-badge), www. adopt-a-cop.org
- Altar prayer response leader
- Annual prayer and evangelism conference coordinator
- Children's prayer leader
- Coordinator of prayer groups
- Day-shift leaders for the prayer center
- Father-and-son prayer experiences coordinator
- Healing teams leader
- Intercessory coordinator for community leaders – matching intercessors with community leaders for prayer; putting an intercessor into every courtroom and in public hearings where church/state and faith issues are being decided

- Intercessory focus and issue groups
- Intercessory prayer team brigade leaders
- Intercessory prayer teams director
- Marketplace 'Salty' groups (contact PROJECT PRAY for a prayer guide)
- Mother-and-daughter prayer experiences coordinator
- Neighborhood prayer evangelism
- Nursery prayer coordinator – blessing the babies: not just babysitting
- Prayer ambassadors ministry – teams of positive, priestly prayers sent out to bless community leaders, both those who are believers and unbelievers.
- Prayer-care teams – used in ministry to shut-ins and others in need
- Prayer chains
- Prayer coordination for the shepherds of the city
- Prayer for city leaders
- Prayer for unsaved family and friends
- Prayer missions – in the city, focused on specific places
- Prayer mission teams – focused on dark places in the city
- Prayer mission teams – for overseas or out-of-town prayer team deployment
- Prayer partners
- Prayer retreat coordinator
- Prayer support for missions – missionaries, unreached people groups, nations, the 10/40 Window
- Prayer-walking
- Prayer watch organizer
- See You at the Pole prayer coordinator (annual event for Christian youth in September of each year, at their school flagpole), www.syatp.com
- Senior prayer partners of youth
- Seven mountains prayer strategy
- Youth prayer leader

Intercessors

Intercessors comprise one of the focus areas. However, they also constitute the bubble of prayer support in which the prayer ministry itself operates. Everything, even the prayer ministry itself, should be bathed in prayer, so find ways to wrap every effort in prayer. It seems strange to suggest that we should 'pray about prayer,' but if we are not careful, we'll replace God's direction for our prayer ministry with 'good ideas' rather than 'God ideas.'

Prayer Force

The entire prayer effort – every individual who is praying at home or is an identified part of the one of the prayer efforts – constitutes the prayer force. The total 'prayer force' of your church is determined by the number of people you can quantify as being a part of some aspect of the congregation's prayer effort. For every stream and type of prayer in the church, how many are you mobilizing for prayer? How many homes are signed up in the neighborhood evangelism effort? How many are doing the work of intercession? How many are taking a watch shift at the prayer center? How many are using the prayer center – by personal visit, email contact or phone call?

The ideal would be every member a part of the prayer force. The practical goal is to mobilize and involve at least 50 percent of the church in some exercise, some prayer ministry – learning or doing, in the course of a year!

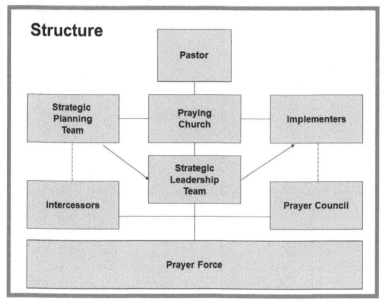

---

1   George Barna, *Building Effective Lay Leadership Teams,* quoted by Cheryl Sacks, 63.

TEN
Prayer Ministry Strategy
The Milestone Process

Any church without a well-organized and systematic prayer program is simply operating a religious treadmill.

– Paul Billheimer[1]

Pray as if everything depended upon God, and work as if everything depended upon man.

– Francis J. Spellman

We ask only for that which would be for the glory of God; for that and that alone, can be for our real good. Second, we ask in the name of the Lord Jesus. Third, we believe that God is able and willing. Fourth, we should continue in prayer 'till the blessing is granted; without fixing to God a time. Patience should be the exercise. Fifth, look out for and expect an answer 'til it comes. If we pray in this way, we shall not only have answers, thousands of answers to our prayers; but our own souls will be greatly refreshed.

– George Mueller

Prayer is calling people to a supernatural worldview. While people continue to maintain a belief in the supernatural God, they have planned and directed their lives and ministries in ways that appear to short-circuit that belief.

– John Quam[2]

How do you begin a prayer transformation process in your church? In the book, *Milestones – Markers on the Journey Toward Becoming a House of Prayer,* there are 15 milestone markers on the congregational transformation journey. They unwrap in seven phases. These are intended to be instructive about the important elements in the process of leading a prayer reformation in your congregation. A caution! On one hand, do not be overwhelmed by the details. These markers are to enlighten and help you on the journey. Do not embrace them legalistically, but do take them seriously. See their holistic nature and allow them to inform your process.

In addition to the book *Milestones – Markers on the Journey Toward Becoming a House of Prayer,* you might also find the book *The Praying Church Made Simple – The Process* and its companion, *PERSPECTIVES*, great resources. These resources focus on the first year and the first three milestones. They are filled with idea materials for dialogue by a developing prayer leadership team.

PHASE ONE: Learning about and Doing Prayer – The Launch (3 Simple Processes)

Milestone One: Launch a Church-Wide Prayer Meeting

Start a Prayer Meeting. Every congregation needs a regular preaching meeting, typically, Sunday morning; and, a teaching/training meeting for discipleship. It also needs a corporate prayer meeting, the church gathered to pray the Scripture, to pray for the lost and for one another, to discern the will of God not only for themselves personally, but also for the congregation. The church-wide prayer meeting is the place a congregation learns to cultivate sensitivity to the ways of God. This is *not* an intercessory prayer meeting. You may need a gathering for intercessors and intercessory prayer. This is a congregational prayer meeting framed in the transformation of the church. In such a gathering, humility and brokenness before God are cultivated. Dependence on God for direction, provision and protection are demonstrated. Here, the congregation waits before God. Listens. Hears from God, and in hearing from God, determination is forged to obey, even if such obedience is costly.

Do this not less than monthly. Weekly or twice monthly is better – but always with a goal of a weekly gathering of the congregation for corporate prayer, not preaching or teaching, not 'praise and worship,' but prayer.

Consider the models you will use. Refer to the *Praying Church Made Simple* resource or the *Praying Church Resource Guide*. A good measurement is to begin with a short season of praise and worship that warms hearts and moves the people to a collective God-focus. Then, use some Biblical passage as a basis for prayer. Teach the congregation not only to read the Scripture, but also to pray it; not only to hear it preached, but also to hear it prayed in faith. Praying the Scripture together transforms and unifies a congregation before God more quickly than any other activity. Then, engage them in missional prayer – for the lost, an unreached people group, a nation, the city or neighborhood around the church. Finally, pray for one another and personal needs. Close with thanksgiving and praise.

Milestone Two: Develop a Prayer Leadership-Learning Team

Look for Teachable Prayer Leaders. Every congregation needs a group of people stewarding and championing both personal and corporate prayer; couples prayer and the family altar; parents blessing their children and youth prayer; prayer groups and prayer for every ministry in the church; intercessory prayer and prayer evangelism; crisis prayer and community focused prayer – and more. Your goal must not be to be a congregation with a prayer ministry, but to become a praying church. That means prayer must permeate the life of the congregation – and that requires intentionality. It is more than prayer as an activity – it is the creation and maintenance of a culture of prayer.

In the typical congregation, there is no group designated to steward and champion prayer. Prayer is too often ignored or taken for granted. As you encourage participation in the congregational prayer meeting, watch who shows up regularly. Identify potential prayer leaders. Meet with this growing group, at least monthly, train and team them. Consider launching a Prayer Leader's Continuing Education (PLCE) effort with other congregations in your area (learn more at www.projectpray.org). These quarterly gatherings use curriculum developed by Project Pray. They expose prayer learning-leaders from multiple congregations to teaching about prayer ministry in bite-sized segments via video clips and discussion guides. They introduce fresh practical prayer tools. They provide time for prayer leader-learners to consider next steps for their team and congregation. If you meet quarterly with other congregations using the PLCE materials, also plan to meet in the intervening two months as a congregational leadership team. Remember, leaders must first be learners. And there is not only a great deal to learn about prayer, but a great deal to unlearn.

The learning here is conceptual. It involves not only learning about prayer but also about prayer leadership. In the next phase, you will engage in exploratory learning. You will learn from congregations who are on the journey ahead of you. You will investigate prayer needs, both in your congregation and the community around you. Here are some resources for your prayer leadership-learning team.

- First, if you launch a PLCE process, you will discover a host of materials that can be reviewed from your participation in the quarterly meetings.
- In addition, the comprehensive *Praying Church Resource Guide* is a 700-page collection of practical materials to assist in the prayer ministry process. In it, you will discover six lessons called "Learning Team" materials. These include videos, handouts and helpful materials to guide your prayer leaders in foundational learning.
- Of course, you can also use this book, *Transforming Your Church into a House of Prayer*;
- Or, *The Praying Church Made Simple* by P. Douglas Small.
- Obtain a copy of *Milestones – Markers on the Journey Toward Becoming a House of Prayer.*

To prevent a narrow focus, you need a curriculum for your prayer leadership training. During this internal learning, using outside resources, that are at times stretching, the group should develop a collective mindset about prayer and the prayer effort you want to unwrap. In the next phase, they will explore living models. Gather these leader-learners at least once monthly for one year or more if necessary.

Milestone Three: The Personal Prayer Life Challenge

Emphasize Daily, Personal Prayer. Congregational prayer expresses collectively the spiritual hunger of a praying people who not only desire their own transformation, but that of their church and their city. Congregational prayer necessitates a partner in personal prayer. Public prayer without private roots is a house without a foundation. The hidden part of our life in Christ allows us to be an able vessel through which Christ works. A church can never be a house of prayer without praying people and praying homes; and a church will never be prayerless if it has praying people and praying homes. The inability of a church to sustain a prayer meeting is often due to personal, private prayerlessness. A missing ingredient in most prayer ministry plans is both the absence of an opportunity for the church to gather corporately for prayer, and an adequate emphasis on personal prayer space (prayer closets), the power of a couple praying together, and the family altar or family worship. The recovery of daily, personal and family prayer is the most challenging aspect of the prayer effort. It is the most difficult stake to drive; and simultaneously, it is the well that will provide the most water. Prayerless people can never lead or sustain a prayer ministry effort. Yet, it only takes a small core of committed prayers with fire in their hearts to start a congregational prayer effort – three to five percent.

Start your prayer ministry effort with a prayer meeting (Milestone One)! This should be a grace-based prayer gathering – not a dutiful obligation, but a delightful opportunity. It should be open to the entire congregation, an invitation to meet with God together as a congregation. Do not make it *problem* centered, make it *Presence* based. The difference is self-focused praying versus God-focused praying. In this prayer meeting you are leading by doing, learning to pray by praying.

In both the church-wide praying gathering and the leader-learning team meetings (Milestone Two), consider the importance of a disciplined, daily personal time with God. Keep coming back to this, gently, but relentlessly, "To lead prayer, we must be people of prayer. How are we doing with our daily devotional time with God?" It cannot be a matter of legalism, a 'have to.' It must be a 'want to.' Sadly, we avoid this due to our own dismal record at daily prayer. This cannot be avoided. You are building a prayer effort without a foundation without the private, hidden life of prayer.

Your weekly prayer gathering should encourage daily prayer time – and eventually, the daily prayer time of increasing numbers of praying people will feed the fervor of the church-wide prayer gathering. Your leadership team should encourage each other on-ward in personal prayer. As you move forward, you will want to challenge the entire congregation to join the weekly, church-wide prayer gathering, and spend time with God daily.

PHASE TWO: Discovery

For about a year you have been in the process, faithfully promoting your regular prayer meeting (Milestone One). Hopefully, you have laced additional prayer moments into your Sunday worship. You may have also taught on prayer and offered additional prayer experiences. However, all of this is strategically short of a public call to transform the church into a house of prayer. Your focus, in the first year, is on leadership development and internal learning (Milestone Two). Frankly, you are not ready to go public without vetted praying leaders and more information about what a house of prayer involves and until these potential leaders have developed healthy and vital personal prayer habits (Milestone Three).

Milestone Four: Research and Discovery

Research and Discovery. There is a veritable reformation of the church taking place across the nation and around the world. The 500-year-old reformation is still on! The next critical component on the heart of the Father is the restoration of the church into a house of prayer. The movement is still on the fringes, but it promises to become a mainstream development. It is the heart of God that His people pray and that His church become a house of prayer to the nations.

There are models emerging. Congregations across the denominational continuum are establishing viable prayer ministries, prayer rooms and prayer centers. A growing number of congregations see the importance of a minister of prayer or prayer coordinator as a staff level position. Pastors are now seeing the vital link between prayer and evangelism-mission. Increasingly, congregations are establishing vibrant prayer meetings. Around the world, where the church is growing exponentially, prayer is driving the process.

You now need to move from internal, conceptual learning to exploring more fully your future as a congregation devoted to prayer. You will want to start a research project, first, to discover the depth of prayer commitment in your own congregation. You may have a sense of where the people are, based on their attendance and participation in your prayer meeting and other prayer opportunities. However, *you need hard data* – not only from the present state of prayer in the congregation but also from the past. You also need to be aware of churches around you that have launched a prayer effort from whom you can learn. These will become your best friends.

The concepts you have studied as a learning team should now allow you to discern between faddish prayer practices and those that are sound, to interpret what you see as you explore and determine practices and ideas worthy of integration into your process. Without prior internal, conceptual learning, your exploration is likely to degenerate into a collection of disconnected, eccentric prayer practices that you then attempt to implement. Be careful.

You are on a journey – that demands a map. You are building a house of prayer, and that demands an architectural plan. You have heard the voice of God calling you, but you may not have a clear sense of what your house of prayer will look like when it is built. It must not be merely an addition, a room added on to the house of praise and preaching you now have. Explore. Dream. Plan. Interview others on the same journey. Learn from their failures and successes.

By the time you start your research, you should be well into your church-wide prayer effort. The core of your potential leadership team should be increasingly stable – although it will still expand and contract. Your team should have established a healthy habit of meeting with God daily, with a growing level of satisfaction in their prayer effort. You should also have a list of questions about prayer ministry. Your team is searching for answers and that signals readiness to begin to explore prayer ministry models. Your stability and depth as a team will now allow you to involve additional people in your research and discovery process, and not lose the culture of humility and unity. As you research:

- *Look first inside* your own congregation. What is the level of interest among those who are members of this church? Explore. Conduct surveys, interviews. Create a prayer resource manual detailing all the prayer ministries and activities that already exist in your congregation. This is probably a two-to-three month project. The manual would list each "prayer ministry" and the person designated as leader. It would note the purpose of each prayer ministry – its focus, its target participants, the frequency and duration of its meetings, the length of time in existence, a vitality rating, a projection for its future including ministry expansion plans and maximum number of participants anticipated.

- *Look back* at the history of prayer in the congregation or in the movement of which you are a part. Get a historical perspective.

- Then, *look out* – find models of prayer in other congregations. Adopt and adapt.

- Now, *look around*, for prayer needs in the community, in the neighborhood around the church, among the friends and family of the members of church.

- And don't forget to *look up to God* – what is He saying to your group about your prayer effort.

Conduct a survey of prayer ministry interest in the congregation.[3] Collect all this data in a notebook – a 'ragged' notebook. This is a for-leader's-eyes-only compilation of existing prayer activities. It should answer these questions:

- Are there regular church-wide prayer meetings? How many attend in comparison to church membership and Sunday morning attendance?
- Are there special interest prayer meetings – for missionaries, unreached people groups, community concerns, and unsaved family members?
- Are prayer requests recorded, managed and taken seriously?
- Are there city-wide prayer efforts?
- Are the existing prayer groups open to new people? Are they closed without knowing it? Are the wineskins of these groups already hardened? What new groups need to be started?
- Are the leaders of these prayer ministries teachable? Is it *'their ministry?'*
- Determine the prayer materials and resources currently available to the congregation.
- Discover the state of the 'prayer communication system.'
- Evaluate the prayer ministries and groups already in place.
- How many active prayer groups are there in the congregation?
- How does the church communicate prayer needs and opportunities to the congregation?
- Is there a 'prayer list?'
- Is there a system to mobilize intercessors for emergency prayer?
- Is there a prayer newsletter?
- Is there a section on the church website for prayer?
- Is the congregation allowed to pray – or do the "professionals" do all the praying?
- What prayer ministries are doing well? Not so well?
- What prayer ministry efforts can you build on? How can they be improved? Become more effective?
- What training is now available or is needed?
- What is being done to encourage prayer – by individuals, families, intercessors, for evangelism?

Learn, explore, survey – but above all, keep praying together as a developing prayer leadership team. *If the leadership team is not a praying team* and is <u>*not open to learn*</u> – *the prayer ministry will fail*. If the leadership team *does not become a team* – the prayer ministry will fail. If they pursue the *"pieces"* of the prayer ministry about which each of them is passionate without a seamless approach to prayer, without regard for the whole – the prayer ministry will fail. If they do not have a clear and long-term sense of where the prayer ministry is to take the church, namely to revival and mission out of personal transformation – then the prayer ministry will fail and competitive prayer options will emerge. If they are not humble, a non-negotiable essential – the prayer ministry will fail! Prayer should change the *ethos* of the whole church.

<u>Don't rush ahead</u> without exploration and research. It will be counterproductive to merely project a plan that is a collage of exotic ideas. Instead, you want an informed plan. Further, you need a leadership team that believes in the plan, and in fact, has developed the plan and is committed to its implementation.

Meanwhile:

1. Your congregation should continue to pray together (Milestone One).
2. You are continuing to identify leaders who are learning together and are teachable (Milestone Two);
3. And deepening their own prayer life (Milestone Three).
4. As your leaders determine to meet God daily, you evidence the fruit of that.
5. You now complete your research –
   - *looking in* (what is the level of prayer and prayer theology in our congregation);
   - *looking back* (what is the congregational prayer history);
   - *looking around* and exploring other congregational prayer models;
   - *looking out* to see the needs of your harvest field, and;
   - *looking up* dependently and expectantly to God.

Now, you are ready to begin to plan forward.

Expand your leadership team
for this exploration stage.

Milestone Five: Planning – Articulating Vision and Mission, Strategy and Tactics

Move from Research and Discovery to Planning. Now you are again ready to expand your leadership team as you unpack the data from your research. It would be a good idea to plan a prayer leadership retreat at this point. You can use this book as a resource and the companion leadership materials available from Alive Publications. If a leadership retreat is out of the question, plan an in-town retreat. At any rate, you will need to take seriously this planning stage and involve elders/council/deacons – whatever church leadership structure you have and other key leaders. It is possible, sadly, that your effort to this point – the prayer meeting, the learning team, the encouragement toward personal prayer, and even the research and discovery phase – has not significantly involved staff and key leaders. The prayer effort has remained a sidebar effort. You cannot mainstream the prayer effort without leadership engagement and endorsement. The planning stage <u>must</u> include them. You are now *getting ready* to 'go public' with your prayer effort.

The research phase should be a three-to-six month process. Don't rush. Be systematic. Lay this foundation deep. <u>Secure leadership buy-in</u>. The subsequent planning phase should not be less than three months. Here you are setting the trajectory of your congregation for years to come.

Values, mission, vision, strategy, and tactics are interrelated elements of effort. By these, you hammer out and declare what is important (values). Out of values comes your intention (purpose)

– the concise prayer mission statement and your expanded vision statement, the big picture of the kind of prayer ministry you want to see in your congregation and what it will look like when it is finished, though it will take years to develop. On the basis of a collective understanding, you project a strategy out of the mission and vision statement – that is the big picture plan (architecture). You plan big, but then unwrap that big strategy (prayer coordinator/general contractor) in little pieces, step-by-step, piece-by-piece (implementers/subcontractors/ministry leaders). The prayer ministry pieces are the tactics.

Values→ Purpose→ Mission→ Vision→ Strategy→ Tactics

Most church ministries lack a big picture vision and a long-term strategy. They lack a clear congregational mission. They engage in one tactical endeavor or program and then another, calling those strategies. A congregation raises up one prayer domino and watches it fall, "This year, we are focused on prayer walking," or, "The family in prayer…," or, "Building a pastor's prayer team." Those are fine, but the big picture (vision) calls for lining up more than a few dominoes (strategy) so that a series (tactics) of learning and doing events trigger and release their energy one into another. Your plan must build momentum to undergird and accelerate change in multiple areas, simultaneously. That is holistic – and that helps you accomplish your long-term goals. Here's why. It is failing systematically. Sequential, consecutive, stand-along tactical programs are not adequate. The church needs systematic change.

As you move through the process, you will begin to practice your stated values. Your mission will become clearer. Your vision will expand. You will, at times, modify your strategic plan. All battle plans experience a change when the enemy is engaged. You will make tactical adaptations on the ground – the architect will help you with structural integrity. Shortcuts will cost you in the end.

Break your strategic plan down into steps forward – create a timetable. Review the sequential action steps and the strategic sequential planning example (Chapter 8).

You learn and do. You train leaders – strategic training. Then you apply the learning and also offer wider learning. Then you test the learning – you do. Again, you assess, teach into learning gaps and restructure. You do out of learning – relearn and redo, expanding teaching and training.

As stated earlier, like a chain, one weak link threatens the integrity of the whole chain. The power of your prayer ministry will not be in one single area – but in how you link the strength of each area together.

Also, notice the growing breadth. You move from training a team to congregational engagement, and then to serving other churches, and to reaching a city.

Focus on Long-Range Goals

Discover the appropriate 'level' of intensity for the prayer ministry in your situation.

- Can you see an aggressive, balanced, integrated prayer process?
- Is there a possibility of having a dedicated prayer room?
- Could you realistically sustain a 24/7 prayer process? In most cases, that is a long-range goal for a church of a thousand or more and is not recommended as an immediate step. A prayer room could be open for use during extended daylight hours.
- You could certainly began to build consistent, daily prayer support for the church and its mission. Dream, but launch a prayer process that is sustainable given the amount of workers that the church can allocate to it presently. Grow into the dream.
- What level do you see your church achieving?
- What function will intercessors play?
- What will the interface of prayer and mission (prayer evangelism) look like?

- How will prayer be organized to support the ministries of the church? And how will prayer be integrated into those ministries?

- How will the church develop a prayer discipleship, teaching-training plan?

- What are the ways and means by which you will teach and encourage personal-devotional prayer? This may be anything from bulletin inserts to additional congregational prayer exercises. It may also include prayer experiences, continued teaching of prayer, both at the church-wide level and in the discipleship arena.

Coming out of this planning phase, you should have:

1. Hammered out your prayer values.
2. Developed a prayer ministry, mission statement.
3. Started forging a prayer ministry, vision statement.
4. Laid out the initial steps of your next year strategy and tactical steps.
5. Set a tentative plan to engage the congregation in a variety of prayer experiences beyond the weekly prayer meeting and Sunday morning experiences. These should reflect the diversity of your planned prayer ministry that will unfold over the next few years.
6. A clear sense of the learning-leaders who are respected as leaders and can now take a more active role in moving your prayer process forward.
7. Confidence in going public with the announcement, "We have determined to make our congregation a 'house of prayer for the nations.'"

Milestone Six: Affirming Leaders (Leadership Structuring and Affirmation)

Affirm a Core Prayer Leadership Team. Armed with research (Milestone Four) and a flexible plan (Milestone Five), it is time for the learning leaders, the exploratory and planning teams to give birth to a permanent prayer leadership team with a prayer-coordinator. You have been cautious. You have vetted your leaders and tested their resolve as well as their appetite to learn and their capacity to change. Now the prayer implementation plan should unfold. This does not mean that no prayer implementation has taken place earlier. In fact, a part of the discovery should have been prayer learning and doing experiences along with the affirmation of existing prayer leaders and the reshaping of existing prayer ministries. What we want to avoid is running headlong into piecemeal implementation without a long-term understanding of congregational prayer needs.

The prayer effort moves forward on two legs – learning and doing, and those, by leading. Now, more than ever, you are moving squarely into the execution phase. What was on the edges of congregational life will now be front and center – you are ready to call your congregation into a full-blown encounter with God in prayer.

The transition from explorers to planners and then to leaders might take place as late as 18-24 months into the process. The typical transition will probably be between twelve and twenty-four months, somewhere in the second year. More important than linear time is sequential time. First pray and learn together. Then, explore and plan. Guard humility and unity. Then lead.

- The senior pastor will serve as the 'visionary leader' of the planning and leadership team.
- The prayer coordinator (praying pastor) will be the point-person in leading the process.
- A person with good strategic planning/thinking skills is also needed (architect).
- An elder (church council member) might be a part of the team or someone appointed to serve as a liaison.

Meet to pray – not just to work your plan! If you don't; you violate the first principle of your process – prayer! Prayer is about a relationship with Jesus, both personally and corporately – not just his work.

The Senior/Lead Pastor must cast the initial vision for the

Church's prayer ministry. A part of the discovery phase will be prayer support for God to speak clearly to the Senior Pastor about the blueprint for prayer ministry.

From the beginning, include the Pastor of Evangelism. When planning your training work with the Pastor of Discipleship and with the director of your missions program. Don't miss the opportunity to learn from congregations around you who are launching prayer ministries. An inside architect or some outside prayer consultant may be needed to work on the fusion of the various elements into one. (PROJECT PRAY or some other prayer-coaching network would serve at the pleasure of the Senior Pastor in the area of helping to translate the vision for prayer into a strategic process in conjunction with the focus – discovery teams.)

Project Learning/Doing Options

Coming out of your prayer planning retreat, the core leaders should now review the plans and projections made by the planning teams for congregational prayer experiences in the next twelve months. Start slowly and deliberately. Do some simple things to raise the profile of prayer ministry! Do a bulletin insert on prayer – monthly. Suggest some books on prayer – and make them available to the congregation. Show videos on prayer ministry to the congregation. The Sentinel Group has a whole series of videos on how prayer is changing the face of cities and, in some cases, nations (www.sentinelgroup.org). Do some teaching and preaching on prayer. Actually pray – form spontaneous groups for prayer after during the Sunday service. Groups of six to eight will be more comfortable than prayer-triads at the beginning.

PHASE III – Going Public: Feeding the Prayer Fire and Finding Leaders

Milestone Seven: Envisioning the Congregation

Envision and Awaken the Congregation. You are now ready to 'go public' with your prayer effort. Of course, for perhaps a year or more, you have been conducting a congregation-wide prayer meeting. You have not been concerned with numbers – and that is an important consideration. At times, in a small church, you may have gone to a prayer meeting in which no one showed up – but, you were there, and you prayed, and you persisted. At other times, those in attendance might have consisted only of the small group of leaders with whom you had been meeting separately. The bottom line is this – you persisted; and, hopefully, you have begun to forge a model for your prayer meeting that is effective. You have had occasional Sunday prayer experiences. You may have exposed the congregation to denominationl or national calls to prayer. In each case, you have not been concerned, to this point, with numbers – the calls have served to uncover those with a heart for prayer and provide opportunities to expand prayer's focus from self-interested praying to kingdom prayer purposes. That small group of leaders with whom you have been quietly praying, learning, then exploring and finally planning is now a vetted leadership team.

Now, you are ready to engage the congregation. Call for an open vision meeting. Previously, you recruited to your learning team quietly and privately. Now, you will openly recruit to your effort. Make an announcement on Sunday morning. Build the meeting, "Those interested in seeing our church become a house prayer; join us for an evening of prayer and reflection." Put on the coffee. Conduct the meeting in your fellowship hall, around tables. Share some of your findings from your exploration. Share some of the prayer experience plans you are projecting for the coming year. Designate certain tables by interest. For example,

THE PROGRESSION

Out of those who come to the prayer meeting and from your learning team; from those you know meet God daily; those who explored and planned, you will now set forth a formal leadership team.

You have seen them under pressure.

You have measured their willingness to learn, their flexibility.

You have determined those who are tactical and those who can think strategically.

You have heard them pray – and that is not about 'pretty praying,' but about passion and depth, scope and vision, Biblical roots and balance.

You have seen the mature, those who can bring the others to consensus, those who repel and those who serve as glue for the group.

It is time to set forth a prayer leadership team.

some might be interested in personal prayer, family prayer, intercession, prayer evangelism, prayer for missions and missionaries, prayer teaching and training, men and women in prayer, prayer for and among singles, prayer for and by youth and children, prayer walking, prayer for the community, the creation of a prayer room/wall, prayer chains, and so forth.

The areas you have identified in your planning should be at the top of your list. In smaller meetings, combine the table discussions – personal and family prayer, prayer at and in the congregation, intercession and prayer evangelism. Keep the seven marks of a praying church in mind in the process.

Your eventual goal is to permeate your congregation with prayer until you have a worshipful prayer ministry with mission at its edge. The height of your structure and the weight it must carry determines your depth. Going deep is more important initially than moving forward and higher. If you have chosen to follow the Milestone model, and the steps outlined here, you have worked quietly, off the radar screen. You have had difficulties, comers and goers, breakdowns and breakthroughs – but you have persisted. You have learned, explored and projected an informed plan.

For almost two years, you have patiently invited members to a church-wide prayer meeting and some came. You may have laced into your Sunday worship additional prayer experiences as well. Your leaders will have grown in their prayer theology – most significantly, from a view of prayer as acquisition, a transaction with God, to a view of prayer as the context for transformation. They now strongly believe that prayer is at its heart worship and at its edge mission, and in between, God meets our needs. It a relationship with a holy God in the context of love and grace that calls for change – in us, our churches and our world. This is a view of prayer you want the entire congregation to come to own.

As you host an envisioning evening for the launch of a new level of prayer ministries in your church; do some of these things:

- Share the stories of what God is doing through prayer.[3]
- Show one of the shorter transformation videos.[4]
- Talk about both the need for prayer and the joy of prayer.
- Describe your vision for prayer ministries in the church.
- Spend a good share of your time praying. Pray individually. Pray into your vision for prayer!
- Introduce the congregation to the 'Seven Markers of a Praying Church,' and the 'Ten Prayer Values.'
- Share your research and your dreams.
  SAY: *We announced an evening to talk about prayer ministries, and I am delighted that you came. What brought*

you here? Let's pray that to God! "God when I heard about this meeting…my heart leaped…I knew you were calling me to this…"

SAY: *What do you envision happening in our church by prayer? Let's pray that to God!* "God, the desire of my heart is to learn to pray…so many of us want a closer walk with you… Lord, would you teach us to pray?"

You could ask these questions and get *"shared"* responses. But, when the people *pray* their responses, the effect is different! Dramatically different.

The schedule might look something like this:

> 7:00 p.m. Welcome
>
> Begin with expressions of thanksgiving and praise
>
> 7:10 p.m. Tell stories of what is happening in congregations that have become intentional in developing a prayer ministry.
>
> 7:25 p.m. Show one of the shorter Transformation Videos (Transformation II - Preview Clip, www.sentinelgroup.org).
>
> 7:45 p.m. Share the vision for prayer ministries in your church.
>
> 8:00 p.m. Pray!
>
> 8:15 p.m. Break into small groups (4-7). Have a leader at each table, representing an aspect of prayer you hope to develop. Ask each member to share – "What is *your passion* for prayer and prayer ministries in this area?" Record key responses.
>
> 8:45 p.m. General Sharing. After a time of interaction, refocus the group. Ask this question – "What is God saying *to us* about prayer in our church and community?"
>
> 9:00 p.m. Prayer – Wrap up and summary by the leader.

Appoint prayer implementation task teams. This is the first wave of implementers. With your key leaders (SLT) at the core, surround them with members of your learning, discovery and planning teams, along with congregational participants interested in some aspect of the prayer effort. With the 'Seven Markers of a Praying Church' in mind, consider additional prayer activities and events that you can sponsor during the next twelve months to engage the congregation in prayer. In the past, such offerings were sidebar events testing interest. Now you want them to be mainstream events. You have vetted key leaders. You have solid research. You have plans bathed in prayer. You have a conviction that the church should be a house of prayer for the nations.

Now your strategic leadership team (SLT) will multiply into a variety of implementation task teams each charged with sponsoring, planning, promoting and leading some event(s) that reflect the diversity of your prayer effort. These task teams are not permanent teams – they are teams set forth to help you launch and broaden a more diverse prayer effort. They are event teams.

Milestone Eight: Church-Wide Enlistment

The Task Teams. In your visioning evening, hopefully, you had an open and positive discussion about the church as a house of prayer. You should have exposed the congregation to the 'Seven Markers of a Praying Church,' and your values, perhaps adapted from the 'Ten Values of a Praying Church' resource produced by Project Pray.

Coming out of the Envisioning Evening, you should have found additional people excited about making the church a house of prayer. Now they have an opportunity to serve on 'task teams.' The task teams will each lead some prayer event or emphasis over the next six months or more. You are testing two things: leadership capacity and congregational readiness.

CAUTION: The envisioning evening is not to set the trajectory. The Holy Spirit does that – and as leaders, you have discerned the direction in which you must move. Now, you need to affirm the congruence between the perceptions of the congregation and the informed plan of leaders. What do congregational members see as the essential elements of a house of prayer? You might find surprising congruence, but typically, you will find a significant distance between the two visions. What you discover will inform how you teach and train into that gap. The evening will help you determine how quickly you can move forward, or how deliberately you must plod onward. Your envisioning evening may leave you thrilled by the interest and affirmation of the congregational participants. Or, it may leave you disheartened by dissonance and confusion, by the degree of commitment to a narrow prayer theology. Be ready for either response. Either way, don't give up.

You are learning from your members and stretching their vision. You are also identifying additional potential prayer leaders in the various areas that you will develop over the next few years. This is a marathon, not a sprint. Your prayer effort is now public. Your goal is congregational engagement. Get 'em praying. Prayerfully work your plan. Assess and make adjustments. Add and subtract.

Learning Components

Earlier we said that your prayer ministry advances on two legs. Your leaders offer prayer learning and doing activites. And then they assess. The cycle is then repeated. With regard to your whole process, here is another look:

Learning

PRINCIPLES – Teaching on prayer! New learning!

PRACTICUM – What do those principles look like applied? How is this practiced? Make your teaching practical.

PICTURES – Give stories, examples, illustrations.

Doing

Do Prayer!

Do a variety prayer experiences, led by the SLT and the Task Teams, spread out over the 'four dimensions' – personal prayer, corporate prayer, intercession, prayer evangelism. If possible, press *more deeply* into each dimension, remembering, your goal is multiple prayer experiences in the next six-twelve months.

More deeply means:

- Beyond personal prayer is couple-praying, the family altar, family blessing ceremonies, families and mission, etc.
- Beyond corporate prayer is men's and women's prayer gatherings, an elder-deacon prayer retreat, Schools of Prayer (Project Pray offers a number of these), prayer triads and quads, prayer groups, etc.
- Beyond intercession is watching in prayer, all-night prayer meetings, prayer calls, teaming intercessors, teaching them to give the gift of prayer, etc.,
- Prayer Evangelism involves teaching the importance of prayer for the lost. You might experiment with prayer for Unreached People Groups, prayer-walking and prayer missions, etc.
- For each prayer experience, appoint a 'task team' to provide leadership. At least appoint a team for each broad category into which you will teach or call for prayer experiences.
- You are now expanding your leadership and eventually your goal is, for example, a leadership team focused on each area in which you want to build a significant prayer stream – personal and family prayer; intercessors; prayer evangelism; prayer groups, etc.

Leading

- As you move through the year, ask, "Where are you in your PROCESS?"

- Ask each team to assess the prayer experience they led.
- Assess, "Are we on track; on schedule? Ahead, behind?"
- Probe the prayer habits of the congregation.
- Has your response been what you thought it would be?
- What are your current PROBLEMS/SUCCESSES?
- Adjust your plan as you move forward.
- Stretch out your timetable, if necessary.

PHASE IV – Expanding Leadership Teams and Long-Term Planning

Milestone Nine: Multiple Leadership Teams

Expand Your Leadership Team. Let's review. You started your effort with a congregation-wide prayer meeting (Milestone One), and from that group, you chose potential leaders from those who were willing to learn (Milestone Two). You met with them, prayed with them, and urged them to develop a consistent personal prayer habit (Milestone Three). You stretched their vision, urged them to explore different prayer models around them (Milestone Four), and then led them through a planning process (Milestone Five). You then, with fresh, affirmed, key leaders (Milestone Six), out of an informed plan, cast vision to the congregation for the enlargement of your prayer effort (Milestone Seven). Then, for almost a year, you offered prayer experiences to the congregation, deepening and widening their prayer practices (Milestone Eight). These experiences and events were led by task teams.

Now, around your Strategic Prayer Leadership Team, you want to finally organize multiple prayer leadership teams to carry forth the various aspects of your ongoing prayer effort. These teams will plan and lead specific prayer experiences and emphases. You will find these team members among the learners-explorers-planners and task team members who helped in Milestone Eight. The events gave you the opportunity to vet permanent team members. Additional team members would be drawn from the pool of people participating in the prayer events of the last year.

Teams recommended:

- Prayer Ministries Coordinator
- Prayer Room/Center Coordinator
- Intercessory Prayer Coordinator
- Prayer Evangelism Coordinator
- Department Support Coordinator
- Marketplace Coordinator
- Training Coordinator

These prayer leadership teams, unlike the SLT that carries responsibility of the whole vision, focus on specific prayer ministry areas. The purpose of these teams is to dream, plan and lead on-going specific prayer ministries and experiences in their area. Your goal is not merely prayer activities, but the creation of a culture of prayer. That will require more than prayer activities – it will require daily personal prayer, at-home, by couples and families. It will require a new level of intercession by mature intercessors, trained and teamed, mobilized and focused on prayer evangelism rather than merely reacting against the darkness. It will require systematic missional praying, prayer groups, prayer teaching and training, perhaps, the creation of a prayer room/center or at the very least, some prayer focus – cross or wall in the sanctuary itself.

Create Your Prayer Council

You have a group of core leaders, and now focused implementation teams. This gives you an opportunity to begin to identify a 'prayer council.' The 'prayer council' will be comprised of the leaders for every prayer ministry *already in existence,* and the leaders of your various implementation teams, prayer ministries you are birthing. These people are the backbone of the current prayer stream of any church but they have rarely been convened.

Sometimes their interests in prayer are so specific in focus that they have not connected with other people of prayer in the same church. By bringing these people to the table, you will advance the process. The goal is a non-competitive, seamless, prayer process in the local church.

Milestone Ten: Diversified Training

Multiple Prayer Planning and Implmentation Teams. You have a Strategic Prayer Leadership Team – a core of leaders. It may be increasingly difficult for them to manage your growing prayer effort. They, or others appointed will lead the Implementation Teams that will carry the burden of a specific aspect of the prayer effort. In addition to leading various prayer experiences and ministries during the year, these micro implementation teams also need to become micro learning teams, learning about, for example, family prayer issues and models, and so forth. They need to pray together, just as the original learning team did during the first year. As they lead specific prayer experiences for the congregation (doing prayer), they will also explore possibilities going forward.

Out of these micro processes, there should emerge a subset of leaders for each area of prayer ministry that you are developing: at-home prayer; family prayer; prayer groups; the proliferation of prayer in the congregation, including, embedding intercessors into every ministry; prayer partners for pastoral and ministry leaders; the intercessory prayer ministry; prayer evangelism; prayer teaching and training; prayer with and for youth and children; a prayer crisis line, and so on. In a smaller congregation, actually the typical church (the average congregation has about 75 present on Sunday morning), combine these areas: at-home prayer; at-church prayer; intercession and prayer evangelism; teaching and training. First, form interest groups around the areas that you want to explore going forward. Then, task teams to lead various prayer experiences. Finally, permanent micro-leadership teams.

Give these micro implementation teams as long as a year to meet together, to pray and learn, to explore, as they also sponsor track-specific prayer experiences, to develop an informed plan for their specific prayer focus. Out of their work, create, for example, a 'personal and family prayer enrichment team,' and an 'intercessory prayer and evangelism leadership team.' Each area demands informed, inspired leaders.

As you did with your core leaders, you are now vetting the leaders of these specific areas of ministry. At first, they served on implementation task teams, focused on prayer activities in various aspects of your prayer effort. Then, they were assigned more permanent leadership of a specific prayer endeavor.

Each micro implementation learning-leader team will find helpful resources to begin their journey in the *Praying Church Resource Guide*. They will also benefit from being a part of the

Prayer Leaders Continuing Education quarterly training meetings.

Keep asking the questions:

- Where are we now in our strategic process?
- What are our next steps?
- What is going well?
- What needs a funeral?
- Are we speaking to all 4-dimensions or becoming absorbed in one or the other?
- What part of our prayer ministry needs help?

Monitor your attitudes! Keep a faith-filled perspective. See the vision! Encourage one another. Keep stories of other churches and their success after perseverance before the team.

Look for early successes! Celebrate them. Don't cross the creek at the widest spot! Introduce prayer experiences and programs that will be received most readily, most naturally. Carefully discern your congregation. Don't shock them with a "spiritual warfare" conference when they are struggling to learn conversational prayer! Find out where they are at, and take your prayer ministry to them.

Go slow! Babies learn to walk with support – and they take one step at a time. They fall a lot too! If you have read this far in this book, you are charged by the idea of prayer leadership! But, you may be in for a shock. Many Christians are not so excited by prayer. Too much change, too fast – will set your prayer ministry efforts back. Teach, then do! Then, assess. How well did we do? How many participated? Are we ready for the next step? Do small events. Develop key leaders for each focus area.

Prayer is something we never stop learning. Like any relationship, it always has challenges, seasons and stages. It is multi-faceted. During this year, offer ongoing regular training on prayer, at least one new discipleship class every quarter. Elders and deacons should also be trained in prayer – regularly. Every department should be penetrated by prayer – and prayer training.

Prayer training should be broad – personal prayer, praying Scripture, prayer and meditation, prayer and heaven's courtroom, the power of entertaining God, intercessory prayer, watching in prayer, lament and prayer, prayer and evangelism, models for prayer, prayer for direction and guidance, prayer missions and treks, there is so much about prayer to learn.

The ways and means by which you teach and encourage personal-devotional prayer may be anything from bulletin inserts to additional congregational prayer exercises. It may include prayer experiences, continued teaching of prayer both at the church-wide level and in the discipleship arena. How will the church develop a prayer discipleship, teaching-training plan? How and what will you teach intercessors? How will you train in prayer evangelism? What training will you offer prayer group leaders? Ongoing, diverse teaching and training, with the recognition that the entire church needs prayer training. Pray for a hunger to learn and embrace the discipline of prayer; and not merely, prayer as acquisition, or prayer for personal enhancement, a far too narrow self-interested prayer theology, but prayer as communion, the context for daily, personal transformation.

Avoid offering popular prayer teaching and training that only perpetuates narcissism and pragmatic prayer. Quick-fix prayer models, 'Step 1-2-3 to your miracle,' feeds the unhealthy obsession with self, and self is what must die for spiritual growth to occur.

At the end of the year of congregational engagement, you want to transition 'task teams,' now vetted, into permanent leadership team for each focus area going forward. You want to reconfirm, not only core leaders, but also members of your prayer council. And you are ready to move in several directions at once over the next few years, each led by a micro team focused on some aspect of your whole prayer process.

PHASE V – Engaging the Four Dimensions

Your year of prayer experiences planned and led by, then evaluated by micro implementation-task teams, your budding prayer council and your core leaders, will now allow you to move forward in multiple directions at the same time with multiple prayer leadership teams around your SLT.

Milestone Eleven: The Family Altar

The Family Prayer Coach and Team. There are two great blessings in the Bible – the blessing on the home, on Adam and Eve (Gen. 1:28), and the blessing of Jesus as he left the earth (Lk 24:49), the 'blessing' that was fulfilled in the coming of the Holy Spirit on the day of Pentecost. In that moment, the church was constituted. These two great blessings are the means by which God's purposes move forward, on these two great institutions, the home and the church. The word bless, *barak*, means knee, it implies prayer. By prayer, we secure God's blessing on both our homes and our congregations. A praying church requires praying homes, and praying homes will also insure a praying church.

As one of your first steps, you emphasized personal prayer (Milestone Three). That is the anchor – daily, personal prayer at-home. You now want to encourage the expansion of personal prayer to couples prayer, the family altar, fathers and mothers praying spontaneously with sons and daughters, formal blessing events, all moving to missional prayer, out of each member's personal time with God. Someone on your leadership team needs to champion and resource personal and family prayer.

Milestone Twelve: Intercession

The Intercessory Prayer Leadership Team. Intercessory prayer is the critical element in mission. However, intercessory prayer cannot be the center of your prayer ministry. Intercession is a utility of prayer. It is the edge of prayer, between light and dark, saved and lost, inside and outside. It is on the line or the wall, where some advance of the kingdom of God is sought, or some push-back by the Evil One is occurring. It is the means by which God opens closed doors, enlightens blind hearts, opens ears, empowers the witness of an evangelist or missionary. It is fraught with warfare, but its heart is not warfare, but the reconciliation of the lost to Christ. Intercession and intercessors need the tethering of worshipful communion. Mobilize intercessors after you have established an understanding of healthy corporate prayer aimed at transformation, after you have articulated a sound prayer theology.

Intercessors are typically the ones praying at home – but not always in healthy ways. And, they are often the ones who will show up at church for a prayer meeting. Note those who have supported the prayer effort. You probably have some teachable intercessors in your leadership team. Now you are ready to identify and mobilize them across the congregation.

Alive Publications has released a small book called *Intercession – the Critical, Strategic, Middle*. And, the book *Entertaining God – Influencing Cities* is also a great resource. It emphasizes 'hosting the Presence of God' as the key to intercessory influence. There are also materials for training intercessors in the *Praying Church Resource Guide*. You will find a great deal of material on intercessory prayer. Make sure you use material that does not emphasize spiritual warfare as 'the essence' of intercessor; nor material that denies its reality. You want to develop worshipping intercessors who know their strength is in communion with God, not railing at the darkness.

Most people have heard of intercessory prayer, but many have a confused sense of what it is. Some see it as belonging to an exotic handful of the more spiritually elite prayers. So they distance themselves from intercession. Some see intercession as a 'spiritual gift' – and they are sure they do not have it and are grateful. There is scant evidence that intercession is a spiritual *gift*, especially one limited to a handful of fervent prayers. That being said, there does appear to be a group of believers who have a special *call* to intercessory prayer. Estimates are that such Christians compose five-to-ten percent of believers. However, all believers are invited into the role of intercession; it is the noblest use of prayer. In intercession, we stand between God and another, perhaps in behalf of their greatest need – to become a follower of Jesus Christ.

Preach on intercession. Teach on it. Identify those who feel a call to the ministry of intercession. Meet with them. Pray with them. Begin to trust them with assignments for prayer. Debrief them.

Eventually, you want to look at teaming your intercessors. See the *Praying Church Resource Guide* for suggestions. As you explore the possibility of teaming intercessors, consider PIT CREWS – small 'personal intercessory teams' for each ministry in your church. In addition, configure as many intercessors as will participate in virtual prayer teams of five-to-ten, depending on your size. These are not PIT Crews, focused on or attached to some ministry effort, they are generally the way you organize your intercessory effort. Create a means to convey prayer requests, needs and news to your intercessors through these virtual teams. You might use email, twitter, texting or old-fashioned telephone chains. At times, you may want to do prayer exercises – prayer chains, prayer conference calls, etc.

Do some prayer walking, prayer missions. Hold extended prayer times. Do a prayer chain. Conduct a 24-7 prayer weekend. You identified a mission field earlier, now engage intercessors to pray into and over that mission field. Take them there. Study the world around your church. Create prayer points. Cultivate a caring church, and that starts by prayer. Care without prayer is humanitarian work. It is noble. But what sets the church's care apart is that it invokes God's blessing on the gift, and invites His Presence to go with the gift. And it is Presence that brings a consciousness of need, conviction by the Spirit that leads to conversion. Don't do care without prayer! For more ideas see *The Praying Church Resource Guide*, Section 7 – "Prayer Evangelism."

Identify your intercessors. Offer training. Training intercessors is perpetual. They will be trained best 'on the wall' in the act of interceding. The Holy Spirit will teach them. Team them. Direct them. Debrief them. Get them engaged in missional prayer, proactively praying, not merely reactively praying. Affirm them.

Milestone Thirteen: Prayer Evangelism

Establish a Prayer Evangelism-Mission Team. Prayer is at its heart worship, and at its edge mission, and in between God meets our needs. Sadly, almost all of our prayer energy today is focused on our own needs. Not only do we undervalue prayer for the sheer pleasure of being with God, we invest far too little prayer in mission. The prayer ministry of the church is not complete unless it has a missional interface and intercessors, as well as having families and the congregation consistently engaged in prayer evangelism. God opens doors by prayer. Any missionary that finds a door unlocked will, on examination, discover the fingerprints of an intercessor on the doorknob.

Intercessory prayer is posited on the understanding of prayer as communion. Establish worshipful prayer as communion with God before you begin to develop the prayer evangelism effort.

The Praying Church Handbook, Volume IV, is specifically focused on "Intercessory Prayer and Mission." It is a collage of

Prayer Ministry Strategy - The Milestone Process

over 1400 pages, written and electronic, on topics related to intercession and mission. A great primer is Steve Hawthorne's annual guide, *Seek God for the City*! The great course, *Perspectives*, produced by the late Ralph Winter, with Steve Hawthorne is the greatest collections of missional materials for ready learning in existence.

The prayer evangelism effort is perennial, relentless, ongoing. Every church needs a mission field near – around the church and its facility; and a mission field afar – a nation, an unreached people group, etc. Every member needs to see themselves as a missionary inside their vocational network. There are five neighbors to whom each member needs to pray for, care about, and when possible, share Christ – their physical neighbors who live next door to them and their vocational neighbors beside whom they work; their family and family-like friends; their circle of acquaintances where they shop and dine, seek entertainment and services and then, that special 'Jericho Road' person who desperately needs a neighbor – a needy person God seems to put in our path.

Milestone Fourteen: Prayer Groups

The Prayer Group Network Leader(s). People learn to pray by praying – there is no other way! Small prayer groups are the best vehicle to accomplish this goal. Form prayer groups around specific themes. The themes might vary – prayer for lost loved ones; mothers praying for daughters; fathers praying for sons; prayer for unreached peoples; prayer for revival and awakening; prayer for city fathers; prayer for the nation and its leaders; singles support and prayer group; witnessing teens prayer group; prayer for community schools; prayer missionaries; prayer for nations; and more. The presenting reason for every prayer group attracts participants, but their underlying value is that prayer groups are the places people learn to pray. The small intimate setting with trusting friends invites people to pray aloud. And praying aloud is liberating to prayer.

At times, you may be approached by someone who wants to lead a prayer group. Be careful. Appoint a mature leader. Here, those learning to pray are affirmed by veterans. They are mentored, raised to peer status, and at times thrust into leadership in another small prayer group.

The prayer groups in your congregation should revolve around a healthy all-church prayer gathering. They should not be a substitute for the entire congregation gathered in prayer, led by the pastor. Healthy leaders are necessary to lead them. Keep the group size to about a dozen. Have a multiplication policy and strategy from the beginning. No prayer groups should compete with the congregational prayer meeting. Prayer meetings morph into church plants. If that is your strategy make that clearn. If it is not – make that clear as well. Create prayer groups in all four-dimensions of your praying church – groups that will feed family prayer, support church ministries, groups of intercessors and for prayer evangelism.

There is a great resource on prayer groups in *The Praying Church Resource Guide.*

PHASE VI – Maturing the Praying Church
Milestone Fifteen: The Prayer Room/Center

Create Your Prayer Center. Everything needs a place. Depending on your size, create a prayer center (larger congregations) or a prayer room (smaller congregations). Create a prayer counter in your foyer for information and a way to connect with the ongoing prayer effort. Create a focal point for prayer in the sanctuary itself – a prayer corner, a wall, a prayer display, a cross, perhaps decorated with the names of lost loved ones and prayer needs, an altar laden with pictures of friends and families with needs, especially those who need God. For a larger church, setup a prayer station in the foyer or in the spring/summer months, a prayer tent outside. Offer prayer before and after your services.

Where, in your facility, are people regularly, visibly engaged, in the call to pray? Where can intercessors retreat for prayer? Where can those in simultaneous intercessory exercises go for prayer? Is there a place where prayer groups can meet not only on Sunday, but during the week? Is the sanctuary dedicated as a prayer room seven days a week? Open and accessible? Made palatable to prayer – lights and worshipful music, or, is it a strange idea that people might come to the church to pray during the week?

Early in your effort, you repurposed the sanctuary as a place of prayer. Your first act was the establishment of a church-wide prayer meeting – typically, held in the sanctuary. You also began to lace into the Sunday morning service special prayer moments. At some point, you will need to determine if you want to establish a prayer room, and how that will be used. Prayer Centers typically demand a congregation of a thousand or more.

As your leadership team becomes a planning team, they will often need a space – for meetings, maps, and prayer and strategy sessions. That need will only increase. Once you identify intercessors and launch prayer groups, the need for a 'place' to meet and pray will intensify.

PHASE VII – Forever

Never Stop Praying. You never stop praying or developing your prayer effort – that is at the heart of building the church. Now, you may want to go back and emphasize the three simple beginning steps again, revisit values and vision, mission and strategy, your tactical plan. It might be a good idea to conduct your research again and compare the level of congregational prayer now to where you were when you started the process.

Keep working on making the church a house of prayer for the nations.

Final Word

Prayer can never be about programs. It is about our relationship with God and how that affects all other relationships! When former Missouri Govenor and Senator Robert Ashcroft was being sworn in as the U.S. Attorney General, his father was only a few days away from death. The senior Ashcroft was a powerful Pentecostal preacher and a great man of God. As the party prepared to leave for the ceremony, someone suggested that they pray. Senator Ashcroft reached over to help his father up, "I wasn't getting up," the elder Ashcroft said. "I was getting down – for prayer!"

When the doctor left the room of Dr. Bacchus with a solemn look, the godly, Christian leader and former college president asked what he had said. "You cannot live more than half an hour," came the reply. Without hesitation, Bacchus exhorted, "Then get me out of bed and place me on my knees. Let me spend the time in prayer for this sinful world." From the position of bended knees, Bacchus ascended to glory.[5]

What I am suggesting in this book is not a prayer program for your church – but a radically different way to see the world and relate to other believers. It is the kind of passion expressed by a young preacher from Zimbabwe:

> I'm part of the fellowship of the unashamed. I have the Holy Spirit's power. The die has been cast. I have stepped over the line. The decision has been made; I'm a disciple of His! I won't look back, let up, slow down, back away, or be still.
>
> My past is redeemed; my present makes sense; my future

is secure. I'm finished and done with low living, sight walking, small plannings, smooth knees, colorless dreams, tame visions, worldly taking, cheap living and dwarfed goals.

I no longer need preeminence, prosperity, position, promotions, plaudits, or popularity. I don't have to be right, first, tops, recognized, praised, regarded, or rewarded. I know life by faith, lean on His Presence, walk by patience, am uplifted by prayer, and I labor with power.

My face is set, my gait is fast, my goal is heaven, my road is narrow, my way is rough, my companions few, my guide reliable, my mission clear. I cannot be bought, compromised, detoured, lured away, turned back, deluded, or delayed. I will not flinch in the face of sacrifice, hesitate in the presence of the enemy, ponder at the pool of popularity, or meander in the maze of mediocrity.

I won't give up, shut up, let up, until I have stayed up, stored up, prayed up, paid up, and preached up for the cause of Christ. I am a disciple of Jesus. I must go 'til he comes, give 'til I drop, preach 'til all know, and work 'til He stops me. And when he comes for His own, He will have no problem recognizing me...My banner will be clear.[6]

1   Paul Billheimer, *Destined for the Throne* (Port Washington, PA: Christian Literature Crusade, 1975) 101.
2   As quoted by Alvin Vander Griend, *The Praying Church Sourcebook*, 29.
3   Here are some websites from which you can often pull inspirational stories. Be careful, not all "Prayer Stories" sites are Biblically sound. And not all stories true. I often check out stories on this site: www.truthorfiction.com/index-prayers.htm. A reliable story site is www.guideposts.com/request_prayer.asp. Another site is www.inspirationalprayer.com as well as www.brethren.org/ac/CallToPrayer/Stories.html.
4   The video I use is "Transformation II – Preview clip." It is shorter than either Transformation I or II and contains excerpts from both. Available from: www.sentinelgroup.org or by calling 800-668-5657 They have a number of excellent videos documenting the work of the Holy Spirit around the world out of prayer.
5   Dick Eastman, *No Easy Road,* 110.
6   Anonymous, from R. Kent Hughes, 62
7   C. John Miller. Outgrowing the Ingrown Church.
8   Vander Griend, 117.

ADDITIONAL IDEAS FOR CHURCH PRAYER

Encourage each ministry area to organize a <u>Prayer Covering</u> – 3-5 people who will be the prayer partners to that ministry: youth, singles, children, nursery, etc. Encourage the leader(s) of that ministry area to take prayer seriously. Use the intercessors that have proven themselves as leaders.

Have a prayer fair! An evening in which ministry leaders and people of prayer come together. Give each ministry leader a chance to share their vision for the coming year. Be creative. Have each one emphasize his/her vision for the integration and need of prayer support for what they are doing. Then partner intercessory support for each ministry. It is wise to limit both the number of intercessors supporting each ministry, and the number of ministries each intercessor can support. You might make some of the assignments by lot – just an idea. Have each intercessor put their name in several baskets that represent the ministries that they personally want to support in prayer. Then draw out the names that will comprise that team.

Depending on the size of the church and the number of ministries to be supported, and the number of intercessors available, limit the size of the teams to 3-5. Don't allow prayer support to be a matter of mere popularity – one ministry with a dozen intercessors and another with none. It is probably good to also limit the number of ministries any intercessor is seriously supporting in prayer to 2-3.

Once the assignments are completed; you may want to allow for a moment of switching teams to align hearts. However, remember – you started the process by allowing intercessors to place their names ONLY in baskets of ministries to which they had a sense of drawing. Encourage them to remain on that prayer team –

for a year. Provide a moment for the teams to convene, exchange phone numbers and emails, agree on a lead partner, and set a time to meet again with the ministry team leaders to hear a larger version of their ministry dreams and begin the prayer support process.

Conduct a Prayer Revival – a week of nightly prayer meetings.

Create a Prayer Chain. It is an old-fashioned, telephone calling plan where one calls another who then calls another – until all have heard. It passes along urgent prayer needs quickly. More complete information can be posted on the Prayer Request section of the Church Website (if you have the capacity for quick posting).

Encourage members to *form prayer triads* – and meet for prayer monthly, if not weekly. These triads are focused on transformational prayer, not transactional prayer. The small, covenantal groupings allow for intimacy and confidentiality. They should be prayerful in nature. And the heart of that prayer should be "to be like Jesus." Once a year, ask each triad to invite a 4th member into their group to experience triad praying for 4-6 weeks. Then, allow that person to spin off and form their own triad. Be flexible. One of the original triad members might spin off, leaving the newest man to become a member of the existing triad. Or, the four might become two pairs, and each find a 3rd member to form two revised triads. Or, a triad may allow a newly developing threesome to meet with them and then spin off to become independent. The groups must reproduce! Or the movement pray stalls and dies. Reproduction forces the group to have an external, missional focus. They are to impart prayer! That should make the modeling of prayer a quality issue.

Form Prayer Cell Groups. These are larger than the triads, typically 8 – 15 participants. They are not as intense as the triads. These informal prayer groups may meet around a prayer theme or cause. They may be joined together by some homogenous factor: couples groups, northside, professionals, educators, singles, young brides, singled grandmothers, friends of Israel – or any other common denominator. They should not be share groups. They should focus on prayer. John Miller in his book, *Outgrowing the Ingrown Church*, says, "Prayer meetings constantly tend downward, to either intellectualistic Bible studies or, anxiety-sharing sessions where religious arguments break out. Christian people and their leaders are ready to do almost anything except get down to praying with power and authority in the name of Christ."[7] Good prayer time always includes worship and simply loving God.

Conduct a Prayer Vigil. A prayer vigil can be any length of time. Participants agree to pray about some cause or issue for some season – 24 hours or a month. A prayer vigil can be held in a location – almost as a lock-in for participants. Or they may arrange a schedule in which each takes a turn on "the watch" from their homes.

Encourage Senior Intercessors. At a church in Michigan, Senior Intercessors adopted a young person for a year of prayer. They prayed for them. Occasionally, they sent notes of encouragement to the young people. But they never identified themselves. Some of the youth learned that "someone" was praying for them – but they didn't know who it was! Annually, a dinner and sharing time is held and the young people get to meet the Seniors who were their secret prayer partners during the year. Kids say, "It's nice to know someone cares!" Or, "It helped me through the year!" And, "It makes me feel special." And the adults? "This has created a special bond between me and this young person." In prayer, you always give your heart away. Another Senior noted, "Prayer is more powerful than I realized!"[8]

DEFINITIONS

24/7: Prayer, 24 hours a day, seven days a week. This can be seasonal or permanent. A church of a thousand or more is usually required to sustain this level of prayer intensity.

Architect: A member of the Prayer Leadership Planning Team or a consultant/coach who helps with critical, strategic thinking in the design of your prayer process.

Church-wide Prayer Meeting: The call to the entire congregation to gather for prayer, typically, under the pastor's leadership to seek not only the 'hand' of God, but also the 'face' of God. This is not a leadership or intercessory prayer gathering, but an every member prayer gathering with a focus on standing before God and hearing God as a congregation. Scripture-based prayer is encouraged, moving to missional prayer, without forgetting prayer requests and personal needs. This is Milestone One in the process. Call the entire church to gather to pray.

Core Leaders: This is essentially the same as your Strategic Prayer Leadership Team. These 3-5 leaders are the driving force of your prayer ministry effort. Up until Milestone Six, all your 'leaders' should be 'learners.' They assist with discovery-research and in developing a congregational prayer ministry plan. That assures vetted 'core' leaders who agree with the mission and vision, the values and strategic process. At Milestone Six, you affirm them and other leaders around them.

Church-wide Enlistment: A further stage in the growth of your prayer effort. It occurs late in Phase III, at Milestone Eight. Prior to this point, you should be selective in recruiting prayer learner-leaders and those who assist with research and planning. With a vetted, stable core of leaders, you are ready to invite members from the congregation, not merely to pray together – you have been doing that – but to assist in leading some aspect of the prayer effort.

Discovery Process: This is Phase II, Milestone Four. This is the research phase. This phase will take at least three months of intensive involvement. You will need to expand your leadership team during this process, bringing around your SLT a group to help with the discovery/research process. You will need survey instruments to measure prayer and prayer interest in the congregation. You will be well served to pay for a mission profile of your community (Contact PROJECT PRAY for more information, 855-842-5483). You need hard data on your harvest field and your harvest force.

Envisioning Evening: This is a tool for church-wide enlistment. On this evening, or a series of evenings, you will invite the congregation to a prayer vision event. You will attract those interested in involvement in your prayer process. You will share the vision and mission for prayer, data from your discovery/research process, and ideas for moving forward. You will recruit volunteers to specific focus areas and from them form implementation/event planning teams.

Ethos: Refers to the 'culture' of the church, not the tangibles or new tools, not to ministry techniques and practical ideas, but to the environment in which they are implemented – the levels of grace and love, kindness and forgiveness, the 'spirit' of the teams. Prayer *praxis* is not adequate; we must change the culture of our churches and leadership teams.

Focus Areas: Focus areas are the micro areas of prayer. They are tied, to an extent, to the four dimensions and the Seven Markers of a Praying Church. Each focus area – personal and family prayer; intercessory prayer; prayer evangelism; marketplace prayer; the prayer room/ center, and even specializations like children, youth/teen prayer, singles, seniors, etc. – will need a leadership team.

Implementation Team: Essentially the same as 'task teams' who are either leading a 'focus area' and developing a plan for that specific area or planning and leading an event, whether it is a learning or doing event. Implementers begin their work in Phase III, at Milestone Eight, as you begin to unwrap prayer events and opportunities in the congregation, testing interest on different fronts. The 'permanent' leadership teams are formed in Phase IV at Milestone Nine.

Intercessors: All believers are charged with the ministry of intercessor, tied to reconciliation. Intercession does not appear to be a spiritual gift, but there are often in a congregation, a small group, who are hard-core intercessors. They usually comprise five-percent of the congregation, no more than ten-percent. Identifying them, teaming and directing them, debriefing and affirming them, can often spark a spirit of intercession in the whole of the church. Intercessors are identified and organized in Phase V, at Milestone Twelve.

Intercessory Prayer Meeting: This is a gathering of intercessors to intercede. It is not the church wide gathering. It is transactional, missional prayer. It often tends to be more intense than the church wide prayer meeting.

Learning Team/Learning Leader Team: In the early going, you build a leadership team by building a learning team. Insist that in the area of prayer, everyone is a learner. Humility is critical to unity. Your initial team will remain a learning team through the first year, meeting to pray and review learning materials. They will evolve into a discovery/research team, then a planning team, and finally, their leadership will be affirmed.

Milestones: Measures of progress in the journey to make a church a house of prayer for the nations. There are fifteen Milestones, unwrapped in seven Phases, typically over a 5-year period in a congregation. Some of the milestones are unwrapped simultaneously, others, sequentially. These are the basis of the book, *Milestones – Markers on the Journey Toward Becoming a House of Prayer,* by PROJECT PRAY. An overview is found in the book, *Transforming Your Church into a House of Prayer – Revised Edition;* and, the first three milestones are the subject of the book, *The Praying Church Made Simple.*

Micro Teams: These teams lead pieces of the larger prayer ministry. They are also referred to as implementers or task teams. They may be responsible for one project or they may become permanent.

Mission: A prayer mission statement is a concise declaration who, what is being done, and for what purpose, with what outcome in view. The mission statement declares what you are called to do, that is, what you 'should do,' where you are going. It is a declaration of organizational direction.

Multiple Leadership Teams: At the heart of your effort is your SPLT, and your Core Leaders, but around them, perhaps with members of the SPLT leading different aspects of prayer, serving as captains of task teams, are multiple leadership teams. These micro teams carry the burden for some specific aspect of the prayer effort.

Phases: The process of transforming your church into a house of prayer is a multi-year journey. We have divided that journey into Milestones, measures of your progress, and grouped those into phases. In some phases, your milestone efforts are sequential, one following another. In other cases, they are simultaneous.

- Phase I – Learning About and Doing Prayer – The Launch (3 *Simultaneous* Milestones)

- Phase II – Discovery (3 *Sequential* Milestones)

- Phase III – Going Public: Feeding the Prayer Fire and Finding Leaders (2 *Sequential* Milestones)

- Phase IV – Expanding Leadership Teams and Long Term Planning (2 *Sequential* Milestones)

- Phase V – Engaging the Four Dimensions (4 *Simultaneous* Milestones)

- Phase VI – Maturing the Praying Church (1 Milestone)

- Phase VII – Forever – Repeat the Cycle with new leaders!

Prayer Council/Prayer Ministries Council: Your Prayer Council is every prayer ministry leader in your congregation.

Prayer Implementation Plan/Strategy: Out of your research and discovery, and using this resources, perhaps with others recommended, such as *The Praying Church Made Simple* and *Milestones – Markers on the Journey Toward Becoming a House of Prayer,* you want to project a multi-year implementation strategy, a big picture plan. Of course, it will be revised, perhaps, numerous times, but this is your blueprint for moving forward.

Prayer Force: The sum total of your prayer efforts, the full force of people and prayer activities in your congregation. It is leaders and planners, strategists and implementers, specialized intercessors and all others.

Prayer Leader Continuing Education (PLCE): The PROJECT PRAY PLCE is a quarterly gathering of prayer learner-leaders from 3-12 congregations for a two-and-a-half hour gathering that involves teaching, the introduction of tools, and time for each congregational prayer team to 'talk-it-over and take-it-home.' It is a 15 session, 43 month program that is designed to encourage congregational prayer teams in the early stages of their journey to make their church a house of prayer.

Prayer Ministry Surveys: Every church needs to measure the depth of and commitment to prayer by its members and leaders, as well as prayer theology and assumptions. A number of instruments have been created to assist in that assessment process. Contact PROJ-ECT PRAY (855-842-5483) for more infromation. These instruments can be used throughout your journey, but they are particularly helpful in the Discovery phase.

Research and Discovery: In Phase II, at Milestone Four, you enter discovery-research. Here you conduct research on the levels of prayer inside the church. You look back at the history of the congregation. You look for models of prayer. You look around for prayer needs in the community. This is when a demographic harvest field assessment is helpful. This information is critical for your planning.

Strategic Leadership Team/Strategic Prayer Leadership Team (SLT/SPLT): We often refer to this team as the SLT. However, you may have a congregational SLT, and therefore, you may need to add the qualifier 'prayer' – SPLT. This group of critical leaders steward the prayer process. In a small church, what we have called your 'core' leaders may constitute the SPLT. A larger church might demand a larger leadership team. At the heart of that SPLT might be a loosely defined team of two or three leaders, that are the very 'core,' the heart of your prayer effort. The SPLT might also be leaders of micro-teams, implementation teams, that carry on the specific areas of your prayer effort.

Strategic Planning Team (SPT): This team is typically a very small group of strategic thinkers – three-to-five. It may be the pastor, the prayer leader/coordinator and a strategic planner, an idea architect, who knows how to strategically, and sequentially, lay out a multi-year plan that integrates learning and doing, building out the four dimensions and Seven Markers of a Praying Church.

Strategy/Tactics: Strategy is the 'big picture *plan.* ' Tactics are the short-term *steps* of that big-picture process – the parts. Strategy is the architectural plan; it guides the contractor. Tactics are subset plans, at times that are a collection of small steps, at others, a single step. This is the stuff of sub-contractors. Tactics push the one domino over – the one program, the one event; strategy lines up the dominoes in order that one program and event leads to another, and that the energy of the one event is carried over into another. Tactics focus on a single endeavor; but strategy aligns and harnesses the various endeavors, noting: this (training) is being done to prepare for that (event/exercise), and that (event) sets up what follows. One failure in the chain and the process is endangered. The architect (SPT) builds in back-up plans.

Task Teams: Task Teams are essentially the same as 'implementation teams' who are either leading a 'focus area' and developing a plan for that specific area or planning and leading an event, whether it is a learning or doing event. Implementers begin their work in Phase III, at Milestone Eight, as you begin to unwrap prayer events and opportunities in the congregation, testing interest on different fronts. The 'permanent' leadership teams are formed in Phase IV at Milestone Nine.

The Four Dimensions: The core of the philosophy of prayer ministry in all of the works of PROJECT PRAY. They are at the heart of the Seven Markers of a Praying Church. The four dimensions are actually two pairs in the prayer process. The first pair is praying homes and a praying church; at-home and at-church prayer. The second pair is intercessory mobilization turned outward in prayer evangelism.

The 'Ragged' Notebook: As you begin your journey, you want to collect, in one place, all the prayer efforts that exist in your congregation. This will include those who lead groups, advocate for prayer causes, etc. It should include formal and informal prayer groups and opportunities. It might include such things as, how many 'Our Daily Bread' resources are distributed by the congregation. Are seniors praying – when, where, how many? Do your teens participate in SYATP (See You At The Pole), a September, public school prayer gathering held in late September annually. This will be invaluable in your planning effort.

The Seven Markers of a Praying Church: Includes the four dimensions – praying homes and a praying church, defined by homes with a family altar and a church with a pastor-led prayer meeting; and identified, teamed, directed intercessors with a definitive prayer evangelism-mission focus – and with those, a pastor-led prayer leadership team, on-going teaching and training, and a prayer room/center.

Values: Values are not the things that you *call* important, but what you are actually *doing!* By doing, you demonstrate the value of the idea. Do you value prayer? Hammer out *idealized* values – what you *should* be doing and how you *should* behave – and chart your course toward transformation as you compare those with what you are actually doing.

Vision: Vision sees; mission feels; strategy draws a map; tactics are the steps to the end goal. Vision dreams of what the church will look like when it is a house of prayer for the nations.

Alive Publications, an outreach of Alive Ministries: PROJECT PRAY, is an independent small publisher that specializes in prayer and prayer-evangelism resources for individuals, small groups and local churches. The ministry also produces resource kits, with companion videos and study guides that accompany several of their books.

PRAYER – THE HEART OF IT ALL

Discusses prayer fundamentals; the four critical elements: at-home daily prayer, the church at prayer, intercessory prayer and prayer evangelism; and how to apply each of these to create a great awakening in yourself, your church, your sphere influence and the world. Book $14.99; Personal and Group Study Guide $14.99; Resource Kit $99.99

THE PRAYER CLOSET
CREATING A PERSONAL PRAYER ROOM

What we seek is more than a place, more than mere words or even a disciplined, noble routine. It is more than the fact that we pray daily or the function of prayer and its benefits – it is relationship that, to be transforming, has be centered in the heart. Prayer is not something we do, it is someone we are with. And that needs a place! Book $16.95; Resource Kit $74.99

THE GREAT EXCHANGE - WHY YOUR PRAYER REQUESTS MAY NOT BE GETTING ANSWERS

The lack of answers to our prayers is not because God no longer answers or does not want to help. It is often an issue on our side – some hindrance to prayer, blockages in our own heart. Learn practical steps to answered prayer! Book $14.99; Personal and Group Study Guide $14.99; Resource Kit $129.99

ENTERTAINING GOD AND INFLUENCING CITIES Prayer is not about words and requests. It is not even the first and foremost about intercession. That will come. Prayer is about hosting God in a world from which He has been excluded. Book $14.99; CD $8; DVD $15

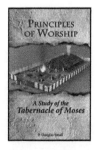

PRINCIPLES OF WORSHIP

A Study of the Tabernacle of Moses. Descriptions of the purpose of each piece as a template for prayer. A study that goes beyond review of details, this study is rich with spiritual insights.
Book $19.99; 4 CD Set $25; 2 DVD Set $25
Book with Powerpoint Resource $80

www.alivepublications.org

THE
PRAYING CHURCH
HANDBOOK

- A collection of substantive reflections on prayer.
- Contributors include global and national leaders, as well as Church of God authors, leaders and intercessors.

4 VOLUME SET

VOLUME I
Foundations
(664 pages)

VOLUME II
Personal and Family Prayer
(714 pages)

VOLUME III
The Pastor and the Congregation
(716 printed pages; 428 pages on disc)

VOLUME IV
Intercessory Prayer and Mission
(732 printed pages; 587 pages on disc)

WWW.ALIVEPUBLICATIONS.ORG

"I can't believe how this has changed my prayer life."

School of Prayer

Schools of Prayer are training courses focused on learning, experiencing and leading in the area of prayer. They are facilitated by P. Douglas Small or through our new associate presenter program.

Our glorious role is help people begin to recover a Biblical view of prayer, one that is not merely transactional and acquisitional, but also transformational.

Project Pray is excited to announce a new avenue for Schools of Prayer. We are training associate presenters to facilitate Doug Small's teachings. Through this partnership we are able to expand our offering to congregations and organizations to experience a prayer reformation. Contact us today to learn about the Associate Presenter Certification.

School of prayer topics include:

The Prayer Closet: Creating a Personal Prayer Room

What we seek is more than mere words or a disciplined, noble routine for prayer. Prayer is a relationship that has to be centered in the heart. Prayer is not something we do, it is someone we are with. And that needs a place!

The Great Exchange: Why Your Prayer Requests May Not Be Getting Answers

Prayer works because God works. It is effective because its hope is in Him and His action. But it also demands changes in us. Learn practical steps to answered prayer!

PRAYER – The Heart of It All

Grow deeper in your prayer life by discovering why God wants us to pray. Discover how to: develop a personal prayer life; pray together as a family; start a prayer ministry in your church; prayer missionally for others and for a Great Awakening.

Schedule your
School of Prayer today!

www.projectpray.org   855-84-ALIVE